LOST IN
THE VALLEY
OF DEATH

PRAISE FOR THE BOOK

"Justin Alexander Shetler went to India in search of adventure and authenticity, and never came back. Was his disappearance the result of a crime, an accident, or a profound spiritual transformation? This mystery beats at the heart of Harley Rustad's gripping and propulsive book, which is part travelogue, part pilgrim's quest, part detective story. The result is the classic hero's journey updated for a hectic, hyperconnected world: think *The Lost City of Z* meets *Eat, Pray, Love*, only set in the Himalayas in the age of hashtags."

—KATE HARRIS, author of *Lands of Lost Borders*

"A compelling read and a fascinating story, which Harley Rustad tells with great flair and even greater compassion. The parade of parents with kids gone missing in India's Parvati Valley moved in parallel to my own plight—each of us facing the same suite of bewildering possibilities, from natural death to foul play to a new life."

—ROMAN DIAL, author of *The Adventurer's Son*

"A mysterious tale of a spiritual seeker, a survivalist on a motorcycle pilgrimage through the Himalayas, who places his trust in a sadhu, only to disappear like honey on a razor's edge. A wonderful book."

—WADE DAVIS, author of *Magdalena* and *Into the Silence*

LOST IN THE VALLEY OF DEATH

A STORY OF OBSESSION AND DANGER IN THE HIMALAYAS

HARLEY RUSTAD

HarperCollins *Publishers* India

First published in India by HarperCollins *Publishers* 2022
4th Floor, Tower A, Building No. 10, Phase II,
DLF Cyber City, Gurugram, Haryana – 122002
www.harpercollins.co.in

2 4 6 8 10 9 7 5 3 1

P-ISBN: 978-93-5489-342-1
E-ISBN: 978-93-5489-350-6

Cover design Joanne O'Neill
Cover images Shashikant Todkar (front),
Justin Alexander Shetler (back)
Author photograph Michelle Proctor

Typeset in 11.75/15 Garamond 3 LT Std

Printed and bound at
Thomson Press (India) Ltd

❶❿◙❂HarperCollinsIn

For Élise

Death is not extinguishing the light; it is only putting out the lamp because the dawn has come.

—Rabindranath Tagore, Indian poet

CONTENTS

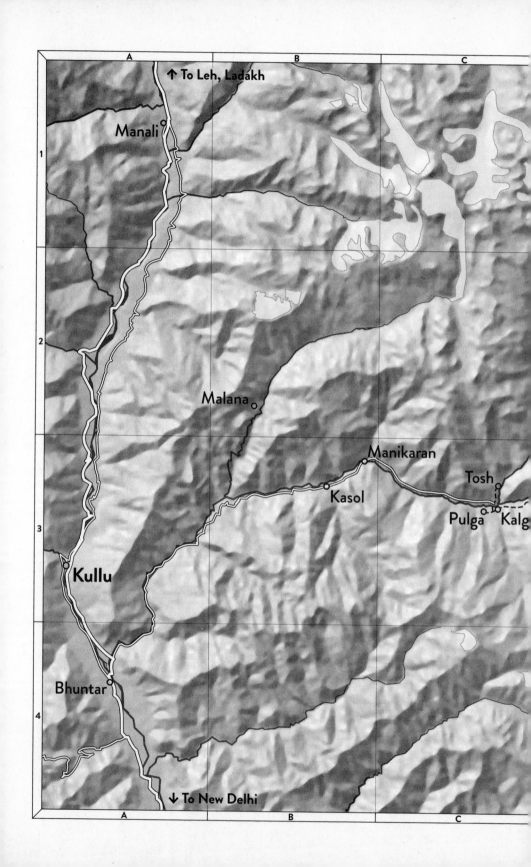

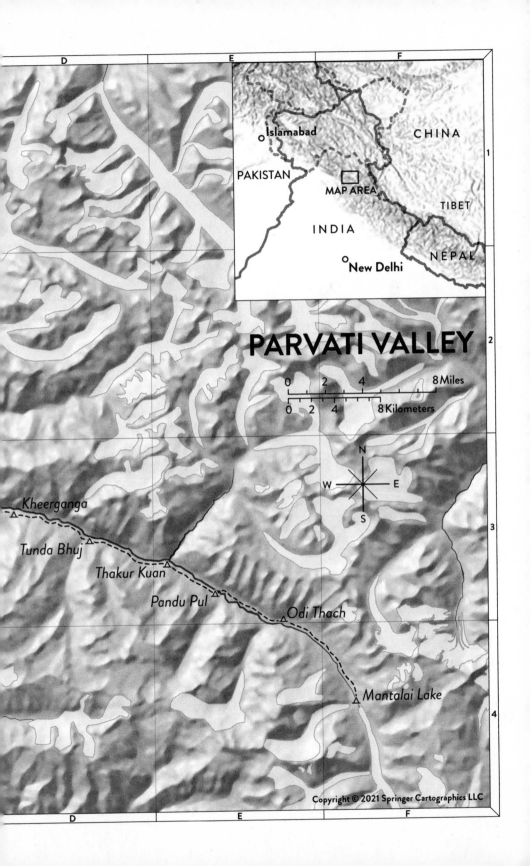

PAKISTAN

Islamabad

CHINA

MAP AREA

TIBET

INDIA

NEPAL

New Delhi

PARVATI VALLEY

0   2   4   8 Miles

0 2 4   8 Kilometers

N
W   E
S

Kheerganga

Tunda Bhuj

Thakur Kuan

Pandu Pul

Odi Thach

Mantalai Lake

AUTHOR'S NOTE

I began investigating the disappearance of Justin Alexander Shetler shortly after he vanished in the Indian Himalayas in the late summer of 2016. I had come across one of the first news articles written about him, published in the *Times of India* newspaper that October, and was immediately drawn into his story. He was American, thirty-five years old, and had traveled around the world extensively before he had arrived in India. He was a trained survivalist and had tens of thousands of social media followers. And he had disappeared while on a pilgrimage led by a Hindu holy man to a sacred lake deep in the mountains in a remote corner of India called the Parvati Valley.

Over the following four years, I conducted hundreds of interviews with Justin's parents, close friends, and acquaintances—from those who had known him as a teenager to some of the last people to see him alive. I wanted to know who he was, what had brought him, eventually, to India, and what he had been searching for. Some of the direct quotations I use in this book are taken from podcasts and interviews that Justin participated in as his status as a minor travel social media star grew. Some dialogue and scenes are pulled from videos shot by Justin and posted online or filmed by fellow travelers or friends. Any other re-created dialogue comes from the recollections, often corroborated, of these sources.

I traveled to the Parvati Valley twice—initially six months after Justin vanished and then to mark the three-year anniversary of his disappearance—to interview local police, mountain guides, guest-house owners, holy men, and shepherds: anyone connected to the path that Justin had taken in his final two months. I interviewed people in the United States, Canada, Philippines, Thailand, Nepal, and India who had shared a meal or a moment with him, who had known him for years or had encountered him briefly. I tracked down backpackers who had met him on the road, each one returning to his or her home country around the world with a memory of a man they couldn't shake.

He was born Justin Alexander Shetler. That was the name on the passport under which he traveled until he disappeared. But most people who had come across him online had known him by his social media profile name, Adventures of Justin. Many with whom I spoke, acquaintances as well as some close friends, had known him only as Justin Alexander. For the last decade of his life, that was the name he preferred in person and online. I was told that Justin had intended to legally and officially drop his birth surname. Those who crossed paths with him on the road—as travelers, tourists, pilgrims—knew him simply as Justin.

LOST IN
THE VALLEY
OF DEATH

PROLOGUE

The traveler had all that he needed inside his cave. It wasn't much but enough to survive. He reclined against the granite wall, bare back meeting cold stone. He had collected fallen wood, anything half dry, from the forest around his cave, stripping some logs into kindling with his machete, and set about lighting a fire. He positioned it near the mouth of the cave so the noxious smoke would dissipate into the night and animals would be deterred from entering. He opened a book; there was just enough light in which to read. It was a book about the search to find happiness in the world.

His cave lay in a forest deep in the Indian Himalayas, a half day's walk from the nearest village or the nearest road, near the head of a slender valley. There were dozens of caves in this forest that had formed in the lee of boulders or by great stones fracturing apart to create caverns. Many caves were tall enough in which to stand and long enough in which to lie down. Some boulders were said to have been dropped by the gods, as who else could move such colossi of stone, while others had been left behind by similarly powerful forces of nature, great glaciers that had retreated up the valley long before. Many people had walked by these caves without a second glance. But over the years, pilgrims and travelers of a certain type had found sanctuary in them, refuge from the elements or the world beyond. This traveler had sought out a cave. It was why he had come to this valley: to find a place in which to retreat and think about his life.

There is power in the Himalayas' many mountaintops. They are purpose made stone, offering paths to realization and a sense of profound achievement of strength, determination, and will at their tops. Mountains have long served as endpoints of pilgrimages: to Mount Everest straddling the Nepal–China border, to Mount Kailash on the Tibetan Plateau, and to Mount Meru in the Indian Himalayas, often called "the navel of the universe." Summits offer perspective, a chance to look back down at your footprints with clarity. Yet for every mountain there is a valley residing below. If the expanse of a desert humbles and the restriction of a forest disorientates, the intimacy of a valley comforts—providing tranquility and a shield from the forces of exposure. In valleys, thoughts don't float away across an ocean or a plain, never to return; they remain to be incubated. Around the world, seekers climb mountains to achieve that clarity or to be closer to their gods, but it is the valleys below in which their intentions solidify and from which they take their first steps. In these sanctuaries pilgrims can bask in the possibility of what lies ahead and above.

In his cave in the valley the traveler crossed his legs and warmed his feet near the fire, drying his black leather boots at the same time. He drank water that he had collected from a nearby spring out of a metal mug, one of the few items he had brought with him. He ate some nuts, dried fruit, and oats that he had purchased at a market down valley and threw a log on the fire. Beside him lay a long bamboo flute that he played during the daytime while sitting in a meadow overlooking the valley below; throughout his travels in India, he had carried it wherever he went. On a rock shelf next to him was a bull's horn that he had collected from the forest outside, as well as a large black feather that had fallen to earth from a Himalayan condor. Not long before, the traveler had tattooed the outline of an eagle in flight across his chest.

Eventually, he lay down on a bed of collected tree needles. Inside the cave there was light, a warm orange glow from his crackling fire and a single candle that he had melted onto the rock by which to read. But the world outside was dark. Thick canopies of pine, walnut, and deodar, a species of aromatic Himalayan cedar, blocked the moon; only the rain found a way through the branches. It was late summer, and the monsoon, in an instant, would shift from a drizzle to a torrent, pelting the mountains and blanketing the valley in heavy mist.

Every year, as consistent as the monsoon, pilgrims and travelers had come to this remote corner of India. They had come to find peace and tranquility, what a Hindi speaker calls *shanti*. They had come to breathe mountain air, to walk ancient forests, and to hike through a valley in the most storied mountain range on earth. They had come to be closer to the gods in a place where Shiva, the most iconic deity in the Hindu pantheon, the great master of yoga and asceticism and the supreme transformer of the world, is said to have meditated for three thousand years. Some of the visitors had traveled peacefully, departing satisfied with their experience and keen to tread elsewhere. But others had not.

The Parvati Valley is a seemingly idyllic corner of Himalayan India, with its big mountain vistas, forested glens, and quaint timber-framed villages clinging to its hillsides. It splinters off a part of the Kullu Valley, also known as the Valley of Gods. Named after a goddess itself, the Parvati Valley hosts its own compendium of legends and mystical stories, a place where gods manifest as dynamic rivers and their actions bring hot springs from deep underground to the surface. But the Parvati Valley has earned its own nicknames: the Valley of Shadows, the Valley of Death. It is a place where every movement exists on a knife edge, where a wrong turn tips a vehicle over an unbarriered cliff edge, a wrong step pitches a traveler into the churning maelstrom of the river, a wrong turn sends a hiker to ranges unknown. Since the early 1990s, dozens of international backpackers have vanished without a trace while traveling in and around the Parvati Valley, an average of one every year, earning this tiny, remote sliver of the subcontinent a dark reputation as India's backpacker Bermuda Triangle. The circumstances of each disappearance are different—the tourist's country of origin; villages visited or paths walked; last known location—yet eerily similar. All feature a spirited backpacker seeking an off-the-beaten-track adventure, a collection of anecdotes from fellow travelers relating the backpacker's final days, a family's anguished search, and thousands of unanswered questions.

This traveler had arrived in the Parvati Valley as many before him had: with a goal and a picture in his mind of what he could accomplish among the mountains and the mist. That picture, at least in part, came to life inside his cave when he carefully placed his phone on a rock, set the timer, and captured a self-portrait as he reclined with his book and his fire. It was one of the last photographs he shared online with his followers on social media. Shortly thereafter, the traveler's name, Justin Alexander Shetler, would be added to the list of those who had entered the Parvati Valley never to be seen again.

PART I

THE WAY

Rise, wake up, seek the wise and realize.
The path is difficult to cross like the sharpened
edge of a razor, so say the wise.

—Katha Upanishad, Sanskrit text

Tell me something you are dedicated to in life and a true
test of that dedication is, Would you die for it?

—Stalking Wolf, as quoted by Tom Brown, Jr.

1
TRAILHEAD

There is only one road into the Parvati Valley. It's a narrow track—roughly paved in parts, washed-out dirt in others—along which rattletrap buses twist and swerve and screech to a crawl with inches to spare as they pass. At several points, vehicles drive under overhanging rock along a route blasted into the mountainside. On one side of the road, the cliff rises, an impassable plane of earth and stone that seemingly touches the clouds; on the other side, it drops precipitously to the milky blue waters of the Parvati River hundreds of feet below. It was at the end of this road but the beginning of a path that Justin set off on his final journey. The hillside hamlet of Kalga was as far as his Royal Enfield motorcycle could take him. He now needed to walk to reach the upper reaches of the valley. The trail into the mountains was clear before him: follow the godlike river that thrashed and thundered in his ears.

On a warm August day, with blue sky and sun offering a welcome relief from the downpours that had drenched the valley and blanketed its forests in mist for much of the summer of 2016, Justin headed for a trailhead. He strolled along a dirt path through Kalga, between two-story wooden guesthouses and apple orchards, toward the edge of the village. Dogs barked, men and women tended their fruit trees in anticipation of the harvest, and multicolored prayer flags fluttered in the humid breeze. Beside Justin walked Andrey Gapon, a Russian man who had spent three months on holiday in the valley. The two had met several weeks earlier, and Gapon had been captivated by the thirty-five-year-old American, who had revealed that he was living in a mountain cave with minimal supplies.

Now Justin was embarking on a four- to five-day hike to Mantalai Lake, a cluster of pools at the top of the valley and the frigid source of the Parvati River. For some, the lake is a place to pitch a tent as one stage of a Himalayan trek. For others, it is the destination—a holy site associated with Shiva. There, as across India, many elements are considered a manifestation of the divine. The very mountains that frame the lake, boasting peaks that pierce through clouds at 20,000 feet, are part of Himavat, the ancient king and personification of the great Himalayan range. He is the father of Ganga and Parvati, goddess daughters who take the form of rivers breaking free from their glacial states and flowing down from the great mountaintops to feed the land. Ganga takes form as the Ganges River, India's singular waterway that believers see as pure no matter how polluted she is beneath the surface. But here the river is Parvati—the goddess of love, harmony, and divine strength; the wife of Shiva and the mother of the beloved elephant-headed god Ganesha. When the Parvati River is calm, it brings forth life and delays death; it nourishes and provides, cools and heals. But when the river turns fierce, it is a deadly force, battering mountainsides and consuming earth as it swells. This duality mirrors the goddess for which it is named. In some of her incarnations, she is benevolent and sustaining, an exemplar of life-giving love. In another, she wears severed heads around her neck, a ferocious and destructive divine power.

Gapon wanted to see off his new friend. As they weaved along the small village's dirt paths, stooping under apple tree branches laden with ripening fruit, they were so deep in conversation that they took a wrong turn and ended up spun around. They laughed. "What an interesting way to start this journey," Justin said, noting the omen of becoming lost before even setting out. When they found the path they knew led to the trailhead, Justin began talking about an idea he had been mulling over: he had been thinking about creating some kind of centralized online memorial for adventurers who have passed away, where their digital trails could serve as eulogies to their lives.

Something wasn't sitting right with Gapon. He could tell that Justin was anxious about the journey that lay ahead. He offered to accompany him to Mantalai Lake; the Russian man was familiar with the route, having just returned from a guided trek to the lake and over a high mountain pass into a neighboring valley. The trek had been challenging but profound, and he would be happy to do it all again, especially alongside someone like Justin. He was disappointed when Justin politely turned down his offer.

Many pilgrims and travelers hire guides and porters to assist them on their trek to the lake, to cook meals and to set up camps, but Justin had been presented with a different opportunity. A sadhu, a Hindu holy man, had invited him on a pilgrimage to the sacred lake, where the man would teach him yoga and meditation and Justin could experience the ascetic life. Justin planned on staying at the lake for ten days, living off the few supplies they were taking and sleeping out under the stars or in boulder caves. It was a journey he wanted to do alone with the sadhu, he told Gapon. He had formed an image in his mind of what the journey would be like. Three days earlier, he had posted online about his plan to trek with the Hindu holy man. "I want to see the world through his eyes, which are essentially 5000 years old, an ancient spiritual path," he had written on his blog and social media accounts. "I'm going to put my heart into it and see what happens."

Around midday, the two men reached the trailhead in a meadow strewn with granite boulders; from there the path snaked off into the forest. Gray langur monkeys with obsidian faces shook the high branches above them. Justin handed Gapon his iPhone and asked him to take his picture to mark the "beginning of a spiritual journey." The American man offered a soft half smile as Gapon took the photograph.

Justin had displayed toughness and determination by spending the previous three weeks living alone in a Himalayan cave with little more than a sleeping bag and a machete. He had revealed trust in his bond with the sadhu who had promised to guide him on his pilgrimage. But it was his heart—his passion to better understand his place in the world—that Gapon admired most in his new friend. Still, even though Justin was clearly a seasoned traveler and an experienced outdoorsman, the Russian man was concerned. The plan was ambitious. Mantalai Lake lay nearly 13,500 feet in elevation in a broad, exposed saddle, with no trees for shelter or firewood to protect against wind and subfreezing temperatures. Justin was carrying neither stove nor cooking fuel in his small brown day pack, so Gapon pressed into his hand a parting gift fitting for someone who valued both practicality and minimalism: a water-resistant red butane lighter. Gapon had used it to light candles while he slept in his own mountain cave and to start the cookstove on his own trek to Mantalai Lake. Justin tucked it into his day pack.

The two men hugged, and Justin turned and began making his way up the path, quickly disappearing into the forest. The Parvati River thundered below.

2
VISIONS

Justin Alexander Shetler was born in the predawn hour of March 11, 1981, in Sarasota, Florida. The city, just south of Tampa, fringes the aquamarine water of the Gulf of Mexico and is shielded by a series of white-sand keys. Adventurous from the start, he began crawling early and adored the water—the bath, the lakeshore, the beach. His mother, Colette Susanne, who goes by Suzie, and father, Terry, enrolled him in toddler swim classes when he was three months old. Terry worked as a carpenter before eventually earning a master's in Oriental medicine, and Suzie was a teaching assistant at a Montessori school, which Justin attended for several years. In raising her son, Suzie encouraged him not only to venture into nature but to be a part of it, to sense it. She taught him to be able to differentiate between a Casuarina pine and a palm tree by touching the trunk with his eyes closed. His first pair of shoes was a tiny pair of suede moccasins that his mother had bought for him; she wanted him to feel the earth under his feet. He collected rocks in an old fishing tackle box. His mother called him "Bear."

Justin was always drawn to high places. When he was ten months old, he startled his mother by climbing halfway up a bookshelf. As he grew older, he clambered up trees, including a giant oak in a field in their neighborhood in Sarasota that they called the "family tree";

when he was upset, he would climb on top of the house and sit on the roof. It was his way to clear his head and to find calm, Suzie thought, but also a way to find perspective on the world, however small it was then, around him. Though he was an independent child, he desperately wanted the connection of a sibling.

When he was eleven, Justin's parents divorced but shared custody. He would spend the week at his mother's and the weekend at his father's. That year, the film *The Last of the Mohicans* was released, and Suzie took him out of school to see a matinee. They ended up seeing the film together seven times. For years Justin idolized the character Hawkeye, a white man adopted by a Mohican chief who gives up much of his European culture to become more connected to the natural world. It was the kind of heroic story of adventure that many young boys might gravitate to. Justin found more legendary figures to revere in books, devouring fantasy series about heroes and magic, immersing himself in fictionalized worlds. He was an introspective boy. In a notebook made of handmade paper that he kept during that time, he copied quotes from thinkers including Laozi, the Chinese philosopher traditionally seen as the author of the Tao Te Ching, and the Buddha. On one page, Justin copied what he called an unknown Chinese proverb:

Thousands upon
Thousands of rivers
Flow into the sea,
But the sea is
Never full—
And if a man could
Turn stone into gold,
Still would his heart
Never be contented.

In elementary school, he had some moments of positivity and others of great frustration. His father told him that he would support him in any way, try to help him find contentment, as long as it wouldn't put his son's life in danger. "I realized that I wasn't helping Justin deal with reality if I was putting myself between him and reality," Terry says. He never wanted to hold his son back.

Two years after the divorce, Suzie moved with her son to South Carolina and then six months later to Montana, with a new partner whom she would later marry. It was there that Justin first experienced the big wild of the American West that he had felt drawn to through books. Suzie had given him a memoir that would end up shaping much of the following decade for her son. "It lit a kind of fire," she remembers. *Grandfather: A Native American's Lifelong Search for Truth and Harmony with Nature*, published in 1993 by Tom Brown, Jr., a wilderness survival teacher from New Jersey, told the story of the author growing up under the tutelage and mentorship of a Lipan Apache scout and shaman named Stalking Wolf. "He was truly one of the ancients, part man, part animal, and almost entirely spirit," Brown wrote in the book. "His home was the wilderness, and in the wilderness he tested all things." Stalking Wolf could read nature, find medicine within plants, and track animals so closely that he could touch them. He could hide his tracks by retracing his steps backward, and effectively vanish from record. The man could walk so lightly and so skillfully through the world that he left no mark. He was there and not there, always present, yet, if he wanted, invisible.

Much of Stalking Wolf's story, as recounted by Brown, has assumed a near-mythic aura. He was born sometime in the 1880s, somewhere in the American Southwest. At ten, he embarked on his first vision quest, during which spirits presented him with the headband of a scout and the staff of a shaman. His elders showed him a path: "To follow his vision he must first spend ten winters training to become a scout, one of the most powerful positions in the tribe. He must then abandon this path for another ten winters and seek the path of a shaman and healer. And finally . . . he would have to leave his people and wander alone for sixty more winters, seeking vision and knowledge, until his vision was reality." Stalking Wolf was reluctant at first, hesitant to leave his people, until one of his elders told him that "a man not living his vision is living death."

As Justin grew older, he tore through Brown's books and wilderness guides, told through the stories of the life and accomplishments of Stalking Wolf and Brown himself. Suzie, recognizing that something was sparking in her son, would drive him to the hills near the Idaho border and watch as he disappeared into the forest with his best friend, an Indigenous boy who lived on a neighboring farm. They would hike, play in the bush, and look for animal tracks. Exactly three hours later, she would see them bounding down the hill toward her. He was never late.

After eight months in Montana, they moved farther west to a small city called Beaverton, a few miles outside Portland, Oregon. Suzie was used to relocating, having grown up in a military family. But the move was devastating for Justin. "Justin felt like he didn't have any roots because we moved," Suzie recalls. Terry remembers his son being "bitter" and "distraught" about leaving Montana. Reflecting on that period of his life, Justin once said, a touch hyperbolically, that at that point he had "probably more houses than years of life." Switching schools and moving towns as he approached teenagehood made it tough to maintain friendships, and when he began at Beaverton High School, he was a reserved young teenager and self-proclaimed loner. He found comfort in music, teaching himself to play his mother's harp, as well as mandolin and guitar. He found his greatest connection with nature.

In the summer after his freshman year, Suzie saw an ad for wilderness and outdoor survival classes in the back of the *Willamette Week* newspaper. She called the number and spoke with a woman named Chris Kenworthy, who had studied under Tom Brown, Jr., in the 1980s. Justin took several classes with Chris and thrived. He was learning, and living, what he had read in Brown's books. Before long, however, Kenworthy recognized that Justin's interests extended beyond what she could offer. She knew of a school, a nature-based educational program, outside Seattle, that might offer him an opportunity to continue to grow and engage with a like-minded community. Kenworthy called Jon Young, a cofounder of the Wilderness Awareness School and the original protégé of Tom Brown, Jr., and told him that she had been teaching a young man named Justin whom she couldn't feed fast enough.

At the end of Justin's sophomore year, Suzie recognized her son needed a change. He had been earning good grades but wasn't happy in the structure of a classroom. She offered him a deal: if he promised to complete his GED one day to earn his high school diploma, she would withdraw him and send him to be mentored by Young at the Wilderness Awareness School full-time. It was an easy decision. Suzie and Terry used Suzie's child support money to pay for Justin's room and board; Kenworthy told Suzie that Justin had also won a scholarship that would cover his tuition. In reality, unknown to Suzie at the time, for years Kenworthy paid the fees out of her own pocket.

When she dropped her son off at the Wilderness Awareness School, a few hours' drive north in the conifer forests of Washington State, in June 1997, Justin was giddy. "It was like a butterfly emerging from the cocoon," Suzie recalls. "He just blossomed and flew. It was so clear that was where he was supposed to be."

The day Justin arrived, Young was holding a class on bird language in the forest, instructing a small group about how birds will signal when a disturbance is approaching by fluttering and chirping two minutes before. As the class went silent to listen, a wave of robins and thrushes flew overhead and Young whispered to a member of the group to set a stopwatch for two minutes. As the seconds counted down, they began to hear heavy footfalls and crashing through the salmonberry bushes. As the stopwatch beeped, Justin emerged through the bracken to find the group quietly waiting for him in a semicircle. Already over six feet tall, he wore his shoulder-length, sun-tinted brown hair tied back in a ponytail. He was surprised to see the group expecting him. "Was I that obvious?" he asked. From that day forward, he vowed to become a master at walking silently in nature. "If you tell me that I needed to climb a ladder from the earth to the moon to get this level of knowledge," Justin once told Young, "I would do it right now."

That summer, Justin moved in with the Young family, who lived on the top floor of a firefighter's house in the small town of Duvall, near the plot of eighteen acres on which the school operated. Friends from the time recall his taste for wearing camouflage and earth tones, as well as his perpetual cheeky smirk and insatiable drive to learn. He officially enrolled in the Wilderness Awareness Community School, an offshoot of the WAS expressly for teenagers, that a woman named Anne Osbaldeston had cofounded. "Here's this super-lit-up kid who was so excited about everything we were doing and already knew so much," Osbaldeston recalls. "I would say at that point, at fifteen, he knew far more than I did about what we were doing." The "school" was little more than a few cabins, yurts, and tarp shelters, which had earned it the nickname "Tarpolonia." Each day brought new tasks and lessons. Bird language was a formative early class—not just identifying species by their unique calls but learning what each bird's intonation and oscillations signaled. The students studied how to craft bow drills and hand drills and employ them to make fire; build shelter in the forest that they would sleep in overnight; identify and harvest edible plants; and practice orienteering and animal tracking at a long sandbar along a nearby river. On the surface, the school was little more than a gaggle of teenagers who met outside to learn about nature, study and read about ecology, and practice wilderness survival skills. But those who attended or taught during that time look back on the school as an outlet of expression that was crucial for some teenagers who might otherwise have found themselves slipping through various social cracks. Osbaldeston places much of that at the feet of Jon Young. "It's like he's an extension cord and he's plugged into the wall and he can plug other people in," she says. "It was as though when people came to the school, they would suddenly light up, to feel connected to nature but also to really feel connected to themselves and their gifts."

Jason Knight, a few years older than Justin during that time, also boarded with the Young family; the two boys shared a bunk bed in the back of the house. They began a friendly competition, pushing each other to complete Young's Kamana Naturalist Training Program, which included completing fifty two-page species journals consisting of drawings of and observations about six different categories including plants, trees, birds, and mammals. Another set of journals that they competed to finish was based on a five-hundred-strong list of tracking observations that was like an enormous wilderness scavenger hunt. Each point was specific: tracks of a coyote standing, tracks of a coyote sitting, tracks of a coyote walking slowly, then walking fast, then galloping; coyote scat that contained mammal parts, coyote scat that contained feathers, coyote scat that contained berries or plants. And so on. "We weren't studying for a test," Knight remembers. "We were trying to learn this stuff so we'd never forget it." Justin was particularly adept at starting a fire; his hand drill set rarely left his back pocket. "It took me nine months to get my first coal," recalls Jon Young's son Aidan, who was three years Justin's junior, "and in the meantime he's just getting coals all the time." Justin challenged himself to learn how to start a fire as fast as someone with a lighter. And he did, Aidan says: "In fifteen seconds he'd have a coal."

The Wilderness Awareness School taught more than survival skills; it often used a rubric that could be applied as a holistic model to a society, a community, or a class. Jon Young came to call it 8 Shields, based on a core of the eight directions of a compass, each one with a role based on an archetype. Justin found his greatest connection in the northeast. It was represented by the sky and birds and was known as a space of great mystery, spirituality, and sacred power. In the cycle of the year, it represented late winter, with which Justin's birthday in early March aligned; in the phase of life, the northeast represented both conception and death, the period of transition and rebirth from one state to another; in the phases of a day, the northeast represented the liminal hours before dawn, in which he had been born.

At the school, Justin finally found a way to express himself as a teenager that felt natural, as well as a like-minded community of mentors and peers who included Doniga Markegard, a young woman his same age who had arrived at the school a year before Justin, in the summer of 1996. "He kind of upped the bar for everybody," she recalls. People around him often likened him to Tarzan for his independence, Rambo for his fearlessness, or He-Man for his strength. Justin was also the trickster of the group, often silently disappearing into the forest to startle the others when they weren't paying attention. But Markegard also noticed that Justin didn't take failure well and was hard on himself when he hit a wall.

Justin earned a reputation for being daring and bold, not only willing but keen to put anything on the line to achieve his goals. The teenagers often dressed in black or camouflage and tried to slink out of their house and through the doors of the twenty-four-hour QFC supermarket in the middle of town without being seen. Occasionally, they elevated the caper by calling the police on themselves with a false tip that people had been spotted lurking around suspiciously; if the group managed to evade the police, it was a particularly celebrated achievement. "I don't think we ever got spotted," Aidan Young recalls.

"Justin was definitely more of a risk taker," Knight remembers. "There was a subset of teens in these programs that wanted to push themselves so hard that they would go barefoot all the time and wear T-shirts and shorts all winter even though it was cold." Justin fit into that subset. After he heard of a legendary challenge that entailed holding a mouthful of water while running fifteen miles without swallowing, unbeknownst to many at the time, he began waking up well before dawn to practice until he achieved the feat. And when an arborist held a lecture at the school, Justin was spellbound as the man demonstrated how after years of training he had learned to fall out of a tree and land safely on the ground by grabbing and releasing branches to gradually slow his descent. The next day, Justin climbed a towering cedar and, near the top, let go. As he tumbled through the branches, he missed several grabs, ragdolled the last twenty feet, and slammed headfirst into the ground, narrowly avoiding cracking his skull open on a pile of rocks. "He should've been dead," Aidan Young says. Justin could be brazen and reckless, but had usually walked away nearly unscathed. "Be careful what you say in front of him" was a common remark among his instructors.

Linne Doran ("Pond of the Otter" in Gaelic) was a focal point of the Wilderness Awareness School. It is a clear, shallow pond with fallen trees visible on the muddy bottom. Around the edge of the pond was where many students selected their "sit spot," returning day after day to a single place to observe and record the natural changes and fluctuations around them. "It seems so simple," says Osbaldeston. "Go sit in a spot in nature every day at different times of day for different amounts of time." But, she explains, the practice gave the students the ability to connect with a place on a profoundly deep level, which, the thinking goes, in turn allowed the place to begin to accept a person into it, as if into a home. It was an ability, Osbaldeston noticed, that many students carried wherever they went in the world. Knight's sit spot was near the creek that spilled out of the pond; Justin's was on top of an old cedar stump on a spur of land jutting out into the water. Some days he brought birdseed that he held in an outstretched hand; the chickadees eventually grew used to him and would happily dart in to eat before flitting away.

"Justin was the prodigy," Aidan Young says, adding that he fit into a lineage that went all the way back to Stalking Wolf. It extended to his physical presence. He was tall and lanky but fit and strong. And his blue eyes left a mark on people. "They were wolf's eyes," Young notes; the only other person he had ever met who had the same eyes was Tom Brown, Jr. "They had that kind of intensity to them."

After two years, Jon Young realized that there was another step for Justin across the country at the epicenter of wilderness education: the Tracker School. Tom Brown, Jr., had founded the school in 1978 in the Pine Barrens of southeastern New Jersey, where, based out of a place called "Primitive Camp," he had trained thousands in survivalism, wilderness awareness, and tracking. Over decades, he not only had established a reputation as an erudite teacher but had built a fierce following of pupils who honed their practical skills and imbibed his philosophy of nature awareness. Brown's legendary story as a tracker and survivalist educator, often recounted in his books and lectures, began in the 1950s. When he was seven, he met a boy of around the same age while out fossil hunting along a creek. The boy, named Rick, introduced Brown to his grandfather, the Lipan Apache tracker and shaman named Stalking Wolf. "He gave us the questions that would lead to our answers, but he never told us an answer," Brown wrote. "He taught me to see and to hear, to walk and to remain silent; he taught me how to be patient and resourceful, how to know and how to understand." At eighteen, Brown decided to put the skills he had learned to a test. He discarded his belongings and clothing and walked naked into the Pine Barrens. He survived by building shelters and living off the land, and emerged an entire year later. "I went into the Barrens naked and I came out 20 pounds heavier, totally relaxed, twice as strong, in tremendous shape," Brown told *National Wildlife* magazine in 1984. Through feats like these Brown's reputation spread, and local authorities began hiring him to help track on-the-run suspects of crimes that ranged from armed robbery to rape. He helped solve several missing-persons cases. After the *New York Times* published an article about one case, Brown was asked to write a book, which he published in 1978. *The Tracker: The True Story of Tom Brown, Jr.* resonated within a particular cohort of people who were feeling a growing disconnect with nature and looking to learn how to reforge their bond with it. The same year the book was released, Brown founded the Tracker School.

As year after year students flocked there to take his courses, Brown was catapulted into legendary status in survival circles. His skills at tracking and scouting were undeniable, but critics have pointed out his appropriation of Native American culture and theology. Some have called him a "plastic shaman." Brown's foundational myth, the story of Stalking Wolf, who died when Brown was a teenager, has also been questioned by many skeptical readers about how much the man had taught Brown and how much had been derived from other individuals or traditions. Most students didn't care, and the stories inspired many thousands of people, including Justin.

In the summer of 1999, Jon Young brought Justin and Markegard, two of his most gifted students, to the school and presented them as the next generation of elite wilderness survivalists. They took a series of introductory classes but were also allowed to dip into and out of more advanced classes at will and live on the Tracker School's land. Justin was based there for a year and a half, during which he completed a dozen courses. Many of the adult students, and even some of the school's instructors, were astonished by his ability and dedication at eighteen.

Many students who came to the Tracker School had a yearning to tap into something bigger. According to several former students, the school also had a darker side that attracted people who were renouncing their lives and looking for a place of support, a place to feel grounded and connected. Dan Stanchfield, who became a mentor of Justin at the school, fit into that cohort. Originally from California, he had been living on a church compound in Iowa, indoctrinated into a community of followers of the Church of the Living Word, also known as the Living Word Fellowship, which he now calls a "nondenominational Christian cult." He abandoned the church in 1995 and, after reading *The Tracker*, embraced a new community at the Tracker School. "Our minds want to create meaning out of everything, our life has to have meaning," Stanchfield says. "And that causes people to fall into so many traps. Life is much simpler than we want to believe it is, but we won't know for sure about anything until we get to the other side." Of the thousands who attended the Tracker School in the 1990s, some came to learn hard survival skills as a way of connecting with primitive traditions, some came simply to escape, and some came to connect with its nature-based spirituality and philosophy.

Tracy Frey, a recent college graduate who became a close friend of Justin at the school, recalls the spiritual elements at the school as prominent, taught side by side with the practical skills. "It is a beacon for lost boys," she says. "It gets them so close to finding something that's actually internal, but not quite. And then they get further lost, because it's so confusing." Justin arrived with a deep and strongly held spiritualism, a belief in the possibility of a bigger current—"The spirit that moves in all things," as it was called in those circles. "He fundamentally believed that there were a lot of people in the world who closed themselves off to this possibility, and he was not going to be one of those people."

Justin had been raised in a religiously fluid and open household. His father, Terry, had been brought up Mennonite on a small farm in

Pennsylvania but had quickly moved away from the faith and, like many in the early 1970s, became exposed to Eastern spirituality and philosophy. After graduating high school, he went to southern California to live in a "hippie commune," where, as he remembers, he did a lot of peyote, acid, and pot. "It was definitely a heavily spiritual experience," he says. In 1972, at the age of nineteen, he was drafted into the air force during the Vietnam War and repaired radio and radar equipment and air-data computers for fighter planes. Two years later, just before picking up his discharge papers, he drove out to Red Rocks Park near the base in Colorado at which he was stationed, climbed up the giant boulders, and watched the sunrise. "Sitting on top of that rock, it looked like you could see to Omaha," he recalls. "The whole great plain stretched out in front of me. And as the sun came up, I just had this vision." He realized that he had been living behind a veil, that he could live in awe all the time if only he could remove the filters.

Terry moved to Sarasota, stopped using drugs, and began a path toward a black belt in the martial art aikido. He also became a vegetarian, moved into an ashram, and started taking yoga classes at a center of the Light of Yoga Society, an organization founded in 1971 that is now the American Yoga Association. For years he practiced yoga for three hours every day. In the summer of 1977, the society organized a trip to India, in which Terry and around forty other Americans flew to Delhi before traveling to Kashmir, where they stayed on houseboats floating on Dal Lake in the capital of Srinagar and toured Hindu sites. "It was eye opening for me in a lot more ways than one," Terry says. The group spent a month in Kashmir, in India's north, where Terry visited Shankaracharya Temple, a hilltop shrine outside Srinigar dedicated to Shiva, and made offerings before a five-foot-tall, glossy black stone lingam, a phallic object that represents the god's generative energy. He performed the rituals and then took a seat within the sanctum of the temple. What happened next shaped the rest of his life. "It was the strongest experience I've ever had," he says. "It just hit me. It was an overwhelming experience that came from being in the presence of that rock." It was both physical and cerebral. "Instead of seeing what I thought was there, it said, 'Well, why don't you look to see what's really there? *See* what's here, don't *know* what's here and try to confirm it.'" He walked down the steps from the temple a believer and looks back on that trip as the pivotal moment in his life. In Justin's family home in Florida, before his parents divorced, the Indian influences remained: on the walls his father had pinned posters of Hindu gods, including Saraswati, the goddess of music and knowledge, and Rama, the principal figure in the Hindu epic the Ramayana, who symbolized individual duty, honor, and responsibility—dharma, the cosmic order of life, the right way to live. There was also a small altar covered in a silk scarf on which Terry had placed a copper vase filled with water, an incense burner, and an idol of Ganesha, the adored elephant-headed god, in front of which he continued to practice meditation, yoga, and read Hindu texts.

The spiritual influence from Justin's mother came largely through Eckankar, a faith that Suzie had belonged to for much of her life. The religion was established in 1965 by an American, Paul Twitchell, based on the belief that every person's soul is eternal, born again and again into a new body. Twitchell gathered seeds from faiths and spiritual teachers around the world, including the notions of karma and reincarnation from Hinduism, creating a religion in which each person can manifest his or her own destiny, through spiritual experiences, to become closer to God. Suzie raised her son under the principles of Eckankar, and of the teachers upon which the faith drew Justin took a keen interest in Laozi, who, as the story was recounted, lived in a mountain cave in the Himalayas, where he meditated for years. Visions and dreams were considered a guiding force to be listened to, respected, and written down immediately upon waking. When Justin was young, he kept a dream journal, replaced by nature journals in his later teenage years.

Suzie never pressured her son to follow her particular path. "Go find your own truth," she would tell him, "because you have to walk in this world yourself." And he did. During his two years at the Wilderness Awareness School, Native American spirituality and philosophy were a constant presence through visiting elders. Gilbert Walking Bull, a Lakota man and the great-grandson of the legendary Sitting Bull, established ceremonial grounds near the school and provided experiences with sweat lodges and spirit quests to the students. "We were studying nature during the week, and on the weekends we were studying spirituality with Gilbert Walking Bull," recalls Doniga Markegard. At the Tracker School, Justin consumed the worldview of Tom Brown, Jr., and Stalking Wolf firsthand rather than in the pages of books. The story of Stalking Wolf—an archetypal wise master who takes up a student and passes on the wisdom of the world—resonated strongly with Justin, as did the notion of a vision quest.

Like Stalking Wolf before him, Brown had embarked on his own quest, as he wrote in *The Vision: The Dramatic True Story of One Man's Search for Enlightenment*. "With each passing event, things became clearer, questions about myself were answered, and I felt a deep connection to that self," Brown wrote. "I suddenly knew who I was, where I was going, and what I really wanted to do in life. There was no more pain or discomfort, my mind no longer fought the imprisonment of the quest, but rather it expanded to become that quest, that wilderness." Brown walked out of the Pine Barrens on the fourth day of his vision quest a changed man. He had seen his way forward: "I needed to choose a pure reality filled with excitement, adventure, and intensity—a life of rapture rather than a life of comfort, security, and boredom like everyone else was choosing." Stalking Wolf and Tom Brown, Jr., had lives of parable and fable, of great deeds seeking greater understanding. Their stories were not only mythic but cosmic. And they were passed on to thousands of young readers such as Justin who had open and insatiable appetites to understand what lies beneath the surface of life.

What he learned at the wilderness schools crystallized into a new worldview in which nature is more than the sum of its individual parts, more than any tree or creature or being, a connectivity that, as Brown wrote, "can be seen best in the flow of its interactions." The goal—through sit spots, awareness training, and study—is to be able to see those connections. "Trying to live a spiritual life in modern society is the most difficult path one can walk," Stalking Wolf once said, as quoted by Brown. "It is a path of pain, of isolation and of shaken faith, but that is the only way that our Vision can become reality. Thus the true Quest in life is to live the philosophy of the Earth within the confines of man. There is no church or temple we need to seek peace, for ours are the temples of the wilderness."

For years, Justin lived and breathed these philosophical and spiritual perspectives. Both his mother in Oregon and his father in Florida fully supported his path. Nature, Terry felt, was the best teacher. Still, even from across the country, Terry noticed that his son was pushing himself into increasingly risky situations to see what he could find at the extremes. "It was spirituality that you get from the near-death experience. Justin realized at a very early age that he could get that kind of experience from doing things that were dangerous," Terry says. "Every time you face death and you win, you're more alive."

During Justin's first summer at the Tracker School, he was brought on to help teach in a new program, the first one geared toward kids, called Coyote Tracks. Tracy Frey led the youth program. "I wasn't going to spend hours and hours studying a single track or sitting for that long," she says. "It was never going to be me, but it was Justin." Justin inhabited every role: mentor, instructor, survivalist. "He was perfectly comfortable in all of his skins," says fellow instructor Brittany Ceres, "so it was very easy for him to put on one of these skins and see it to the absolute fullest." One of Justin's young students at the time was Liam Purvis, who recalls Justin often emphasizing that "pushing the edge" of ability and comfort would spark greater understanding of the world.

"Safety, security, and comfort are euphemisms for death," Tom Brown, Jr., often said during classes, former instructor Tom McElroy remembers, and it was a maxim Justin didn't just hear but put into action. "When my greater fear told me no, Justin would just go for something," he says. Justin grew close to McElroy, a twenty-one-year-old instructor at the Tracker School who had a few years of taking and teaching classes under his belt when Justin arrived. They bonded fast and often embarked on multiday animal-tracking expeditions in the Pine Barrens. He remembers that Justin was starry-eyed about Brown's philosophy, holding a well-formed idealism about living off the land as well as what pushing yourself to extremes might reveal. Many friends from that time remember that the instructors lodged in a large cottage, an old Boy Scout camp, and that one winter Justin sought a test. "We all have these nice rooms in the lodge but Justin, just outside the front door, built a little leaf hut that he would sleep in, even in the middle of snowstorms," McElroy recalls.

When not based in New Jersey, Justin traveled with Jon Young and a group of students to assist in wilderness awareness classes around the United States. In Idaho, they taught a class on wolf tracking and were hired to collect data on wolves that had been released in the state. Justin used every day, every opportunity, to test himself and glean as much as he could from the instructors, his pupils, and the land around him. He just wanted to learn, and if he felt someone could offer him something, he would open himself to it. It was a side of him that Frey felt protective of, like an older sibling; in an end-of-class note scribbled in one of Frey's Tracker School notebooks, Justin called her "the big sister I never had." "People got him to do all kinds of stuff, because he would do it," she says. "I always wanted to make sure he was safe."

In August 2000, Young, along with Markegard, Knight, and Justin, were scheduled to return to Idaho to continue the wolf census. Justin was driving Knight's pickup truck along Interstate 80 in Nebraska with one of Young's daughters in the passenger seat and Knight sleeping in the bed of the truck under a canopy. Knight remembers being jolted awake. "It felt like being in a blender," he recalls. The truck was flipping and rolling. "I don't remember how I ended up on the side of the highway," he says. Knight ran to the vehicle, which lay on the driver's side, and as he began assisting the young woman from the cab they spotted a semitruck barreling down the highway toward them. They jumped from the wreck to safety seconds before the semi hit the overturned truck with Justin still inside, carrying it hundreds of feet down the highway. They ran down to the wreck. After seeing Justin pinned inside the pancaked cab,

"We thought he was dead," Knight recalls. The state trooper who had arrived on the scene said that over his career he had never seen someone survive a car wreck that bad. Knight remembers Justin writhing and screaming with pain at the hospital. He had fractured vertebrae in his back and sustained a head wound that required fifteen staples. His body was covered in cuts from the shattered windshield glass.

When he returned to Oregon to recover, he confided in his mother that as the driver of the truck, he felt guilty that he had put his friends in danger. He didn't remember what had happened in the seconds leading up to the crash. That particular stretch of highway had a history of deer collisions, the state trooper had told Knight, but Justin agonized over the possibility that he had momentarily fallen asleep. He told his mother that he had thought he had died and was being brought back—that in that moment of purgatory someone or something had told him that this wasn't his time to die. It shook him. As he recuperated from his injuries, he became more brooding and reflective.

Justin spent only a few weeks convalescing at home before joining the tail end of the wolf-tracking trip in Idaho and then returning to the Tracker School. His long hair had been buzzed, revealing the staples in his skull, but Frey could see that the accident had left more than just physical scars. She remembers holding him for an hour the day he returned, reassuring him that it was okay to take time to heal as he cried. He barely talked for days. "This was the first time that he realized he wasn't invincible," in McElroy's estimation.

The accident also marked a dramatic turning point in Justin's spirituality. "He was constantly given the message that he had a higher calling, and a higher purpose," says Frey. "And then he almost dies." In the wake of the crash, he began to abandon everything he had believed in. "There was an emptiness inside of him that he couldn't fill, and he kept searching further and further and further," Aidan Young believes. "He was so skilled and so brilliant that he could do anything, but I think he was looking for something on Earth that ultimately was missing inside—and trying to fix it from the outside in. It was after that accident that it started, that he felt totally lost." The incident might have brought him closer to the divine and turned him into more of a believer, but instead Justin lost faith, becoming cynical about the existence of any form of higher power, which he long felt had been looking out for him. It marked a final push away from Eckankar, his mother recalls, and fully onto his own path to spiritual fulfillment. One day, when he had laid at home recovering, he had said, "God is too big for me." The concept was too overwhelming, too enormous for him to get his head around. "He wasn't able to embrace it," Suzie says. "He couldn't frame it. He didn't have a context."

The accident stayed with him in other ways. Every so often, a piece of windshield glass that had been embedded under his skin rose to the surface. The first few times it happened, he visited a doctor to have the shards excised. Eventually, he would hand a friend a piece of obsidian that had been knapped razor sharp to cut it out. The trauma from the accident lingered. "It's like he couldn't escape this thing that called everything into question for him," Frey recalls. Aidan Young observed that Justin had never shed his role as a mentor and positive influence. "But the thing for me that changed," he says, "and I never saw it again, was that twinkle in his eye. His default had been always happy. After that accident, I never saw that person again."

Justin trained his focus on finding a new kind of freedom. He could go anywhere with the skills he had learned. While working in New Jersey, he lived out of his car or in a primitive camp in the woods and would take the train to New York City to visit museums, where he would study Native American artifacts and history and scribble observations and notes into his journals. He sometimes slept the night in Central Park. He began searching to find the small, tangible pieces of knowledge that he could understand and digest and feel, pieces that would make up something bigger than himself. "In some ways, before that," Frey says, "he may not have ever really questioned his place in his life or on the Earth—or however you want to describe it." She believes Justin would have led an adventurous life without such a forced reckoning but that the accident amplified the intensity. "It gave it all more meaning. Maybe there was also some added seeking: 'What is it that kept me on this Earth?'"

LET IT GO

Justin spent three years based in New Jersey teaching and studying wilderness skills at the Tracker School. While on the East Coast, he visited his father in Sarasota more often than before. In Florida, he took a course in massage therapy while working as a server at a Chili's restaurant and even nervously worked a few shifts as a stripper. "That was the most lost I had seen him," Tracy Frey recalls. Then, in 2003, he and a group of friends, including Frey, Markegard, and McElroy, moved to California. Justin landed in Redwood City, a leafy community an hour south of San Francisco, where he ended up living for six years, sharing a house with a new group of friends. He got a job at the Riekes Center, a community space for kids and teenagers that offered after-school programs in physical education, art, music, and eventually the kinds of wilderness skills that Justin had been mastering. "He was the consummate mentor," says founder Gary Riekes. "He listened and cared deeply, almost to a fault, about people less fortunate than him." Aaron Alvarez was a freshman at a high school nearby when he met Justin at the Riekes Center; his school didn't have a playground or field, so he began taking classes at the center every afternoon. The youngest child in his family, Alvarez had moved from Mexico to California when he was thirteen. Justin took him under his wing. "From the Riekes Center's point of view, he was my mentor," Alvarez says. "From my point of view, he was more of a brother." On weekends, Justin took him camping with his friends. It was a relationship that Alvarez feels "changed the course of my universe" and provided a mentorship that became a sanctuary from any kind of violence or darker paths that he could've been caught up in. The pressure of joining a gang at that time was real, Alvarez remembers.

They often had long talks about books. In school, Alvarez had been assigned to read *Siddhartha*, Hermann Hesse's 1922 novel set in South Asia during the time of the Buddha. Siddhartha, a handsome and strong young man, the son of a high-caste family, is unsatisfied and restless. He seeks knowledge and spiritual connection and so abandons his privilege and his belongings and steps onto the long road of a wandering ascetic. He wants to rid himself of both pain and pleasure, to find simplicity and meaning. He fasts and meditates and studies to bring him closer to achieving nirvana, to finding the "right way." He visits the Buddha, and although he hears and treasures the sermons of the "Illustrious One" and watches others become followers, Siddhartha does not. Instead, he realizes that his own path is distinct and that he must begin anew without looking back. But Siddhartha becomes tempted and distracted by both sex and money and for a time veers off his path onto one of comfort and affluence. Years pass, and a weariness grows in his heart, and a feeling of being trapped by his worldly possessions and power. One evening, he returns to the forest and to the path, remade once again into a youth. He makes his way to a river that he had crossed once before as an ascetic and decides to stay with the ferryman. There he begins to see the unity, the interconnectedness of nature, and that, as the ferryman says, "the river is everywhere at the same time, at the source and at the mouth, at the waterfall, at the ferry, at the current, in the ocean and in the mountains, everywhere, and that the present only exists for it, not the shadow of the past, nor the shadow of the future." He remains for the rest of his days beside the river, in a liminal space between two worlds, helping others cross from one side to the other.

Alvarez had been brought up Christian but was curious about the themes in the book. He remembers that Justin, who knew the story inside and out, had shared how deeply he connected with Siddhartha's tension between a life of privilege and a life of asceticism, and his desire to find his own unique path toward higher understanding. "I remember that he was always trying to search for enlightenment," Alvarez says. "That's what his term was." Justin felt that by understanding, studying, and experiencing other people's beliefs, he would accumulate the knowledge he needed to be able to tap into something bigger than himself. Gary Riekes saw Justin's path, in part, as a spiritual one but also one that was altruistic. "He also had a naivete to him, with how he saw the world and how he trusted people," he says. "He wanted to do good, and see the good, in this world."

2006 was a pivotal year for Justin. That summer, a local high school, in association with the Riekes Center, embarked on a class trip to Nepal to film a documentary about cultural exchange called *Namaste Nepal*. Justin joined as the crew's medic after earning a certification as a wilderness emergency medical technician. The group of American students and teachers visited temples in Kathmandu and trekked into the Annapurna Mountains. It was during that time that Justin began reopening himself to spiritual experiences. In Kathmandu, he witnessed the mystical sides of Buddhism when he met a lama, a Buddhist monk, who was believed to be the reincarnation of the grandfather of the group's guide. Later in the trip, he visited a cave above Ngawal village in the Annapurnas that was said to contain a self-arisen image of Padmasambhava, the legendary Indian Buddhist master also known as Guru Rinpoche.

While the group was in Ngawal, tragedy nearly struck when a local toddler fell out of a second-story window and cracked her head on the cobblestones below. Everyone panicked. Justin picked her up and, with the permission of her family, ran with her to the nearest clinic, in the village of Manang, more than six miles away along a rough mountain trail. To hike it, as some trekkers who are looking for an alternate and less crowded route do, typically takes around five hours. Justin and twenty-four-year-old Kishwor Sedhai, one of the group's Nepali guides who accompanied him, completed it in around half the time. They arrived in Manang, Justin cradling the toddler in his arms, and handed her off to the doctors. The girl was flown to Pokhara, the nearest city, where she made a full recovery.

The trip opened Justin's eyes to a wider world and gave him a new sense of purpose. He quickly began planning his first solo international trip, traveling to Thailand that winter. While on a train from Bangkok to the northern city of Chiang Mai, he met Sitthikorn Thepchanta, who was then working as a tourist guide. Justin asked if he knew where he could train in Muay Thai kickboxing, and Thepchanta found him a trainer and an apartment to rent. Every morning during the two months Justin spent in Chiang Mai, the new friends would jog to the Muay Thai camp together and train. Thepchanta then invited Justin to visit his home in a small village outside the northern city of Lampang. While staying at the family home, surrounded by thick jungle and iridescent rice paddies, Justin was in his element. "He absolutely loved it," remembers Thepchanta, whose father took Justin fishing and whose mother took him chili pepper picking and showed him how to cook green chicken curry. Eventually, Justin asked Thepchanta if he could call his parents Mom and Dad as well. They were thrilled. "I've never had a *farang* son before, so why not!" Thepchanta recalls his father saying, using the Thai word for someone who is white.

"We talked about Buddhism a lot," Thepchanta recalls. Justin was drawn to the notion that a good life comes not from prayer but from positive action and that one's ego must be controlled. While visiting a Buddhist temple in the region, he spoke with a monk "about how to stay calm, and how to deal with your life issues, how to deal with emotions," Thepchanta remembers. Justin appreciated Buddhism's acceptance of suffering and pain as an innate part of life and the idea of a path that leads through the accumulation of knowledge and the renunciation of desires to liberation from this suffering. He asked how one might become a Buddhist monk, and Thepchanta mentioned options for curious backpackers to partake in a ceremony in Chiang Mai where they shaved their heads and lived like monks in a temple for as little as a few days. Justin dismissed that as too touristy. When Thepchanta mentioned Justin's interest to his parents, they offered a more appealing option, taking him to their local head monk to receive a blessing so he could become a monk in their village. Justin threw himself into the process. He learned prayers and memorized 222 rules that he had to recite in Pali, the sacred language of Theravada Buddhism. On January 1, 2007, he passed the daylong initiation process and became a Buddhist monk. Around eight hundred people from the village attended the ceremony, Thepchanta recalls.

Every day for nearly a month after the ceremony, Justin would rise well before dawn, don orange robes, and practice chanting. According to tradition, Buddhist monks don't cook for themselves but instead rely on donations from the community. So after his chores at the temple, he would walk barefoot around the village and people would place a small portion of rice or curry into a large silver bowl in exchange for a blessing for good health. Thepchanta's parents were honored that their "son" was the first foreigner in the village to become a monk. "It was very special for the people in the area," he says. "They loved him. They loved to see this. They loved to see a total stranger from the Western world interested in their daily life and Buddhism."

Justin and Thepchanta formed a strong bond that would last a decade. Justin would continue to return to Thailand and to the village and what he called his "adoptive family" regularly, even after Thepchanta moved away to work in Australia. Justin would show up and immediately be invited into a family home for dinner. "He'd be on the floor eating sticky rice, eating bamboo shoot curry, eating grilled chicken, eating pork curry with them," Thepchanta says. "Over the years, he became a part of the community."

Justin's experiences abroad influenced his life back home in the United States. In the fall of 2006 he had responded to a Craigslist ad posted by a guitar player and a bass player who were looking for a lead singer. Justin had been musical since he was a boy, and over the years he had casually written songs and performed at talent shows at the Tracker School. Adding a drummer, the foursome formed a band that billed itself as "If Incubus, Tool and The Red Hot Chili Peppers had a musical orgy, blacked out, and woke up the next morning, standing there would be PUNCHFACE, the high-energy alternative rock band from the San Francisco Bay Area." Over the following two years, while Justin continued to work at the Riekes Center, Punchface played gigs around the Bay Area, beginning at church celebrations and town square festivals and eventually booking shows at clubs. Justin was the consummate rock front man, strutting for the crowd and putting every bead of sweat he could muster into each performance. The band released its first album, *A Different Kind of Fame*, in 2007. The music video of its song "Celebrate" was stitched together with fan photographs from celebrations around the world and went on to be viewed more than 100,000 times on YouTube—no small feat for a regional band on a video-sharing platform that had launched only two years prior.

Justin was Punchface's lyricist and, like many songwriters, dropped hints as to his true feelings. In "Liberate," he wrote about feeling trapped:

> *I am an elephant shackled to a short chain*
> *When I was young I strived to define my range*
> *Pushed and pulled, found struggle was bringin' me pain.*

In "Firefly," he alluded to concepts he had been introduced to in Nepal and Thailand—of minimalism, reincarnation, and enlightenment:

> *I choose a life, a life beyond me*
> *But first must rid myself of all*
> *So there is nothing to impede*
> *And I'm unstoppable*

To fall, to lose, to die, unleash, be reborn
So I'm dying to let this
Firefly, illuminate my mind
Find a place in me to reside
Light me from the inside.

"Everyone who played music in the Bay Area knew Punchface," according to Layla Brooklyn Allman, a daughter of Gregg Allman, the lead singer and songwriter of the Allman Brothers Band. She first met Justin when she was twelve and singing at a church center in Redwood City. At the time she was trying to step out of her father's shadow by writing her own songs and performing, but she kept hitting a wall of people who assumed that she had earned any recognition or any stage because of her parentage. "Justin was really kind to me at a time when other musicians weren't," she remembers. "They thought I was a rock star daughter who had everything handed to her." Justin, however, saw her as a talented young musician and singer. When Punchface booked a gig, he often ensured that Allman and her band opened for them—including at Bottom of the Hill, one of San Francisco's foremost indie rock venues. Justin embraced his new image, often appearing onstage in a muscle tee with a bandanna around his neck, and with fake tattoos: a sunrise on his right shoulder or the word LIBERATE along his arm.

In January 2009, Punchface toured Japan, playing about a dozen shows. Through the following spring and summer, the band consistently played gigs around San Francisco, including an EP release party at Bottom of the Hill that March. Allman was impressed by Justin's tenacity and dedication: "He meant business. It wasn't a hobby. You could tell this guy wanted to do this for a living." A local magazine noted, "To their fans it may seem like the band has gone from 0 to 60 in 10 seconds flat, going from sweating it out in a small practice space to being a band that can pack big venues overnight." Their live performances arguably peaked onstage at Slim's, a legendary venue that has hosted Green Day, the Black Keys, and Radiohead. Punchface filled the six-hundred-person-capacity venue.

But the band's decline was as precipitous as its rise. Fractures began to appear, and by the end of 2009, Punchface had largely dissolved. Justin took it as a personal failure. His most serious romantic relationship until that point, with a Japanese woman he had met on tour—a relationship that had led to a surprise engagement—was also ending over pressure to find a more prestigious job. The breakup of his engagement was devastating, his mother recalls. Justin had been slow to start dating. Although he had had a few relationships in his twenties, this was the first time he had committed so fully and openly.

In early 2010, Robert Gutierrez, an entrepreneur based in Miami, met Justin through mutual friends in San Francisco. Justin struck him as confused and floating, trying to pursue a career in the navy, training by swimming and running every day. "He was in the process of moving from his life into what he thought was going to be a SEAL team member," Gutierrez remembers. Some friends were under the impression that Justin was ultimately turned down because he had never acquired his GED; others heard that at twenty-nine, he was considered too old. Gutierrez recalls dissuading Justin from joining the military, pointing to its lack of freedom and flexibility. Justin made such a strong first impression on Gutierrez that he offered Justin a job: to move to Miami and work for a startup he had founded called iProof, which offered services to both brands and consumers to track and authenticate high-value goods prone to counterfeiting, from luxury clothing to expensive bottles of wine, using RFID tags or QR codes. The position was attractive, to be the traveling face of the organization marketing and promoting the brand abroad. "Why not take a chance?" Gutierrez recalls asking him. Justin accepted, abruptly quit his job at the Riekes Center, and relocated to Miami. He was based there for nearly three years, renting an apartment in South Beach, a neighborhood bustling with nightlife, palm trees on every corner, and aquamarine water and white sand always a short walk away.

Justin would often spend six weeks straight on the road with Gutierrez on round-the-globe trips, flitting from Miami to Los Angeles, across the Pacific Ocean to Australia, then up to China, across to Italy and France, and back to the United States. They pitched the business in meetings with representatives of wine labels in Australia, apparel companies including Zegna, Dior, Armani, and Louis Vuitton, and Britney Spears's perfume. The job was a departure for Justin, one that offered endless opportunities to see the world and a salary on which he could eat at Michelin-starred restaurants and stay in luxury hotels. For someone like Tracy Frey, who had remained friends with him in San Francisco, the transformation was surprising but his devotion to his new life was not. "He stepped into that persona and didn't come out for a while," she says. "It wasn't fleeting. It wasn't like he shrugged it off when he got home at night. He was all in." It was a transformation and a dedication of a kind many friends had witnessed before, from survivalist living in his car to band front man, from calm mentor to wild partier. "He put aside the nature man and began traveling the world high style," his mother says. He traded his band clothes for suits, his outdoor survival gear for luxury watches and shoes. But Suzie also remembers him often calling her in confusion. "Am I selling out?" he would ask. He would update her on his job and the latest cities he had traveled to—Beijing, Paris, Milan, Sydney—the exclusive clubs he had partied at, and the extravagant lifestyle he could now afford. Suzie would laugh and tell him that it didn't matter what he was doing as long as he felt happy and was being true to himself. But she could tell something was missing, something unresolved that was moving toward the surface.

He felt guilty about his newfound affluence. When Suzie visited him in Miami once, she came across paperwork that revealed he had been supporting a number of foster children, as well as sending money to his "adoptive" family in Thailand and to several people in Nepal, including Bishal Kapali, whom Justin had met in Kathmandu while playing pickup street soccer and whom he had financially helped open a shop there. They shared a "natural connection," Kapali felt, as if they "had known each other for a long time." In spite of the age difference—Kapali was fourteen when they met—the chance encounter sparked a friendship that would last years. "He became my godfather," Kapali says. "Whatever I am right now, it's all because of him."

Although Justin loved being on the road, it frustrated him that he never had the chance to connect with the people or cultures of the places he traveled to. Often, while on a business trip, he would leave Gutierrez on a Friday only to show up for a Monday morning meeting with stories of sleeping in a cheap hostel somewhere, meeting backpackers in clubs and bars, and exploring a city in the middle of the night. "He wanted to have that young mentality, to be energized by interactions with younger people," Gutierrez says; in 2011, Justin turned thirty. "He didn't like the idea of getting old."

During a business trip to Milan, Justin connected with Stefano Vergari, a photographer who showed him around the city. They kept in touch regularly and crossed paths in person whenever they could; Vergari recalls Justin once referring to him as one of his best friends, a comment that surprised the Italian man, considering that they lived on different continents. Vergari remembers Justin becoming increasingly dissatisfied with his well-paid job and his life in Miami, lamenting that "the dark side was tempting me." He told Vergari that he felt stuck on a path that wasn't truly fulfilling, that he wanted a new life. Justin once sent him the Wikipedia page for *Memento mori*—Latin for "Remember that you must die"—a term commonly used to describe a symbol that represents the inevitability of death. He had come across the phrase while exploring catacombs during a business trip in Paris and had been taken with the concept.

Gutierrez recalls a moment when Justin had opened up to him about his future. "I'm not going to live past forty," he had said. He could never visualize what his life might look like after that, whether he felt fulfilled in his job—or would in any job—or if he wanted a long-term relationship and a family. While living in Miami, he met Ashley Keenan on the dating site OkCupid, and they ended up seeing each other for around a year. When Justin wasn't abroad for work, they practically lived together at her apartment. He adored her young son; on Easter morning he left rabbit footprints in flour around the apartment for the toddler to excitedly follow. Keenan's life was grounded and balanced, but a divide grew every time Justin went on the road. She felt there was something deep down that he was struggling to work on emotionally. When he talked about having a family of his own, he imagined having a child with whom he could travel the world, which struck Keenan as a fantasy. "He did live in between these two worlds. He wanted to be the husband who stayed at home and was great with kids, but he also couldn't be that guy." She could tell he was wrestling with questions of identity, who he was and what he wanted. "It wasn't so much that he was a complicated person," she says. "He had so much internal struggle that he was just constantly in pain."

Keenan admired that outwardly Justin always tried to find good in anyone, but it worried her that he would sometimes blindly accept people into his life. She could see in him a tendency to trust people he shouldn't. "That person is not worthy of your friendship, not worthy of your time," she would tell him. Justin told her once that a "little brother" living in Nepal was opening a shop in Kathmandu and he wanted to send him money to help. "How do you know what he's going to do with the money?" she asked.

"I don't know," Justin responded.

"What happens if you find out that the shop doesn't exist?"

"Well, that's okay, too."

When she asked him if he could live with being wrong, with his trust being misplaced, his answer was always yes.

Their relationship ended in the fall of 2013. Justin was feeling depressed about work: after nearly three years based in Miami, the glitz of the salary and lifestyle his job afforded had worn off. "There's some people in this world you can say that in high school he knew he was going to get married, have two kids, be an insurance agent, and become president of the company," Gutierrez says. "And that guy puts his head down and nothing is going to get in his way. Justin wasn't like that. The only thing that Justin really focused on was adventure."

That summer, Justin traveled to Thailand once again to visit his "adoptive family," and he posted online about teaching wilderness survival to a US Marine Corps Scout Sniper platoon that had given him a plaque in gratitude. "With sincere thanks and appreciation for all of your hard work, professionalism and truly world class instruction," the plaque read. "We are better professionals from all that you have taught us . . . and we look cooler in front of the ladies." The words must have felt personally gratifying: though he had seen his dream of joining the Navy SEALs evaporate, he had been asked to train a platoon of marines in bushcraft and survival.

At thirty-two, Justin was feeling restless. His window of traveling the world the way he wanted was closing, he believed; he could live for years off the sizable nest egg he had saved. He called his father and said he felt that his life was speeding away from under him, that he was losing control of his destiny, becoming more successful by typical standards of measure yet less happy with every passing day. From teenagehood onward, he had had an inconsistent relationship with his father. For long periods of time, they had been distant and estranged. His parents' divorce—the years after which, Suzie believed, had been "rough" for her son—was a split based largely on trust that had degraded. From a young age, Suzie says, Justin had known that his father had been unfaithful. There was one period in his life, when he was attending the wilderness schools, when it appeared that he preferred, or at least intentionally chose to promote, the notion that he was estranged from his parents: several friends remember that he barely spoke about his parents, and one close friend from those days had assumed for years that he was an orphan.

The often wide distance between Justin and his father, geographically as well as emotionally, was hard on Terry, too, who notes that there were times he had felt like a failure as a father. He recalls a moment when his son was around five years old, playing near the street in front of their house in Sarasota, and his ball bounced in front of an incoming car. Terry, seeing his son about to run to retrieve the ball, stopped him not by grabbing his arm but by hitting him. The fact that he had reflexively hit his son mortified him. Even though their father-son relationship had waxed and waned over the years after Justin and his mother had left Florida, there were many times in his life when Justin desperately tried to seek his father's approval, Suzie recalls. "Every child wants to be loved by their parents," she says. "They will do almost anything to try to defend their parents or stand up for them or try to find the right. Because in the end, they want love."

When Justin called his father for advice, Terry reassured his son that he could choose any life he wanted. But he also offered a caution. "The biggest delusion is getting what you want," he told his son, before paraphrasing William Blake's "If the fool would persist in his folly he would become wise." The perfect life, Terry told him, is but an illusion, and it can be devastating when your dream materializes but isn't what you thought it would be. But that doesn't mean you don't persist. It's the striving, he imparted, the constant curiosity to better understand the world, that makes one truly happy. It was a notion that Terry had always tried to encourage in his son. He was proud to see him taking it to heart.

In December 2013, Justin quit his job. "I didn't realize that when he said he was leaving, I mean literally he dropped everything," Gutierrez says. "He was itchy." He recalls Justin placing an ad on Craigslist to the effect that he was moving out of town and anybody who needed anything should come by his apartment. Every object—from an Armani suit to a high-end espresso machine—that represented his more materialistic life was cast off for free. "He gave it all away," Gutierrez says. "He didn't want the possessions to possess him." Justin once referred to his years in Miami as "fun" but "necessary," the latter word used with a touch of derision. Gutierrez, when he looks back on working with Justin, calls the time a "hiccup" in the man's story. Whether the moment represented a return to a familiar minimalist and self-sufficient lifestyle or a first step along a new path, he knew that Justin would embrace his new life fully.

Justin stuffed a few essentials into the panniers of an army green Royal Enfield motorcycle he had purchased and once again looked west.

FIRST 4 STEPS

"I'm 32, and last week I retired." The words that Justin used to inaugurate his travel blog in January 2014 seemed to embody the "I quit my job to travel the world" trope or the "Financial Independence, Retire Early," or FIRE, movement that gained popularity in the 2010s. But he was quick to clarify that "retirement" didn't quite fit the stage in his life, which he felt was more aptly described as a transition into a place where he was "free to live the life of my dreams."

In the debut post on his reinvigorated blog at adventuresofjustin .com, which he had purchased the year before quitting his job, he wrote that he had been "struggling with a growing sense of dissatisfaction" with his life and feeling "trapped by this lifestyle that I bought into, and I wasn't proud of who I had become." The post has an air of someone new to revealing his life and feelings online. "Just writing [about his previous high-flying and fortunate lifestyle] makes me feel like a tool," he wrote, recognizing that some readers might interpret his being able to choose such a life as privilege. A deeper read reveals someone exhaling a long-held breath, half calm release and half burning excitement, while taking the official first steps onto an open road with every turn of his own making. He had done what his heroes had done: broken free, stepped back, and set out. He wrote that he was "running away from monotony and towards novelty; towards wonder, awe, and the things that make me feel vibrantly alive." He concluded, "People ask me what I'm afraid of. I am afraid of a life unlived; afraid to look back as an old man and wish I hadn't wasted it on forgettable things or trying to be someone else."

On January 12, he posted to Instagram and Facebook a photograph of a small gray day pack next to his motorcycle. "The adventure begins. As of today I am officially homeless and these are my only possessions." Minimalism was key, a set plan antithetical, a motorcycle ideal. Hitchhiking would have meant being forced to follow other people's plans and paths. Driving a car would have meant being enclosed and shielded. A motorcycle, by contrast, offered complete freedom to turn whichever way he pleased and an intimacy with the road and the passing landscapes. His choice of a Royal Enfield, rather than a motorcycle more familiar in the United States or one built for long-distance touring, was ultimately romantic. The Enfield had a look: rugged, vintage styled, military. He named it Battle Cat, in part after the green feline steed of the superhero He-Man, a childhood favorite.

Among his few possessions, tucked into the panniers strapped to the side of his motorcycle, was his bible: *Vagabonding: An Uncommon Guide to the Art of Long-Term World Travel* by Rolf Potts. Justin recommended the book to many who crossed his path in person and online. "For some reason," Potts wrote in one passage that particularly resonated with him, "we see long-term travel to faraway lands as a recurring dream or an exotic temptation, but not something that applies to the here and now. Instead—out of our insane duty to fear, fashion, and monthly payments on things we don't really need—we quarantine our travels to short, frenzied bursts. In this way, as we throw our wealth at an abstract notion called 'lifestyle,' travel becomes just another accessory—a smooth-edged, encapsulated experience that we purchase the same way we buy clothing and furniture." The book was a manual and a source of inspiration but also a validation.

Justin began his journey, however, not leisurely but determinedly. He sped across the southern United States to reconnect with old friends on the West Coast. He spent a couple months camping in parks, Joshua Tree National Park in California and Red Rock Canyon National Conservation Area in Nevada, before quickly looking abroad. In early March, he left his motorcycle behind and flew to Indonesia. "One way flight to Bali. My Indefinite World Travel Adventure begins," he posted to Facebook. "Everything I own in the world is in my carry on bag and I'm not sure where I'll sleep when I arrive. This is what I've always wanted." He arrived with intention: he skipped the resort towns, googling "Indigenous tribes in Southeast Asia" and clicking on a link. "Taking an overnight boat to the Mentawai islands, 100 km off the west coast of Sumatra," he posted. "For the next 10 days I will be deep in the jungle living with the Mentawai, a tribe who still lives with their traditional culture relatively intact. I am really hoping to learn more jungle survival skills as well as experience a beautiful and ancient way of life before it is gone." For a week and a half, he lived in a traditional longhouse, caught fish and crab, gathered wild coca leaves, and learned how to make poison-tipped arrows.

He once again returned to Thailand and then flew to Nepal, where he went trekking in the remote, arid Mustang Valley. Formerly known as the Kingdom of Lo, Mustang was long a restricted area for travelers due to its border with Tibet. "It's a land of outlaws and bandits, where nomads still live in yak hair tents and feed their dead to the giant Himalayan Griffons," Justin wrote online. He was in his element, exploring places where "people live as they have for thousands of years, no english signs, no guest houses, no phones or wifi." The trip culminated in crossing Thorong La, a 17,769-foot pass, wearing flip-flops. "I'm the happiest I've ever been," he posted. Back in Kathmandu, he reconnected with Bishal Kapali, who took him to Pashupatinath Temple, one of Kathmandu's holiest sites and the oldest Hindu temple in the valley, famously used for cremations. As they watched the pyres burn, Justin asked him about the meaning of life. Kapali flipped the question back onto Justin, who replied that he knew one day he would die and he had a short time to complete everything he dreamed.

He returned to the United States via Turkey in time to make the pilgrimage to Burning Man, an annual art and performance festival and self-reliant community staged in the Black Rock Desert in Nevada that has billed itself as a "crucible of creativity." In the early months of 2015, he embarked on another international trip, this time to South America. He traveled to Colombia and attended a gathering of shamans in Brazil; he hiked to the mountaintop Inca citadel at Machu Picchu in Peru and cycled along Bolivia's Yungas Road, also known as "Death Road," navigating carefully along the cliff-cut route so as to avoid the 2,000-foot drops. At the northern edge of the Atacama Desert, the driest nonpolar desert in the world, he visited the Salar de Uyuni, the world's largest salt flat, where he posed for one of his most memorable self-portraits. The flat's thin film of liquid perfectly reflects the blue sky and pillowy clouds, and Justin, standing naked, arms at his sides like a solider at attention, fixes his eyes on the indiscernible horizon. When he posted the photograph to Facebook, someone reported it for containing nudity; he proudly noted that the social media company's censors had deemed it inoffensive and let it stand.

For those who knew Justin well, that period of his life was a welcome return to the person they knew. It looked as if he had finally found the Goldilocks zone of his life, old enough to be independent but young enough to actively pursue adventure. Freedom, he once said, was his "highest ideal."

Everywhere Justin traveled, he shared his story online. He wrote on his blog occasionally, but the blogging world had been shifting to social media and he followed suit, updating his Facebook account regularly and posting to Instagram under the handle @adventuresofjustin. The persona that Justin embraced—the ascetic vagabond—was in many ways a return to a younger identity, one that had started to emerge at the wilderness schools. His presence on social media hadn't begun that way. When he had made his first posts to his fledgling Instagram account in February 2013, they had reflected his glamorous life traveling the world for iProof, with photographs from Paris, Hawaii, Shanghai, Milan, and the Virgin Islands. He posted about lavish globetrotting and partying at exclusive clubs. He shared one photo of his Panerai Radiomir watch, which retails for upward of $10,000, alongside his Louis Vuitton belt. He posted photos at Thailand's infamous "tiger temple," snacking on scorpions in a bazaar and looking out of his Shangri-la Hotel window.

After he quit his job and turned to a life on the road, the tone of his social media posts abruptly shifted. His message did, too. He changed the bio on his Instagram account to "I'm a nomad, adventurer, and ninja of sorts. Everything I own fits in one bag. The world is my home and this is my story." His posts of expensive clothing were replaced with ones of a bracelet made of woven vines that an Indonesian shaman had tied around his wrist; posts of world-renowned hotels were replaced with ones of camping on a dark-sand beach cooking Dungeness crab over a fire. Armed with an iPhone, an eye for photography, an alluring story, and a will to explore, he played the social media game well. His profiles were open to the public and he captioned his posts with popular hashtags such as #adventure, #wanderlust, #discover, and #travel. He wanted his posts in front of as many eyes as possible, even if many of them were there for his shirtless pictures. And it worked. His follower count began to grow by the hundreds, then the thousands. He became something of a minor travel celebrity. He had found content and a story that was resonating with people looking for inspiration to step out their door and seek a new kind of fulfillment, a different definition of success.

While on the road, he found friendship among like-minded travelers and maintained community through social media. Some people gravitated to his stories, while others were drawn to what his adventures represented. He was minimalist but not rejectionist. His smartphone didn't disgust him; it enabled him; it was a tool to tell his story and amass an audience. "I feel like belonging is a basic human need," he once said, "and with the Internet I can stay social and build a community because the people I choose to associate with is purposeful." Everywhere he went, he shot footage on his iPhone or camera, editing clips together with background music to create videos that he uploaded to his blog and his social media accounts. He appeared to be creating short versions of one of his favorite films, *Baraka*, a 1992 documentary that featured 152 locations in twenty-three countries. "I saw the film Baraka when I was 13 and it profoundly affected me and the course of my life," he had written on Instagram upon landing in Indonesia and watching in person a Balinese ceremony that had been featured in the film. Justin's videos—set in Nepal, Thailand, and around the United States—were arty and well put together, and they played well with his followers. Over the years, they racked up half a million views on YouTube. His social media accounts caught the attention of travel websites and podcasts with names such as Love Affair Travel, OpenWorld, and Flowstate.

In each interview he gave, he recounted the story of his attendance at the wilderness schools, his international travels, and his new self-determining life on the road as if he was establishing a foundational narrative. He often glossed over his years working in Miami. "I wasn't really proud of who I was or what I was doing," he said in one podcast, noting that he had sighed every time he introduced himself as a tech entrepreneur. "None of my heroes are tech entrepreneurs; they're all adventurers."

Justin fit into a long tradition of peripatetic seekers who found freedom in movement and solace in new horizons, who stepped back to understand their place in the world and how they might fit into society. In 1857, Henry David Thoreau, best known as the author of *Walden*, wrote in his journal about his withdrawal to Walden Pond, "You think that I am impoverishing myself withdrawing from men, but in my solitude I have woven for myself a silken web or chrysalis, and, nymph-like, shall erelong burst forth a more perfect creature, fitted for a higher society." To withdraw was to transform and reemerge brighter and more fully formed. One of the most storied examples, who met a mysterious end, was Everett Ruess. Born in 1914 in California, Ruess hiked and wandered the American Southwest, writing and painting, until his disappearance in 1934 at just twenty years old. He left behind a trove of letters to his family and friends that contain hints into his psyche and personality, what had disquieted him and what had spurred his explorations into the deserts and badlands. As David Roberts noted in *Finding Everett Ruess: The Life and Unsolved Disappearance of a Legendary Wilderness Explorer*, the "young man's ecstatic vision of the wilderness, tied to an insatiable wanderlust . . . drove him to one solitary challenge and ordeal after another." One of Ruess's most quoted lines comes from a 1932 letter to his brother, scribbled as a postscript: "I'll never stop wandering. And when the time comes to die, I'll find the wildest, loneliest, most desolate spot there is."

Half a century after Ruess, another young man fatefully committed to disengaging from societal pressures, testing himself, and living off the wild. Christopher McCandless was a twenty-four-year-old recent college graduate when he renounced his possessions, donated his savings to charity, and set off to travel around the United States. Two years later, he trekked alone into the Alaskan bush, where he met his death from apparent starvation. Ever since Justin had read Jon Krakauer's 1996 best seller about McCandless, *Into the Wild*, he had been fascinated by the young man's story—the angst and restlessness that had pushed him, what he had tried to tap into and tried to accomplish. "I'm not trying to cut myself off from society like he was," he said in a podcast interview. "I do have a lot of respect for the guy. That said, I think it's too bad we don't look at the many examples of people who went 'into the wild' and lived to tell a great story."

Like Ruess and McCandless, Justin grappled with the name he was born with. McCandless had famously forged a new identity, opting for the road alias "Alexander Supertramp"; Ruess, in many of his letters to family, adopted several fabricated noms-de-plume that his biographer David Roberts attributed to a "brooding" teenage attitude and Ruess himself admitted stemmed in part from a frustration with the difficulty of the pronunciation of his birth name. Justin, too, was unsatisfied with his name. When he was a young boy, his mother remembers, he had once tried going by Alex, but it had never stuck. Shortly after moving to San Francisco, he had started dropping his last name, Shetler, in earnest, presenting himself simply as Justin Alexander. Some friends say that he simply preferred Alexander as a surname or that he thought it rolled off the tongue better as a stage name for Punchface (all of his songwriting credits are under the name Justin Alexander). But other close friends point to that period of his life as one in which a deep rift emerged in his relationship with his father. In 2006, that foundational year in San Francisco when Justin first traveled internationally, Terry was convicted of sexual battery while working as a massage therapist in Florida. It deeply affected Justin, according to close friends, and his rejection of his surname appeared, in some measure, to stem from a desire to blaze his own trail free of any complicated family history. "I think [the surname change] was his way of saying to his father that he did not forgive him," a close friend of Justin confided.

The shift, for Justin, wasn't a fleeting phase. He kept using his middle name long after the band dissolved and he moved away from California. While working for the startup based in Miami, his business cards carried his full name to match the passport under which he traveled, yet "Justin Alexander" was how he presented himself online. After quitting his job, for a time he changed his name on Facebook to "Justin Alexander Supertramp" in a clear nod to one of his heroes. Several acquaintances and friends from that period of his life had no idea that his last name was anything other than Alexander.

Beneath the beguiling tales and photographs that Justin posted online was a person pushing himself as hard and as far as possible. In one podcast interview, he described his life as "walking that razor's edge." He was referencing W. Somerset Maugham's 1944 novel *The Razor's Edge*, which recounts the story of an American man who had embarked on a spiritual journey in India. The protagonist, Larry Darrell, has returned from living for five years in India, part of which he spent in an ashram under the tutelage of a yogi named Shri Ganesha.

Darrell was steadfast in his journey until he "received illumination, that state when you have at last burst the bonds of ignorance, and know with a certainty there is no disputing that you and the Absolute are one."

Justin was drawn to such stories, aspiring to live life as if he were a protagonist in a grand narrative. "He wanted to do greater-than-life things," Tom McElroy, Justin's friend from the Tracker School, says. "He wanted to be his own childhood hero." Justin's heroes had stalked wild animals, they had lived in solitude in caves with nothing, they had gone on desert walkabouts. And they had always made it through. He surrounded himself with stories of bravery and courage and risk but ultimate survival, and he built a suit of armor that felt impenetrable. "My heroes were all these nomadic mystics who survived in the wilderness," he once said in a podcast interview. When he was a teenager at the wilderness schools, he had heard a legend of a community of Apache who had been living somewhere in northern Mexico or southern Arizona in complete isolation and disconnection from the outside world. It was an apocryphal story, but Justin scoured maps to see if there was enough territory for this possibility. It was a spirit of living that he sought to emulate. "We all grow up with heroes," he once said, "and what you focus your attention on is what you become."

He adored Mark Twain's *The Adventures of Huckleberry Finn*, Jack London's *The Call of the Wild*, and Thoreau's *Walden*—stories of survival, testing, adventure, and independence. He wasn't, however, a fan of Jack Kerouac's *On the Road*. Ever since he was young, he had felt particularly drawn to the works of the comparative mythologist Joseph Campbell. In 1988, when Justin was seven, PBS had broadcast a six-part TV interview series between Campbell and the journalist Bill Moyers about the formation and power of myth. His father had taped them on the family's VCR and watched them with his son many times over the following five years. When Justin was a teenager, he had read Campbell's seminal work, *The Hero with a Thousand Faces*, and gained a new understanding of how myths are created and made. In the book, Campbell illuminated "The Hero's

Journey," a trajectory common to heroic protagonists that has been realized in popular works from *The Lord of the Rings* to *Star Wars*.

The first step is the hero receiving a call to adventure, to a "fateful region of both treasure and danger" represented "as a distant land, a forest, a kingdom underground, beneath the waves, or above the sky, a secret island, lofty mountaintop, or profound dream state," Campbell wrote, "but it is always a place of strangely fluid and poly-morphous beings, unimaginable torments, super human deeds, and impossible delight." The call to adventure appears as a signal through a place or a person. "Whether small or great, and no matter what the stage or grade of life, the call rings up the curtain, always, on a mystery of transfiguration—a rite, or moment, of spiritual pas-sage, which, when complete, amounts to a dying and a birth."

The hero accepts the call and takes the first steps on his quest. He meets a guardian, a guide, or a teacher, then faces a series of tests and trials, both physical and personal; he quarrels with monsters, battles his own fears, and challenges his skills. All the while, the hero is tempted by sirens or doubts to abandon his quest and reckons with the legacy of a father figure. After passing the tests, the hero reaches the apotheosis of his journey. There is a confrontation with his past, whatever he holds in most fear or pain, whatever element has been ruling or dominating or lurking in the shadows of his life. In that moment, "the wall of Paradise is dissolved, the divine form found and recollected, and wisdom regained." Here lies enlightenment, il-lumination, knowledge, awakening—a fulfillment of the quest and a great realization. The hero's old world is shattered, and he is born anew.

"Most of the influences in my life have been mythological," Justin once asserted in a podcast interview. "I like the idea of creating an amalgamation of all of your heroes, the best qualities of each, and then striving to be that." As a young boy his ideal was Hawkeye, then Stalking Wolf and Superman, and then, in his twenties, was a collection of myths and deeds and heroic personalities that took the form of an amorphous archetype: strong, confident, capable, adven-turous. It became himself, or rather who he wanted to be.

Over time, Justin's stories began to acquire their own near-mythological quality. There was the time he carried the injured toddler in Nepal, running for hours—some who have heard the story say days—to take her to the nearest clinic; there was the time he went into the wilderness in Idaho, or, as some recall in Montana, with nothing more than a knife and emerged weeks later wearing buckskin clothing; there was the time he was beaten up, or possibly even stabbed, in Bangkok while trying to save a young woman from harassment. Shortly after quitting his job, he found himself at a Los Angeles restaurant talking with Jonathan Goldsmith, the actor who was appearing on television commercials as "The Most Interesting Man in the World" for a long-running advertising campaign of Dos Equis beer, who remarked, "I think you might *actually* be the most interesting man in the world." Justin illegally climbed the most famous bridges in the United States, he became a Buddhist monk in Thailand, and he crossed snow-covered Himalayan passes in flip-flops.

It was all part of a story that Justin wanted to build, a story that, as he saw it, was just beginning.

In the summer of 2015, Justin rode his motorcycle along the cliff-edge highway between Los Angeles and San Francisco that hugs the coastline of the Pacific Ocean. He arrived in Big Sur, the most renowned section of the road, to pass the Fourth of July holiday weekend with some friends. He had returned to the United States from South America that March and spent the spring on his motorcycle riding from Florida to California. "Years ago, all I wanted was to get out of the country and see the world, and I still do, but what I was really seeking is freedom from monotony," he wrote on his blog. "America isn't a place to escape, rather it's the mindset we must abandon. This is my time to rediscover home with new eyes; and what a beautiful home it is." He had just spent months vagabonding around California. He visited Slab City, an off-grid, anarchic community in the middle of the desert known as "The Last Free Place on Earth," a spot that Christopher McCandless had passed through two and a half decades prior; he slept under the stars in Joshua Tree National Park among the spiky yucca trees; he hiked to the top of Mount Whitney, at 14,505 feet the tallest mountain in the contiguous United States; and he climbed one of the towers of the San Francisco–Oakland Bay suspension bridge, dressed in black to evade security.

When he rolled his motorcycle into the parking lot of Big Sur Bakery, a shake-roofed restaurant with a twinkling-light patio in the shade of conifers, an iconic pit stop along the coastal highway, he was excited to reconnect with some old friends he had met in San Francisco. The stranger in the group was Jonathan Skeels, a New Zealander who was working in the United States as a financial consultant, who had ridden his motorcycle north from Los Angeles with Justin Chatwin, a Canadian actor best known for playing a principal role in the TV series *Shameless*. Skeels remembers that Justin had been wearing a bandanna and vintage-style motorcycle goggles on his head—looking every bit the owner of the retro-styled Royal Enfield bike parked outside—and that he had been charming but quieter than the rest. "You had to hear his stories from other people. It wasn't him telling me about how he went out into the wilds of Montana, or how he slept on the top of bridges." Skeels had noticed a shyness in Justin that didn't match how he presented himself online.

Chatwin had crossed paths with Justin before, once in the Mohave Valley south of Las Vegas, while the actor was shooting a film among a group of like-minded motorcycle travelers; and again at a café in Los Angeles a few months later. At that point, Chatwin went where the acting work took him; he moved around a lot, attracted to those who shared his restlessness. "I had a fascination for drifters," he recalls, looking back on that time, telling me about meeting Scotty Kerkes, known as "Scooter Tramp Scotty," a self-proclaimed "motorcycle gypsy" who had been driving around North America since 1995, and Billy "Panhead" Burrows, who had been traveling the United States nonstop by various means since 1976. In Justin, Chatwin saw some of the forces that drove those perennial travelers, but he also sensed something else. "He had some sort of God-sized hole in his chest that he was trying to find the answer to fill," he says.

As the evening in Big Sur stretched out, someone at the table offered Justin, Skeels, and Chatwin a cabin to crash in for the night. They drove south, a trio of motorcycles weaving slowly along Highway 1 through a fog bank that obscured the coastal view and turned the roadside eucalyptus trees ethereal. They pulled over at the Esalen Institute, an exclusive retreat center that offers a mixture of spiritual workshops, addiction recovery services, and relaxation facilities and purports to be "neither a school, nor a church, nor a spa, nor an inn, nor a monastery" but rather a combination of them all. They hopped the fence and dipped into the retreat's hot pools.

Farther down the coast, they slept the night in the small cabin, in the middle of which Justin hung his own travel hammock and another for Chatwin. Before they fell asleep, Skeels spotted a large insect crawling across the floor, but as he moved to squash it, Justin quickly shooed it out the door. "That's my first memory of gentle soul Justin," Skeels remembers. "Wouldn't hurt a fly." They woke up to celebrate Independence Day with a view of the Pacific Ocean surf crashing against the cliffs below. Over the weekend, Skeels continued to be struck by the man's gentle character and compassion. It was a feeling of meeting someone who is not quickly forgotten.

When Skeels headed south, back to Los Angeles, Justin and Chatwin rode their motorcycles north. The actor was in a rush to get to a job in Vancouver, but Justin tried to convince him to tag along a bit longer. To Chatwin it seemed as though Justin was lost, desperately trying to fabricate a grand narrative for his life. "I just didn't feel like he was following his own path. He was following someone else's path." The name that came to his mind was Christopher McCandless. Chatwin left Justin with a warning: "Beware of the myth you chose. You don't want to end up like him."

After they split off, Justin snaked his way slowly north, riding along the Avenue of the Giants, surrounded by towering redwoods, camping on the beaches of northern California's Lost Coast, and soaking his body in Umpqua Hot Springs in Oregon. "In wilderness

I am a king; free to roam," he wrote online. "The stars are my ceiling, and I fall asleep tracking their arc." He visited his mother near Portland and in Seattle cashed out a retirement fund to purchase an expensive Sony digital camera, choosing a model recommended by his Italian photographer friend, Stefano Vergari. In Washington State, Justin returned to Linne Doran, the "Pond of the Otter" where his sit spot was, and to the Wilderness Awareness School's octagonal meeting hut. He visited Aidan Young, who had been following his old friend's travels online since he had left San Francisco and the Riekes Center. Young thought Justin might take some time to see a number of old friends still in the area, but Justin packed up his things after a couple of days and continued on his way. It was as if there was nothing for him in looking back. "That passion that we all saw that he had," Young says, "where he would pursue things so deeply and so intensely, I felt like that passion came from a lack of home within." In an August 2015 post about his motorcycle trip around the United States, Justin observed, "I think people are drawn to travelers in general, but there's just something about a motorcycle. They ask where I'm from and what I'm doing. The first question isn't an easy answer because I don't feel like I'm from anywhere in particular. I mean, I'm from a lot of places, and none feel like home." Instead, he wrote, he felt most at home on the road.

"To let the mountain slide," Henry David Thoreau advised, "live at home like a traveler." But Justin's mountains loomed large on his horizon, holding mysteries and knowledge accessible only to those who had the will and the determination to begin a climb. The closest thing he had to a home was his motorcycle or his tent, a park or a hostel for the night. Yet he tried as best he could to find or create fragments of belonging wherever he went. That was the point of the sit spot: to connect deeply with a place in order to understand its movements and intricacies. "I've experienced so little of this beautiful world, and the call of the horizon is strong," he wrote in a Q and A for a travel website. "Maybe home is something I'm looking for, and I just won't know until I find it."

Before Justin left Washington State, Young recalls, the two men had a conversation that stuck with him for years, in which Justin had spoken about immortality. "What it means to be immortal," Justin had said, "is the mark you leave on the world and others." If you have an impact on someone and he or she takes that influence and passes it on, your spirit, in that way, can never die.

Justin continued on his journey, camping in Idaho's Sawtooth Mountains, Montana's Glacier National Park, and Wyoming's Yellowstone National Park, where he picked up a roadkill rabbit and cooked it over a campfire. He rode southwest across Nevada until his motorcycle gave up. In a small town outside Reno, while his bike was in the shop, a stranger offered him a couch to crash on for the night. When he woke in the morning, he found that his rucksack, filled with every one of his valuables, was gone. He was chased out of the house by an ax-wielding methamphetamine addict, he recounted in a long blog post about the incident. His new camera, his laptop, and his camping gear had been stolen, as well as numerous sentimental items, including a hard drive containing ten years of travel photographs and journals. It was the third time he had lost his travel writing: while living in New Jersey he had lost a backpack full of his wilderness and personal journals, and in the summer of 2014, he had lost a phone that contained a journaling app in a river.

The latest loss was a bigger blow, one that dented the armor of his carefree, trust-filled adventurous spirit. "As a traveler I have come to rely on the kindness of strangers many times," he wrote about the robbery. "I feel foolish and totally defeated. I can't even write anymore. I've have [sic] nothing." Once his motorcycle was repaired, he drove off along Highway 50, nicknamed "the loneliest highway in America."

In the waning months of 2015, Justin remained mainly in southern California, venturing on his motorcycle only as far as the red sandstone formations of Sedona, Arizona. He had lost his objects of sentimentality and memory and was left with nothing more than what he needed—a reminder of what for him was important in life. When he passed through Los Angeles and reconnected with Layla Brooklyn Allman, she could read the impact of the incident on his face. The robbery had shaken him, but he quickly accepted the challenge of forced asceticism as a new trial: without a tent, he slept out in the city's Runyon Canyon Park, using his day pack as a pillow and his leather motorcycle jacket as a blanket. "Shhh," he wrote online. "I prefer illegally camping in city parks instead of wasting 50$ on a cheap motel in Hollywood. Crickets, police helicopters, and a small family of Great Horned Owls sing me to sleep." He posted a picture to Instagram of his bivouac site, taken not with his expensive camera, which had been stolen, but with his iPhone.

Justin and Allman shared drinks at a bar in LA and sat in her jeep afterward, listening to some music she was working on. They had kept in touch whenever Justin had passed through the city and she had followed his travels online, but it was the first time, seeing him in person again, that she worried for her old friend. She found him deeply melancholic and worried he was masking a deep-rooted pain. "There was a good dose of escapism that seemed to motivate the lifestyle he was leading," she says. He looked exhausted and appeared to be teetering on an edge. It was a brink she recognized well. She had seen similar forces in her family and friends, musicians driven to succeed by their relentless, unforgiving ambition that had become destructive. She likens it to a form of addiction: "I come from a family of addicts, alcoholics, legends, psychos. A lot of people never take their foot off the gas. And I saw a lot of that daredevil streak [in him] of always wanting more. That can make extraordinary things happen, but it can also make bad things happen."

In some ways, she felt that the robbery had hardened him. It wasn't the invulnerability check that it might have been but rather a confirmation that he could make it through any situation with little more than a bruised ego. There was a steeliness in his resolve to push on, not to let a single incident tarnish or curb his dreams. But she felt that he was beginning to move beyond survivalist, outdoorsman territory into something entirely different, "taking on a new energy," she says. "This was the time I saw him when he seemed the most sad to me. I had this little twinge of 'Is this getting out of control?'"

It was a question that friends and acquaintances alike posed during that time of transition. That fall, Justin had come across a survival video posted by Tom McElroy and sent him a message. They hadn't spoken for years, and McElroy was surprised to hear from him. McElroy had parlayed the skills he had learned into a business running survival classes around the world and consulting for outdoor TV shows, through which he was beginning to make a name for himself. McElroy mentioned that he would soon be offering a class on tropical island survival in the Caribbean. Justin quickly signed up and posted about the class. Several women, McElroy remembers, who knew Justin only from Instagram, signed up immediately, as did another who had once met Justin on a dating site.

Justin flew to the Caribbean with a stopover in New York City, where he went on midnight expeditions climbing buildings and cranes. He shared misty pictures from hundreds of feet up, crouching in black with the Empire State Building and One World Trade Center in the background. "This is a felony punishable by 7 years in prison," he crowed online. "This is definitely not me." He then spent two weeks on the island of Saint Croix taking McElroy's class. The course covered many skills that he had already mastered, but in his mind he was forming a plan that would soon take him to a place where island survival would come in handy.

As they were wrapping up the class, a student nicknamed "Hoff" (for his likeness to David Hasselhoff) confided to McElroy that he felt bad for Justin, who was clearly struggling to make sense of his life. The comment took McElroy aback; everyone else in the course had idolized Justin as a knowledgeable, capable survivalist and accomplished traveler. But that man, who was older than the rest of the group and had a family, saw through the facade. He recognized Justin as a midthirties traveler who hadn't found his place in the world and was committed to finding out why. In that moment, McElroy began to wonder if his old friend was simply trying to live an adventurous and unchained life or if instead was he running from

something. "When you're trying to live out your childhood hero's dreams, there's a point where you're living out somebody else's
dreams," McElroy says, "even if it's your younger self."

After Justin returned to California, he picked up his motorcycle
and drove to southern Nevada to meet Amanda Sansoucie. They had
met over Instagram that summer and had casually begun seeing each
other; he visited her twice that fall and winter. The last time, just
before Christmas, they drove out to a range of mountains near her
house and slept out under the stars. But she found their relationship
confusing. When he visited, they were extremely close; when he left,
he would go silent. He was clearly drawn to Sansoucie, a member of
the Native American Chemehuevi tribe; they spoke most about spirituality, she remembers. He told her about visiting Buddhist temples in Thailand and Nepal, and how he had incorporated certain
aspects, including reincarnation, into his system of belief. "I think
he was trying to find himself," Sansoucie says. "He was in a spot in
his life when he realized he was getting older, he realized he didn't
have anything solid like a home or a family. Justin talked about how
everything in his life was so fleeting—the places he visited, the people he met." It seemed to her that he was seeking a kind of awakening, a moment of realization when his life's path would unfold
before him. The reason he so intentionally sought out sacred places
or tried to touch the sacred in natural spaces, was in the hope that
they would spark a moment of clarity, the hope that he could connect
a purpose with his travels. "It was almost as if he was waiting for
something convincing enough to bring him to the other side."

Justin shared with Sansoucie his latest plan, one that had been
forming in his mind for months. It would be a trip larger and longer
than any he had ever taken. It would entail at least a year on the road,
and, maybe, if he could manage, it would be indefinite. It would
begin with a return to familiarity: to the remote islands of Maritime
Southeast Asia, to visit his adoptive family in Thailand, and to re-
unite with some old friends in Nepal. But then he planned on taking
a step into the unknown, to India. He dreamed of buying another
Royal Enfield motorcycle in the country of their origin, where they

hold iconic status, and riding it into the Himalayas, home to an endless spiderweb of roads that lead over mountain passes, to hilltop towns, and into plunging valleys—enough options to fill many lifetimes of wandering. One route in particular piqued his interest: the rugged, remote pass at the very northern tip of the country that leads into the arid, Tibetan-influenced region of Ladakh. It was similar to the Mustang Valley in Nepal that he had explored two years before. As Justin described his itinerary, Sansoucie got the sense that the trip was a means to determine the next steps in his life. "He had shared that he was at a point in his life where he wasn't too sure if he was doing what he was supposed to be doing, because at times he felt like a child running from adult responsibilities. Part of that trip was to figure out if he had pushed something out or if he was on the right track."

Justin bought a one-way ticket to the Philippines. Before he flew out, he posted a quote by Jack London:

I would rather be ashes than dust!

I would rather that my spark should burn out in a brilliant blaze than it should be stifled by dry-rot.

I would rather be a superb meteor, every atom of me in magnificent glow, than a sleepy and permanent planet.

The function of man is to live, not to exist.

I shall not waste my days in trying to prolong them.

I shall use my time.

Justin didn't know where exactly his trip might take him, how much time it might last, or where it might end. In one of the podcast interviews he gave while motorcycling in the United States, he quipped, "Maybe I'll be single, traveling around the world for the rest of my life as an old man. Or maybe in some random country [I'll] fall in love with a little village and disappear forever."

5
ALOBAR

Justin jumped. He arched his back and tucked his legs behind him, his arms outstretched like a bird as he plunged into the aquamarine pool at Kawasan Falls, a remote set of waterfalls and pools in the thick of the Philippine jungle. Some of Justin's followers noticed something new in the photos he posted from the falls, a large tattoo—a black outline of an eagle—that spanned his chest, its wingtips touching his shoulders. He had visited a tattoo parlor shortly before departing the United States but had waited to show it off. The eagle, one of his favorite animals, had always represented something special to him. The tattoo could have been an homage to what the bird represented in many Native American traditions: strength and bravery, balance and mystical power, and, in some legends, their role as messengers between the earthly and spiritual worlds. But the eagle's generic symbolism also seemed to fit: the epitome of freedom. Several friends who knew him well were surprised to see the tattoo; for years he had been averse to them, even though he had sported fake ones while performing for Punchface. He was initially embarrassed by how his tattoo had turned out, telling one friend that it "looked more like a pigeon than an eagle," but he soon embraced it, later telling a fellow traveler that it was a kind of "talisman on his skin."

In the posts from Kawasan Falls, he lamented being forced to hire a guide and wear protective equipment while he explored the canyon and complained that the once hidden and secluded spot, in part thanks to its eminently Instagrammable location, had become overrun with tourists. "I had imagined exploring this place solo and without a life preserver or helmet and felt like just another tourist," he complained. "I'm an adventurer, there's a difference." When one of his followers probed about how he saw the difference, Justin clarified, "Adventurers thrive on danger and the unknown. If you'll check the rest of my instagram, I think you'll see why I don't describe myself as a tourist. I mostly live outside, am homeless, close to penniless most of the time, never stay in resorts, don't hang with foreigners, and make every attempt to make my own way in the world. Adventuring is not a vacation, it's a lifestyle." Tourists might quickly flit from sight to sight, while travelers might linger and develop relationships; adventurers, as in Justin's mind, push themselves into situations they know will be uncomfortable—a return to the root of the word *travel*: "travail," a painful or laborious effort.

When he traveled, Justin's position as an outsider and visitor undoubtedly stumbled into the "noble savage" view, seeing peoples who were least touched by the modern world as sources of foundational—often utopian—principles of life, survival, and respect for the natural world. "I grew up wanting to be a Native American," he would later post on Facebook. "When I was a kid I had dreams [I] was a young Lakota warrior killed in battle." His interest in Native American history and traditions, as well as those of other Indigenous cultures around the world, appeared to come from a place of genuine interest, but also naiveté. Justin's first childhood idol, Hawkeye from *The Last of the Mohicans*, had, after all, tried to occupy a space between the colonial and Native American worlds. Though the term "cultural appropriation" arose in the 1980s, it is likely Justin never heard the phrase in the late 1990s at the Wilderness Awareness School or the Tracker School. Some former students from the Wilderness Awareness School remember the spiritual aspects, including sweat lodge ceremonies, as conducted separately by visiting Indigenous elders. But that still didn't shield the Tracker School in particular from criticism of profiting off the knowledge and traditions of communities and cultures that had long been exploited. It is likely that Justin, in his admiration, believed he was honoring a culture, blind to the possible implications and problematic undertones of his stated aspirations.

Justin was born into a certain degree of privilege, afforded opportunities because of class, race, and gender that allowed him a foundation often taken for granted: freedom. It was a state he sought yet in many ways had had all along. With enough money, something he was always adept at finding, he could go anywhere. Yet as much as he was seeking, he was also running—from relationships, from growing old, from responsibility, from mundanity. Perhaps his inherent privilege was the root of his constant feeling of dissatisfaction: to achieve what he sought, many times he shed his life, abandoned what he had built, pared his possessions back to what was necessary, and started anew.

Though Justin's search was in part a quest for authenticity in others, it was also an attempt to ward off inauthenticity within himself. He created an image online that he struggled to keep up with, one that pushed him to travel to more and more remote destinations; yet all tourists, by the very fact of their arriving in a place, have an impact on its perceived authenticity. Communities are transformed, in some cases to reflect tourists' desire to experience the "authentic," for the benefit of the visitor. He had seen countless photographs of the jungle pools at Kawasan Falls over the years and had dreamed of visiting them. The reality didn't match his fantasy; they had become everything he tried to avoid: crowded, noisy, touristy, inauthentic. At the end of the day, however, his guide invited him to his family home to celebrate a relative's second birthday. Justin ate roast pig and tropical fruit and relished the spontaneity of the moment, proclaiming, "This is why I travel solo." He next outlined a plan to visit the southern regions of remote Palawan Island, the jungles around Mount Mantalingajan. "Tomorrow I will hire an interpreter and hike all day to reach a small remote village." He was worried about contracting malaria and dengue fever and even about running into Islamist terrorists, who he had been told might be in the area. "If it were safe, it wouldn't be much of an adventure would it?" he wrote online. "I should be back online the 27th." Like clockwork, he was—posting pictures and videos and stories about his stay with the Tao't Batu tribe.

After a couple of weeks in the Philippines, Justin flew to Thailand, where he met up with the psychologist and author Christopher Ryan in Chiang Mai. They had become friends over the previous year. Justin had torn through Ryan's book, the *New York Times* best seller *Sex at Dawn: The Prehistoric Origins of Modern Sexuality*; its explorations of polyamorous human history resonated with him. Justin had once photographed himself sitting on his green Royal Enfield motorcycle, naked, with a copy of the book strategically positioned so that when he uploaded it online, it passed Instagram's censors. Justin had reached out to the author, and that summer they had met in a park in Portland, Oregon, where Ryan had interviewed him for an episode of his podcast, *Tangentially Speaking*, in which he interviews people with an atypical approach to life. The episode was accompanied by a standfirst noting that Justin "travels the way it should be done." The episode was so well received that Ryan offered to interview Justin for a second episode. Looking back on the friendship that blossomed out of those interviews, Ryan says he had felt as though he were looking into a mirror. He had traveled extensively when he was around the same age as Justin, and felt that they shared a similar spirit and ethos. They kept in touch regularly, and were happy to reconnect in Thailand.

In Chiang Mai, they finished recording the second podcast episode, which they had started in Los Angeles, and Justin spent a few weeks with Ryan and his wife. Ryan looks back on two moments often. In the first, they were riding motorcycles to Pai, a town situated in an emerald green valley, when Ryan noticed Justin shifting on his bike up ahead. "I realized what he was doing is that he had put both his feet up behind him on the seat, in sort of a yoga posture," Ryan remembers. Justin then let go of the handlebars and, letting the motorcycle coast, stood up on the seat. Ryan was stunned and later chastised him for the stunt. "That was a common thread in our friendship," he says; he had always felt a protectiveness toward the younger man. "He added to the danger level in ways that I found frivolous. And that made me angry. Because the more I felt affection to him the more vulnerable I felt."

In the second memory, they were traveling by *songthaew*, a truck that had been converted into a shared taxi, to visit a temple complex. Justin opted not to sit on one of the wooden benches inside the covered cab but instead to stand on the truck's bumper and hang off the metal frame as if he were riding an old San Francisco cable car. Ryan pulled out his phone and recorded the moment. As the vehicle whipsawed along mountain roads, the wind lashed Justin's shirt and he smiled broadly. It was a moment that Ryan feels summed up the man: ecstatic in a spontaneous moment of adventure yet, once he realized a lens was on him, inclined to flex his arms and pose. He was in the moment but couldn't hold back from also observing himself in the moment. "So many spiritual traditions are trying to bridge that separation," Ryan says, "that chasm of my immediate experience and myself experiencing myself experiencing it." He points to a notion that exists in several forms of meditation, based on Buddhist practices, of "the observer," a kind of alternate form of perception free of ego, an ability to self-reflect objectively. "Maybe for Justin, the risk, the danger, was a way of trying to escape that observation of himself."

Justin's social media following had been growing steadily, and he had begun to see how an online presence could serve as a platform for inspiration. Several times he tried out homemade proverbs in posts and interviews to see how his followers might respond: "You can't have an adventurous life if you don't push yourself"; "Fear is your only captor"; "What's better than a $10,000 watch? A lifestyle where time doesn't matter." They harkened back to the handmade paper journal he had kept as a young boy, in which he had copied inspirational quotes and then begun to write philosophical proverbs of his own: "One who does not give credit to others cannot give credit to themselves" and "A man without an imagination is a man without purpose." The newly minted aphorisms appeared designed to test the reach of his social media presence. What Justin shared online was more than mere updates and observations; he often wrote declarations and statements about the nature of modern travel and tourism, of spirituality and religion, of following dreams and finding freedom. They weren't the intimate words one might record in a diary or the warm thoughts of a letter to a family member or a close friend. He did occasionally publicly share excerpts from the private journal he kept on an app called Day One, typically when he wanted to share his immediate thoughts after a travel blunder or incident. Those entries weren't carefully crafted stories but were rawer and more unpolished, full of emotion, anger, and frustration.

What Justin shared online was only a part of his story. It was what he wanted his followers to know, to see, to be impressed or inspired by. His projected life could be as glamorous or as successful or as adventurous as he had the time and the money to create and curate. In his 2014 trip to Nepal's Mustang Valley, the one when he had hiked over a mountain pass in flip-flops, he had been ostensibly alone—a solo traveler with just a "sleeping bag, a water filter, camera, sandals, knife, and a toothbrush," as he had written. He had visited a remote village, where he had drunk yak butter tea, and had run into Nepali soldiers patrolling the Tibetan border. There was no mention of having to purchase permits, as required by law; there was no mention of a companion. But in fact he had made the journey with at least one European tourist, and they had hired a Nepali guide for their trek into Mustang. The story was only "I" and never "we," and the video he filmed and later posted reinforced his desired image of a solitary adventurer, a lone renegade in dangerous territory.

By 2016, the world of social media "influencers," largely on Instagram, was growing at an exponential rate. Brands were realizing that compensating, whether in money or in goods, people with large followings, captivating stories, or attractive aesthetics in exchange for a product post was in many cases a far more effective and relevant means of promotion than traditional marketing. The posts were cleverly designed to appear like genuine, honest recommendations rather than paid pieces of advertising. Many consumers were unaware that their favorite fashion icon, athlete, celebrity, or world traveler was being sponsored to promote a company. It wasn't until 2017 that the US Federal Trade Commission released guidelines directing social media users to disclose any affiliation with a brand or company or any financial incentive to post a recommendation or a review. Before then, the sector had enjoyed little regulation, oversight, or transparency.

Justin tiptoed into that arena cautiously. He had idolized one couple, a friend recalls, who were managing an Instagram account to which they posted heavily edited pictures of their world travels and wrote paragraphs about finding happiness through companionship and adventure; the couple appeared to live a carefree life on the road, but it was actually being funded by promotions and advertisements. Several times after quitting his Miami job, Justin toyed with the idea of monetizing his own following. He once contacted Royal Enfield North America to inquire about sponsorship, possibly to fund his travels or provide spare parts for his motorcycle. It responded that he didn't have enough followers yet or, at that point, enough of an established brand. Instead of an official deal, several companies simply reshared some of Justin's photographs on their social media platforms, undoubtedly pushing more followers his way. Some companies, including one that made lightweight travel hammocks and another that made motorcycle accessories, used his photos to promote their brand. Whenever Justin began to entertain the possibility of turning his social media presences into a modest business to keep him on the road, he would pull back, either unaware of how to navigate such exchanges or uncomfortable with its transactional nature and how that conflicted with the spirit of his travels.

That January, while in the Philippines, Justin had decided to expand his social media reach, opening a Facebook page devoted solely to his Adventures of Justin brand, linked to his blog, and separate from his personal page. Leah Lañojan, a Filipino woman he had met at a street festival in the city of Cebu, who happened to work as a social media manager, convinced him that it would benefit his outreach. Lañojan mentioned that she could help him find sponsorship for his travels or monetize his accounts. While envious of their freedom, Justin had long been critical of Instagram travelers who posted from far-flung locations and amassed hundreds of thousands of followers. They lacked substance; they were simply visiting lavish resorts and posting pictures for fame and money; their goal wasn't to inspire people, to give followers a window into a different culture or location, or to do good while on the road but rather to passive-aggressively invoke jealousy. It was an issue that he clearly pondered enough to write a long post on Facebook elaborating on his take:

> Some people make money from blogging. It's just not the route I want to take. I hate mixing art and comme[r]ce; it changes my relationship to the art in a way that I don't like. Also I hate advertising or commercials and don't want to go that route on social media. . . .
>
> I, like most people, am afraid that people won't like me, who I am, what I do, what I value. Creating art is expressing myself. It is the most vulnerable I can be and I fear rejection. I worry that people will think I'm self absorbed if I post videos or photos of me living my legend. Or I'll make people jealous. Maybe I should just do my shit and mind my own business. What is my real purpose in all this?

The timing, however, was right. One travel website had called him "the most interesting person on Instagram," another the "World's Coolest World Traveler," and another had named him one of "13 Inspiring Travelers to Watch in 2016."

"He didn't spend that currency to get anything," says Ryan. The tension between the fulfillment Justin felt through travel and the validation he received online, Ryan could see, pained him and made him feel trapped and pulled in conflicting directions. His name was growing online, but was it truly him? Ryan saw in his friend an "alienation from himself, a schism between the star and the audience. I think he was trying to resolve that," he says. "He was always onstage, performing for himself. And he was perpetually disappointed, he was perpetually not enough." But there was little that was going to stop his search. In Thailand, the two talked about the downstream effects of the nomadic life he was trying to build, and Ryan advised his friend that that kind of existence wasn't ultimately going to make him happy. "You're reaching for something you're never going to fully grasp," he remembers telling Justin in Chiang Mai. "Your life doesn't just belong to you. Your life belongs to everyone who loves you, and if you're careless with that, you're careless with their love."

Ryan looks back on that issue—Justin doing things for the way they appear, rather than the way they are—as a core foundation of his friend. "I feel like Justin was in some ways the ultimate product of social media. I don't think he could ever get out of the frame."

Before leaving Thailand, Justin once again visited his "adoptive family" in their village near Lampang. His friend Sitthikorn Thepchanta also returned home in time to witness his younger brother, Noom, complete his own monk's initiation ceremony. On March 11, Justin celebrated his thirty-fifth birthday, eating grilled chicken, prawns, and fish. It was a celebratory visit all around, but Thepchanta remembers something Justin had said during their last night together, drinking cold Chang beer in Bangkok before Justin flew out. He had asked Thepchanta about the concept of reincarnation.

"I don't know," Thepchanta said with a smile, "I'm not there yet."

Justin laughed in agreement. "Why don't we make *this* life better," he said, "rather than worry whether a next life is real?" They clinked their green bottles together.

"Do you know that the path you are walking is a very dangerous path?" Thepchanta then hesitantly asked him.

"I know," Justin replied. "Whatever happens to me, brother, I will go with a smile on my face."

Toward the end of March, Justin flew to Kathmandu, landing just in time for Holi, Hinduism's most vibrant festival, during which revelers douse one another in multicolored powder until everyone in the streets is haphazardly tie-dyed from head to toe. This time, the country that he had visited twice before was in a state of recovery. Almost exactly a year prior, in April 2015, an earthquake with a magnitude of approximately 8 had shattered communities in Kathmandu and destroyed entire villages near the epicenter northwest of the capital. At least eight thousand people had died. Friends Justin had made ten years before, some of whom he had been supporting financially, had been slowly and painfully rebuilding their lives and their country in the wake of the tragedy. He arrived determined to help.

Justin found his way to Alobar1000, a popular hostel down an unpaved alley in the heart of Thamel, the city's buzzing tourist district, and around the corner from a small urban park called the Garden of Dreams. Tashi Ghale, who had helped coordinate the documentary *Namaste Nepal* that Justin had assisted with in 2006, had opened the guesthouse in 2012. Inside the yellow-and-green hostel, dorm beds cost a few dollars per night. Ghale named the guesthouse after the protagonist in Tom Robbins's 1984 novel, *Jitterbug Perfume*, the story of a fictional ancient Indian king named Alobar who forsakes his lineage to embark on a quest to find immortality by meditating in caves, and ultimately lives to be a thousand years old. "I thought that resonated a lot with most travelers," Ghale explains, "trying to find the meaning of life as they move around the world." He was used to seeing international tourists arrive in his country on such paths; they came either for trekking or for temples, for seeking high elevation or for high enlightenment. When Justin arrived in 2016, he stood apart. "I think he didn't want to do anything easy or traditional. He wanted to do things different and unique, where he can find the true meaning of life."

Ghale had organized a ragtag team of international volunteers to help build a primary school in a remote village that had lost its school during the earthquake. Justin signed up. He met some of the group on the popular rooftop patio at Alobar1000, where backpackers sat on cushions on the floor, drinking cold beer and dining on a dish of spiced lentils and rice called *dal bhat* or banana pancakes. There, Kishwor Sedhai reconnected with Justin exactly ten years after they had saved the toddler who had fallen from the window in the remote Himalayan village. One night they sneaked past the fence that encircles Swayambhunath Temple, Kathmandu's famous hilltop "monkey temple," and climbed the hundreds of stone stairs for a view over the twinkling lights of the city. After a few days in the capital, Justin, along with several other volunteers, including Sedhai, traveled northwest to what remained of the village of Bhachek, six miles from the epicenter of the earthquake. There Justin spent nearly a month sharing a green repurposed army tent with international volunteers who were helping construct a new school out of timber, mud, cement, and rebar.

When the school in Bhachek was nearly completed, Justin returned to Kathmandu and to Alobar1000. An American backpacker, Hank Stowers, remembers sitting on the hostel's rooftop balcony when a man with a familiar face walked in. Stowers did a double take: he had been following Justin's travels on Instagram for months. "It was exactly the kind of stuff that I would have wanted to be doing," he recalls. "I wanted to travel with the same vigor and tenacity as Justin. He inspired me to do that. I swam across rivers to run away from cops, I rode on the roofs of buses, and a lot of other things that I wouldn't have done if I hadn't seen someone else doing it." On the rooftop terrace, Stowers plucked up enough courage to approach Justin and introduce himself as a fan. Over the next couple hours and during subsequent conversations at Alobar1000 and around Kathmandu, they swapped stories and travel tips. Justin shared with him his expertise with packing light and making do with little while on the road. "A big theme in all of our conversations was the nature of traveling, how to seize every moment and have fulfilling experiences, but also how to avoid manufacturing your experiences." Stowers had wondered about the authenticity of the person behind the profile: it became clear that Justin was more shy than he presented himself online, but he appeared to be every bit the adventurer he purported to be.

A main topic of conversation was India, where Stowers had just completed a college study abroad semester in Bangalore and to which Justin was headed shortly. They discussed Gregory David Roberts's novel *Shantaram*, which has perhaps inspired more Westerners to travel to India than any other in recent years. The book, in part based on the author's life but largely fictionalized, follows the story of Lindsay, or Lin, who escapes from prison in Australia, flees the country, and ends up living in Bombay for years in the 1980s. Lin's exploits blend illegality with altruism: one moment he establishes a free clinic in Bombay's largest slum, the next he's counterfeiting passports and selling drugs to tourists. After its publication in 2003, *Shantaram* quickly became a must-read backpacker bible, weighting the packs of countless international travelers to the subcontinent in large part because of the book's romantic notions of eking out a life as a foreigner in India. Stowers remembers Justin saying that Lin would be a cooler character "if it weren't for his constant sense of self-importance and disregard for others." Yet there was evidence that Justin idolized at least the superficial aspects of Lin's story. When he was posting on Facebook about his plans for India, one follower warned about overstaying a visa in India. Justin lamented, "The days of Shantaram are over I guess."

Justin told Stowers that he was growing bored with the hostel life and was planning something bigger. "India seems to churn out larger-than-life adventures, and that's what he was looking for," Stowers recalls. But Justin was also fearful about the country. During one of their conversations, he confided that "India is where I will find the other wall." The comment struck Stowers, so much so that he wrote it down in his travel notebook. "I think that his old life in a professional, capitalist setting was the first 'wall,' a barrier to his personality that would either force him to turn away, or kill him. I think that India was 'the other wall' because he knew that there wouldn't be artificial boundaries for him there. The immensity of India can swallow you whole, and you have to set the limits for yourself there, because no one will set them for you. I think that for Justin, that wall was something he was seeking—a space where he could find his own limitations, his own barriers to total self-determination and autonomy. I think he wanted to know where his limit was."

Through Justin's travels, he cultivated transitory connections. His love of animals filled a small hole. Over the years, while on the road, he took in many kittens and puppies that he found near death on the streets, brought them back to his hostel room, and nursed them back to health. He cared for them as long as he could before moving on. In Kathmandu, he picked up a skinny puppy in an alley and brought it back to Alobar1000, but, despite his getting advice from a vet, it didn't survive. "I woke up next to her on the floor. She wasn't moving, her mouth and eyes were slightly open," Justin posted. "She died right next to me, moments before I woke up." He carried the body across the city and buried it under a rock at the foot of Swayambhunath Temple.

It was clear that he longed for deeper attachments. He had been in several significant relationships with women over the years, and he also had at least one serious relationship with a man that had lasted around a year. While working in San Francisco and Miami, he'd had profiles on several dating websites, including OkCupid, and had later joined apps such as Tinder. When he went on the road, he would often set his "location" to the next city on the horizon in the hope of making a connection for when he arrived. After he quit his job, most of his relationships were in some part long distance and either fleeting or casually maintained. He was torn between craving companionship and seeking independence. His social media use appeared to wane the deeper he moved into a relationship, but when he was single he returned to frequently updating his accounts and followers with new adventures, new exploits, and new stories. Yet the comments about independent travel, minimalism, and freedom that he posted failed to convey the reality of his desire, sometimes anguished, for connection and love.

Several people with whom I spoke outlined a similar pattern: they had met online, fallen in love quickly and passionately, and connected in person when possible. One of those was Linda Borini, an Italian American artist living in Los Angeles, who finally met Justin in person in the fall of 2014 after connecting on Tinder and messaging for months. "It was very obvious in that moment that even though it took us so long to get there, a seed had been planted," she says. But Justin was in a relationship at the time, so they kept in touch initially as friends; later, after he became single, they made an effort to cross paths whenever possible. When he flew to the Philippines, he left his motorcycle in her care, and before long they had made plans to reconnect in Nepal. Borini had visited South Asia a handful of times before and jumped at the opportunity, meeting him in Kathmandu in the middle of May. Her first night, they walked the city with Kishor Sedhai and Jacqueline Woo, an Australian traveler who had helped build the Bhachek school. The group weaved through the dark streets to Pashupatinath Temple, the city's cremation temple, and around 1:00 a.m. sneaked inside and watched the funeral pyres burn orange in the night. Empty of the daytime crowds, it felt as if they had stepped back in time. While creeping through the complex, Justin passed a pile of rags and clothes along one wall before realizing that it was a person.

A hand appeared, of a woman, that reached out to him; then a voice, singing in Hindi, cut the silence. Her eyes were black. "It was like a bundle of bones rising from the dead," Borini remembers. Justin was immediately, visibly affected. He wanted to help the woman.

"She's lost," Sedhai told Justin. "She's in another world. She's been taken."

Justin remained shaken by what he had seen at the temple. Borini spent hours in their guesthouse room the next day, talking with him about the woman, but she couldn't figure out what exactly troubled him so. "It seems like you're afraid of something," she said to him. "What are you afraid of?" He said he was scared of reaching a point in his life where he lost his mind. He said that his traveling and constantly exposing himself to ever more adventurous or dangerous experiences and situations was a way of testing that fear. He looked at her like a young boy, she recalls, and asked, "Is that what's going to happen to me? Am I going to be taken by evil?"

The moment of vulnerability surprised Borini, knowing how much effort it took for Justin to open up about his feelings. She didn't even know his last name was Shetler until he was filling in an application form for a trekking permit in the Annapurna mountain region and opened his passport; she had known him by only the name he went by online, Justin Alexander. Over the following weeks, the woman at the temple continued to haunt Justin, as he and Borini rode the bus west to the lakeside city of Pokhara and began their hike into the mountains.

One day along the trail, two men began talking with Justin, and the next thing Borini knew, he was following the men through the forest to find a "cousin" who could procure them hash. "All for the spirit of adventure," in the words of Borini, who had no choice but to follow. The man and the deal never materialized, but she remembers the two days they spent in a remote teahouse situated on a picturesque mountain plateau as the best moments of their month and a half in Nepal together. In her mind, Justin's decision to follow two strangers to try to procure drugs confirmed his assertion that the adventure and the story were king, that danger can lead to pleasure. That May, the travel website HighExistence published a Q and A with Justin in which he rebutted the notion that travel was only about finding happiness. "I think many of us are 'running away' from a life of certainty and towards discovery of the unknown," he said. "Traveling isn't all happiness. If you're searching for happiness, you're searching for a vacation. Traveling is often exploring things that make you uncomfortable: physically, ethically, emotionally, metaphysically."

It was the low season for trekking, the weeks inching closer to the arrival of the monsoon, with few tourists staying in the teahouses where the pair lodged and ate. They were fast walkers but often didn't hit the trail each day until 3:00 p.m. They talked a lot, Borini remembers, chiefly about where he was going with his life. But once she began probing deeper, she sensed a great frustration in him. She wanted him to open up, to express himself clearly, but his uncertainty and his curiosity were also what she loved about him. Many people remain stuck in a kind of purgatory; they are happy to an extent but ultimately unfulfilled in work or love or life. Justin may have been uncertain, but he wasn't afraid, at the very least, to ask questions and search for the answers.

Back in Kathmandu, Justin began preparing to depart for India. One evening they wandered the city's laneways and bought a pirated DVD of a documentary about sadhus, the Hindu ascetics who have renounced their possessions to wander a path toward spiritual fulfillment in the form of *moksha*, freedom from the endless cycle of reincarnation. Some wear saffron robes and their hair in matted locks in the image of Shiva or smear their body in white ash; some are masters of yoga and meditation and profess all manner of saintly abilities. They are often called by the honorific "Baba," meaning "Father." The accounts of Alexander the Great, who brought his Greek armies across the Indus River in 326 BCE and invaded modern-day India, documented "gymnosophists," a name for wise men who went naked. They may have been *parivrajaka*s, wandering ascetics, or *sramana*s, seekers who laid down the fundamental constructs, including reincarnation and *moksha*, of what eventually became Hinduism. Marco Polo, in his travels during the late thirteenth century, encountered in India what appear to have been sadhus, "who live to an extraordinary age, even 150 or 200 years," who practice "great abstinence in eating and drinking" while "going perfectly naked." Polo noted that they took a vow of sexual abstinence as part of their devout spiritual path and that if they "appear to take any pleasure in these endearments, are rejected as unworthy; but if they show themselves totally indifferent, they are then retained."

Of all of India's attractions, nothing has proven more magnetic than its spiritual people, its masters of religion and thought, of poetry and punditry, and of personal development and transformation. The curious continue to come to immerse themselves in the soft chants and wild invocations of the spiritually convicted and to marvel at their dedication. Many sadhus (*sadhvi*s if female), practice *tapas*, expressions of austerity or devotion, from meditation to much more extreme tests of exertion, self-flagellation, or fatigue. One man sat in the same spot for twenty-two years; another remained standing for seventeen years. In 2004, Mohan Singh, known as "Ludkan Baba," or "Rolling Baba," rolled his body eight hundred miles in an attempt to connect New Delhi to the Pakistani city of Lahore to promote peace between the two countries. It is not unreasonable for travelers who encounter such expressions of faith to feel awe in the practitioner's presence or be inspired to incorporate even small elements of such extreme devotion into their own day-to-day lives. Some spiritual tourists seek those with otherworldly, near-supernatural powers: yogis who claim to have the ability to levitate, mystics who can cure illnesses or communicate with animals, sages who can predict the future. Some come to learn how to meditate or how to abstain from sex or other pleasures; some come to sit at the feet of a guru, a great teacher, to guide them on a search for the meaning of life.

Justin and Borini watched the documentary about sadhus in their guesthouse room. "He was enthralled," she remembers. "He was so attracted to the idea of understanding this culture." Borini had first visited South Asia in 2010 on a four-month work contract in south India, a trip that she had extended as long as her visa would allow. "I knew that it was going to open a can of worms and that I was going to have to keep going back," she says. "It broke me. I spent six months there, and I would have never left. I had never been in an ashram. I had never sought out a guru or anything. But just being in India was the experience." But during one of her trips, while staying in the hill station town of Simla, she had met a sadhu who, after a couple of brief conversations, bluntly said, "Okay, it's time to open up. Take your clothes off." It was a disillusioning moment, to say the least. Borini considered urging Justin to be wary of potential spiritual charlatans in India, but she knew that he wanted to have his own experiences, so she held back. "India is what India is," she says. "It's this spiritual land where you inevitably end up having a journey regardless of your intentions. It will break down your ego and make you feel like you have so much to learn, constantly." Justin was itching to go. He wrote online, "I can't imagine where I will be after India let alone [in] 10 years."

Borini flew back to Los Angeles, and Justin, with a six-month Indian tourist visa in hand, packed up and bought a bus ticket to the Indian border. Tashi Ghale, the owner of Alobar1000, offered a warning to his friend before he departed, telling him to tread softly both with his feet and with his mind and that "people can use spirituality as a means to take advantage of you." Ghale had witnessed the transformative nature of a quest like that he saw blossoming in Justin but was keenly aware that it could also consume people so profoundly that it left them overwhelmed. "Nothing is sugarcoated or packaged properly," Ghale says. "Everything that you see here is raw—the pain, the poverty." And going to India, to which many travelers in Nepal head next, can be an immense step. "India is like a final exam if you are taking a course of life. It can be so heavy, it can be so pressuring, it can be so challenging."

Many travelers who have stayed at Alobar1000 have left their mark, scrawling on the white and pale blue walls. There are quotes and messages and mantras, drawings of the Hindu god Ganesha and of the Om symbol. In one corner, someone had transcribed a quote from a letter Christopher McCandless had written in 1992: "Nothing is more damaging to the adventurous spirit within a man than a secure future. The very basic core of a man's living spirit is his passion for adventure. The joy of life comes from our encounters with new experiences, and hence there is no greater joy than to have an endless changing horizon, for each day to have a new and different sun." Justin took a picture of the quote, shared it to Instagram, and then added his own quote to the guesthouse walls in thick black capital letters: "BE KIND, AND DO EPIC SHIT." It wasn't poetry, but it was fitting for the age of Instagram. Underneath, he added his @adventuresofjustin social media handle and a drawing of his eagle tattoo.

Justin left Nepal with a new tagline for his adventures. In many of his posts going forward, it became his hashtag. The message was clear: Follow me.

PART II

THE ROAD

*My heart began to beat like mad because I'd suddenly
become aware of an intense conviction that India had
something to give me that I had to have.*

—W. Somerset Maugham, *The Razor's Edge*

*All India is full of holy men stammering gospels in
strange tongues; shaken and consumed in the fires of their
own zeal; dreamers, babblers, and visionaries: as it has
been from the beginning and will continue to the end.*

—Rudyard Kipling, *Kim*

6
PILGRIMS

On a steamy, predawn August morning in 2008, I arrived in India for the first time. Twenty-three years old and wide-eyed, I landed in New Delhi with a one-year visa and a plan to use nearly every day of that backpacking around the country. I held few concrete goals or items on my itinerary except to explore a country that had long sparked curiosity in my mind.

I was a teenager when I first felt the country's pull. I remember reading Mark Twain's travelogue *Following the Equator: A Journey Around the World* and feeling as though a rope tied around my waist had been tugged. "You soon find your long-ago dreams of India rising in a sort of vague and luscious moonlight above the horizon-rim of your opaque consciousness," Twain had written in the late 1890s, "and softly lighting up a thousand forgotten details which were parts of a vision that had once been vivid to you when you were a boy, and steeped your spirit in tales of the East." For me, those tales had begun with my father, who had spent six months traveling in South Asia as part of a three-year trip around the world in the late 1960s. I had grown up on his stories from his foundational trip through southern and eastern Africa, Southeast Asia, and the Middle East, but it was those from South Asia that had most captured my imagination: eating a mouth-scorching boar green curry in Ceylon; hiking through a snowstorm in the Hindu Kush; sipping golden tea in Darjeeling. He had traveled with a history book rather than a Lonely Planet guide; had taken rolls and rolls of pictures on his film camera that he shipped home; and had lived off money orders sent to general post offices in cities a few weeks before he arrived.

He was in India at the same time as the Beatles, who, along with Mike Love of the Beach Boys and other celebrities, were meditating in egg-shaped stone meditation pods in the foothill town of Rishikesh on the banks of the Ganges River. There the band wrote numerous songs, many of which were released on the self-titled record commonly called "the White Album." "Everything you need is here/ And everything that's not here is not there," John Lennon later wrote in "The Happy Rishikesh Song," which was never officially released. Though the Beatles eventually departed under a cloud of accusations of sexual impropriety launched against their guru, their time in the Himalayas reportedly weaned the group off LSD and, as the *New York Times* noted, "seems to have opened a floodgate of creativity and got them out of what threatened to be a creative rut." With the spotlight on the transformation, healing, and personal growth of such celebrities, many thousands of curious minds hoping to achieve a similar experience flocked to India.

The Beatles generated a cascade of new attention for the "Hippie Trail," a legendary overland thoroughfare for people looking for an intrepid journey to connect Europe with South Asia via the Middle East from the mid-1950s through the late 1970s. Flying was expensive, so those travelers took low-cost trains and buses, hitchhiking whenever possible. Many in a generation that freely questioned its role in society and rejected the status quo in politics, society, and religion felt that acceptance and connection would be found in India. As Rory MacLean wrote in *Magic Bus: On the Hippie Trail from Istanbul to India*, those travelers "aimed to learn and extract pleasure from 'the foreign.' Most of all, they traveled to be transformed." After an Australian couple, Maureen and Tony Wheeler, took the route in 1972, they collected their notes and recommendations and, the following year, stapled together a guidebook and called it *Across Asia on the Cheap*. It included practical information about transportation, lodging, and food and was the first publication of what would become the global guidebook company Lonely Planet. The wealth of information, bound together in a single volume, gave structure to a trail that was not yet a trail, turning what might have felt like an impossible cross-continental expedition into a manageable journey. As the route's popularity grew, all-inclusive "overlander" buses ferried tourists across the continents, often terminating in Kathmandu, Nepal, where they congregated in hostels and cafés along what was known as Freak Street. The road was long and bumpy, but it traveled through some of the most storied terrain in the world: past the great mosques of Istanbul and Tehran, through the legendary Khyber Pass, and into the markets and forts of Lahore and Delhi.

The first printing of *Head East*, another guidebook published the same year as *Across Asia on the Cheap*, encouraged people to "Leave the West for just a little while, free yourself to do whatever you want to do or feel. You'll never be the same again once you've drunk the freedom of the world. The peoples of the East may not have the material wealth of the West, but they do possess everything else—especially a soul." Some of the travelers went to see the world, some went for cheap hash, but others crossed the world for sincere, purposeful reasons: they fundamentally believed that India would open their eyes, fill in a spiritual blank space in their lives. The Hippie Trail was marketed as not just an exploration of the world but a probe of its spiritual facets along a pilgrimage to the birthplaces of Hinduism and Buddhism, a chance to walk the land of reincarnated monks and wandering sadhus and connect with the teachings and symbolism— antimaterialism and minimalism, yoga and meditation—of Shiva, Vishnu, and the Buddha. There were many spiritually curious travelers who arrived in India during that time and found what they were looking for. But there were others who, upon finally arriving in South Asia, found the destination not what they had imagined, not what they had built it up to be. Some, at the end of the long road, even took their own lives.

My father left India after four months entirely enthralled. He flew to Southeast Asia and Indonesia, where he passed seven months, before returning to India to bus, train, and hitchhike through Pakistan, Afghanistan, Iran, Iraq, Syria, and Jordan to Turkey—following the Hippie Trail but in reverse. In our family his stories were legendary, often turning into lessons or parables in a blink. I grew up in awe of my father's travels, in particular in India. It was an inevitability that I would one day follow in his footsteps. By 2008, I had graduated from university, worked for a year roofing houses in Vancouver, Canada, and, without deliberation, begun planning a trip. I may not have realized it at the moment, but I was looking to India to provide a moment of clarity for what I wanted to do with my life. My undergraduate degree felt useless. I had no career ideas. I was, in many ways, lost.

Within days of my arrival in India, I was at the foot of the great Himalayas, watching as monsoon mist burnt off to reveal the range's peaks. My father stood beside me. It was my hope, here in the country he so adored, that we would find our way back to the close relationship we had enjoyed when I was a young teenager. If anywhere in the world could challenge and push us while offering a setting of shared interest, it would be India. We spent the first six weeks of my ten-month trip together in the country's north and west. India had changed dramatically in the forty years since my father's first visit. The country was booming—its population, its economy, and its tourism industry. In the early 2000s, the country had officially launched an "Incredible India" (stylized as Incredible !ndia) marketing campaign in a bid to promote itself as a premier tourist destination. The ads buried the country's poverty, environmental issues, and inequality under dazzling footage of elegant train journeys, mountaintop getaways, and ashram retreats and included targeted advertising for travelers who might be interested specifically in adventure, nature, or spirituality.

That year my father had turned sixty-five and wanted to test both his body and his mind on a two-week unsupported trek in India's far-northern region of Ladakh. I sought out those mountains to embark on a trek with him, to learn about his past—as a traveler and a father—as a way to understand my own road ahead, my future. Ultimately, he and I failed in our attempt to hike the Zanskar Valley, forced to turn back after several days by the onset of altitude sickness. We were both humbled, and both felt defeat. But for me the failure stung harder: I lost an opportunity that I had built up in my mind as the ideal moment, of clouds parting deep in these storied mountains, to connect with my father.

For millennia, India has rested in faraway consciousnesses as the source of ancient religion and mysticism and as a destination for awakenings in their myriad forms and names: nirvana, *moksha*, enlightenment. From around the world, inquisitive pilgrims of all ages, backgrounds, and religious persuasions have flocked to India to embark on journeys of self-discovery, exploring the roots of notions such as karma and reincarnation, in the hope that they will be transformed.

This perception arose from a long history of outsiders magnifying the region as a place of impossible beauty. The first European emissaries, missionaries, and travelers who began crisscrossing the globe returned from the lands that later became India with images of color, vibrancy, and riches unfathomable at home. On Marco Polo's homeward journey from the Far East in the late thirteenth century, the Venetian traveler disembarked and visited several regions of India's south, a land where, he wrote, "Every thing necessary to support life abounds," a place he called "indeed the noblest and richest country in the whole world"—a bold statement by one so well traveled. He noted that one region produced "the most beautiful and valuable cotton cloths in the world; also the thinnest and most delicate, resembling our spiders' webs." He saw magic in a conjurer "who enchanted the fishes, depriving them of the power to injure the persons who dive under water for the pearls" and fauna unparalleled, "an abundance of wild animals, particularly monkeys of various shapes, some of which would almost seem to be men. There are cats of a very peculiar and wonderful species, lions, leopards, and ounces [snow leopards] in great numbers." These stories—of tropical landscapes and cloud-piercing mountains, of warm spices and healing herbs, of fine textiles and glittering jewels, of magic and mysticism—became the bedrock of India's image for centuries.

By the twentieth century, India's spiritual teachers, its orange-robed gurus and wise yogis, became the country's traveling face around the world. A student in Berlin, an actor in Los Angeles, or an artist in London could hear an address by a Buddhist monk or partake in a mass meditation with a Hindu priest without leaving his or her city. Those who looked east with curious eyes memorized the story of Siddhartha Gautama, a prince who had renounced his title and possessions and began a long wandering in search of spiritual fulfillment before sitting under a tree for forty-nine days and becoming the Buddha. They idolized the story of Mahavira, the twenty-fourth and last *tirthankar*, a spiritual teacher or prophet, of the Jain religion. Also born into royalty, Mahavira forsook his family, property, and possessions at age thirty to devote the rest of his life to the pursuit of Kevala Jnana, the Jain state of omniscience. They studied the ancient Hindu and Buddhist texts, or sutras, or the Sanskrit epics the Mahabharata and the Ramayana, looking for inspiration.

Those who were inspired by the tales of asceticism, enlightenment, and transcendence turned their eyes to India in the hope of walking similar paths. If the likes of the Buddha and Mahavira had achieved an awakening there, why couldn't they? For many, India was seen as the source of it all—where it had all begun, and, for many, where their own journey might culminate. Throughout the twentieth century, hordes of travelers flocked to the country—donning the saffron robes of a Hindu sadhu or the white dressings of a Jain priest, the muted woolens of a Buddhist nun or the elegant robes of a Muslim imam—and embarked on a journey to "find themselves." The literature that had emerged from and about India in the late nineteenth and early twentieth centuries, written largely by colonists or travelers from the West, proliferated notions of pilgrimage, mysticism, and spirituality in the minds of those looking in from the outside.

Some scholars have placed the early-twentieth-century wave of spiritual tourists at the feet of Helena Blavatsky, a cofounder of the Theosophical Society, a group devoted to comparative religion and philosophy. Founded in 1875 in New York City, the society shortly thereafter relocated its headquarters to Adyar, in south India, under Blavatsky, who was originally from modern-day Ukraine. "Blavatsky and her followers came upon a groundswell of changing sentiment towards India and particularly its religious traditions, and popularised it," wrote Alex Norman. "They added to the already developed Romantic notion of India as the mystical locale, *par excellence*. . . . With her writings, regardless of their veracity, India moved from being a colonial location and seat of mercantile possibility, to being one of sacred geography and spiritual possibility. In particular, she helped cement the notion of India as a place of self-realisation and self-transformation; one that had been developing for some time."

As more and more international travelers visited India, they brought home experiences and teachings, blazing a shining trail for more travelers to follow. Transcendentalists, members of the mid-nineteenth-century movement led by Ralph Waldo Emerson, which advanced notions of individual freedom above society and the value of the natural world, found inspiration in Indian classical texts including the Bhagavad Gita, a seven-hundred-verse epic poem, part of the Mahabharata, that explores moral and philosophical dilemmas inherent in war, spirituality, and life. Emerson called the Bhagavad Gita "the first of books; it was as if an empire spake to us[,] nothing small or unworthy but large, serene, consistent[,] the voice of an old intelligence which in another age & climate had pondered & thus disposed of the same questions which exercise us." Henry David Thoreau, a mentee of Emerson, was also greatly influenced by Indian spirituality, mentioning ancient Sanskrit texts including the Vedas, the oldest collection of Hindu scriptures, produced sometime between 1500 and 1100 BCE, and the Laws of Manu throughout his works. He once alluded to the way Walden Pond, which served as the setting of his most famous work, is linked—both literally through the melting of ice and movement of water, and symbolically through those who perform rituals at its banks—to India's holiest waterway: "The pure Walden water is mingled with the sacred water of the Ganges."

Whether through teachings or texts, India became a spiritual beacon for those who were unsatisfied or untethered, curious or uncertain, who set out along paths that often ended at the bare feet of a guru. In Sanskrit, the word *guru* roughly translates to "moving from darkness to light," and for every persuasion and interest, India has provided a guru with a welcoming hand. Tourists looking for guidance can take their pick. For humble self-realization and love there have been Neem Karoli Baba and Shri Mataji Nirmala Devi; for yoga, Tirumalai Krishnamacharya, known as "the father of modern yoga," as well as B.K.S. Iyengar and Bikram Chowdhury; for selflessness, there were Sri Ramakrishna and his disciple Swami Vivekananda, both revered in India for their teachings; for music, Ravi Shankar; for miracles, Sri Sathya Sai Baba; and for a simple hug there is Mata Amritanandamayi Devi, known as the "hugging saint." And for Transcendental Meditation there was Maharishi Mahesh Yogi, the guru made legendary by the Beatles.

Through the second half of the twentieth century, every seeker of wisdom was influenced by those who had previously walked the road. Memoirs such as *A Search in Secret India* by Raphael Hurst, published in 1934 under Hurst's pen name, Paul Brunton, offered a personal story of an international traveler experiencing an enlightening moment in India. In the company of the Indian sage Sri Ramana Maharshi, Hurst, a British bookshop owner born in London, experienced an awakening. "I find myself outside the rim of world consciousness," he wrote. "The planet which has so far harboured me disappears. I am in the midst of an ocean of blazing light. The latter, I feel rather than think, is the primeval stuff out of which worlds are created, the first state of matter. It stretches away into untellable infinite space, incredibly alive."

No book, however, had such an impact as *Autobiography of a Yogi* by Paramahansa Yogananda. Originally published in 1946, the year before India gained its independence from the British Empire, the book quickly found resonance around the world, particularly in the West. Ravi Shankar told the *Guardian* that he had given George Harrison a copy of the book, which had sparked his interest. The book follows Yogananda's journey throughout India and abroad in a search for enlightenment. Born in the dusty transit town of Gorakhpur, India—near the birthplace of the Buddha—he arrived in 1920, at age twenty-seven, in the United States, where he introduced thousands to Eastern spiritual teachings and practices.

Autobiography of a Yogi has been credited with popularizing concepts including yoga and meditation, interwoven into Yogananda's message of "self-realization" through transcendence of the ego and acceptance of the true soul, to the Western world. The book arrived at an opportune moment. "As the American people were being buffeted by the thunderous wrath of two world wars and a major depression," Columbia Business School professor Hitendra Wadhwa wrote, "he exhorted them to practice yoga so they could discover that the spiritual anchorage they were seeking was already with them—in fact, it was *within* them." Studded with principles and parables for life—Yogananda's desire to seek the Himalayas is tempered by the words of his own guru, who says, "Wisdom is better sought from a man of realization than from an inert mountain"—*Autobiography of a Yogi* had an influence that cannot be overstated. The book has sold more than 4 million copies and, in 1999, was named by Harper-Collins one of the one hundred best spiritual books of the century.

Yogananda's story became nothing less than a guidebook for those looking to India in the hope of attaining spiritual fulfillment. The book inspired Steve Jobs, decades before the creation of the iPod or iPhone, to save enough money while working as a technician at the video game company Atari in Los Altos, California, to fund a trip to India to meet a guru. The guru he sought was a Hindu mystic named Neem Karoli Baba, born around 1900, who had been a wandering ascetic until he had built an ashram near the north Indian hill town of Nainital. "For me it was a serious search," Jobs told his biographer Walter Isaacson. "I'd been turned on to the idea of enlightenment and trying to figure out who I was and how I fit into things." Jobs arrived in India in 1974, but when he reached Nainital, he learned that Karoli Baba had died a few months earlier. The guru's ashram was nearly abandoned. Even without meeting his guru, Jobs spent seven months in India before returning to the United States, to Silicon Valley, and he returned transformed. When he called his parents from the Oakland airport asking to be picked up, they barely recognized their son. "My head had been shaved, I was wearing Indian cotton robes, and my skin had turned a deep, chocolate brown-red from the sun," Jobs told Isaacson. When he walked back into the Atari offices asking for his job back, he arrived barefooted and wearing saffron robes like a sadhu—a far cry from the later image of the clean-cut, black-turtleneck-and-jeans-wearing visionary behind the most iconic technology company ever. When he died in 2011, according to Isaacson, the only title that was on Jobs's personal iPad was *Autobiography of a Yogi*, which he was known to reread every year. At his memorial service, each attendee received a mysterious brown box that contained not Apple's latest tech innovation but a copy of the book that had so influenced Jobs's life.

Some seekers, such as Jobs and Harrison, returned home galvanized and incorporated what they had learned into their lives. But others arrived in India and never returned from their journeys. Malcolm Tillis lived in India between 1973 and 1984 and during the later years became particularly fascinated by "the many Westerners who have taken the plunge, left the bright lights of home and are now living fulfilled lives in this vast, fascinating country," he writes in the introduction of the reissue of his book *New Lives: 54 Interviews with Westerners on Their Search for Spiritual Fulfilment in India*, first published in 1989 as *Turning East: New Lives in India*. He toted his Olivetti typewriter across India to find those people and to document their stories. "You will find a former Nazi youth supporter who served a jail sentence after the 2nd World War, two reformed heartbreakingly disturbed teenage rebels," he wrote. "There are also some exceptionally brave people who abandoned successful careers— even their families. A few, however, arrived in India with their married partners—one couple with their 4 children, all six committed

Buddhists. You will also find ascetics living alone in isolation, and saintly souls who knew instinctively from childhood there was a richer life waiting for them to find and unfold."

Many of Tillis's interview subjects offered accounts similar to that of Hans Hablützel, who, in 1952, left his home in Switzerland at twenty-three in search of a guru in India. He told his family and friends not to try to contact him so as to not interrupt his spiritual path. Outside Calcutta, he found a guru who told Hablützel when he arrived that he had known he was coming and had been waiting for him. Hablützel studied under his guru for twelve years—during which he gave him the name Swami Jnanananda—until the older man's passing. Hablützel then began a long wandering around India that ultimately culminated in the Himalayas, near the glacial source of the Ganges River. After decades of study, Hablützel became a yogi, inspiring hundreds of followers in his own right. "People often ask me why I have chosen this path," he told Tillis. "From my early days I wanted to know the purpose of life, what one can attain within a lifetime. If I become an artist, what is the ultimate art? If I become a poet, what is the ultimate poem? If I become a musician, what is the ultimate music? I tried all these things; very soon I realized there is no ultimate. So then I wanted to know the purpose of this life which is made up of so many moments: what is a moment of life—a moment of consciousness—a moment of existence?"

Contentment, Hablützel claimed, is the secret to happiness and the only way to achieve this is not to search for happiness, but to instead step back: "To forget the world makes man a pilgrim; to forget the next world makes him a saint; to forget the ego gives him self-realization; forgetfulness of the forgetful is perfection." But there are dangers lurking, known as "the Five Thieves"—lust, anger, greed, infatuation, and ego—that weaken and inhibit a person's capacity for satisfaction. They are found in Hinduism, Sikhism, Buddhism, and Jainism and can be overcome through devotion. "All spiritual practice is to enable us to eradicate these evils," Hablützel said; someone who has mastered these evils will be "detached even when they are present in his environment." The way forward is to look forward.

"For anyone who has renounced the world," he said, "there is no past."

The 2001 documentary *Last Hippie Standing* chronicled the lives of those who had built a new life at the end of their rainbow. "Maybe they died and maybe they're still living under a tree somewhere or sitting in a cave," one man named Swami William, dressed in orange robes, said in the film. He said he first came to India from the United States in the late 1960s: "I think perhaps it was just the most exotic, the most different from Protestant America, the most different thing, the most unusual, the most colorful. And those people growing up at that time, seeing that—and this is a cliché, I suppose—the materialism of American culture didn't provide spirit. The youth of America in the sixties, in their twenties, had everything. And it wasn't enough because everything was things, and there wasn't spirit and mystery and creativity and magic."

For seekers with a certain conviction, one step is always first: renunciation. Former lives hold baggage and trauma and burden, whereas with a change into saffron or white clothing and the shaving of a head, a new life can be born. One of this cohort was an eighteen-year-old American, William A. Gans, who in 1969 traveled along the Hippie Trail to India, where he adopted the sadhu way and a new name, Baba Rampuri, as he recounted in his memoir, *Autobiography of a Sadhu: A Journey into Mystic India*. Rampuri claimed he had been the first Westerner initiated into the Naga sect of sadhus, renowned for walking naked save for ash covering their bodies and armed like their warrior ancestors.

Foreign travelers such as Gans, all largely inspired by pursuing spiritual growth in India, took up residence in ashrams or found remote corners of the Himalayas in which to live quietly. In the 1960s and '70s, one of the most storied corners was the temple of Kasar Devi and the surrounding Kalimath Ridge. Located in the mountains of Uttarakhand, the ridge became a beacon for freethinking international travelers, many of whom lived there for years. Alfred Emmanuel Sorensen was one of the first. Born in 1890 in Denmark, he arrived in India in 1930 at the invitation of Rabindranath Tagore, an Indian poet and musician who in 1913 had won the Nobel Prize in Literature, the first non-European to do so, and whom Sorensen had met in England. "I have come [to India] with no conscious purpose and with no concrete idea of giving or of getting—but as a wanderer, a happy pilgrim, who know that the goal is everywhere," Sorensen wrote in his journals, later collected in the book *Dancing with the Void*. In his first few years in India, he became an initiated Buddhist monk and was given the name Sunyata by Ramana Maharshi, a renowned guru who attracted many followers from the West, who called Sorensen a "rare-born mystic." After exchanging his European garb for the robes of a sadhu, Sunyata traveled throughout India as an ascetic, visiting temples and gurus and spiritual sites. The family of Jawaharlal Nehru, who would become India's first prime minister in 1947, offered him a caretaker position on a piece of land in the hills near Kasar Devi. Sunyata would end up spending forty years in India, based largely in a cavelike stone hut that he built on Kalimath Ridge. "I was contented in Denmark," he told his biographers, "though I could see that others regarded me as an oddity. In England, I felt freer. In India, I felt at home. But in Himalaya, I feel closest to heaven."

Sunyata lived a simple life in his hut, as well as in an even more secluded cave higher up the mountain. "In Himalayan solitude," he said, "one does not think or talk about any ailments, diseases or ego woes. Within me, there are no sin complexes, frustrations or grievance complexes." As his reputation grew, seekers from around the world were drawn to the ridge: the poets Allen Ginsberg and Gary Snyder visited in the early 1960s, as did the musicians Cat Stevens and George Harrison. Others included the writer D. H. Lawrence, the psychologist and psychedelic advocate Timothy Leary, and the renowned Buddhist academic Robert Thurman, who brought his young daughter Uma to the ridge in the early 1970s. The eccentric congregation of writers, artists, inventors, poets, and spiritual seekers who flocked to Kalimath Ridge led to a nickname, "Crank's

Ridge." It was also known as "Hippie Hill" for the thousands of backpackers who followed the famous and turned the remote mountain refuge into a subculture outpost in the Himalayas.

By the late 1970s, the legendary Hippie Trail had come to an end, when the Iranian Revolution and the Soviet invasion of Afghanistan severed the overland path and heightened the danger for travelers. India, however, retained its draw for seekers. They took new routes, by land and by air, believing that any rough road was worth it if it led to the glimmering pinnacle they felt lay at the end. They had questions, and India, they believed, held the answers. The country was seen as a place of transformation, and they went to be transformed.

In 1985, Régis Airault arrived in India to work as the resident doctor of psychology at the French Consulate in Bombay, the commercial center on the country's southwest coast now called Mumbai. At the time, travelers from France, upon arriving in India, could visit the consulate to place their passport and return plane ticket into safekeeping. Airault, therefore, had the opportunity to speak to those travelers, often in their twenties or early thirties, soon after they landed in India, excited about their forthcoming travels, as well as after several months in the country, before they returned home. He began noticing a curious condition in some of the French travelers, particularly among those who had spent longer periods of time in the country: a spectrum of behavioral and psychological changes that later became known as "India Syndrome." The condition has cousins around the world: religious tourists to Jerusalem are struck with a spontaneous psychosis upon visiting the city, certain that they are hearing God or in the presence of saints; visitors to Florence are physically overcome, even hallucinate, upon viewing the beauty of the city's art.

In India, Airault would be dispatched to examine travelers who had lost their bearings, had become disoriented and confused, or had found themselves in manic and psychotic states. The contrast was shocking. "I would see them perfect when they arrive and after one month, I would see them totally unstable," he recalls. Initially, what Airault observed was blamed solely on drug use, but many of the travelers were also exhibiting symptoms such as depression and isolation, stemming from a feeling of disorientation in an unfamiliar land or culture. In rare cases, others were later diagnosed with acute psychosis, delirium, and delusion. At its most powerful, India Syndrome could be all-consuming, leading to a complete detachment from reality or an overwhelming disconnection from familiarity. Airault came to call that group "the travelers who were lost forever."

Over the decade that followed, the French psychiatrist traveled back and forth between France and India researching and compiling notes and observations into a thesis, which he adapted into a book, published in 2000, called *Fous de l'Inde*—Crazy About India—which revolves around a central question: Does India itself bring forth these transformations, or do people go there determined to be transformed? He argued that India possesses a collection of forces, unlike those found anywhere else in the world, that can spark these personal changes: "More than any other country, India has a way of stimulating the imagination and stirring intense aesthetic emotions which can at any moment plunge the traveler into utter anxiety," he wrote. "For this reason, our 'experience' of India can be somewhat ambivalent. This depends on each person's personal history, their 'impulse to travel' and past traumas which have been buried deep inside. The subconscious has a way of bringing us face-to-face with them at certain times of our lives. Because India speaks to the unconscious: it provokes it, makes it boil and, sometimes, overflow. It brings forth, from the deep layers of our psyche, the buried."

Airault distinguished the symptoms of India Syndrome from common culture shock, the experience of travelers either feeling an intense connection to a new and different place or feeling an extreme rejection and disconnection from it. Culture shock often manifests within days of arriving; India Syndrome, rather, typically emerges after weeks or months of residing in the country. He notes that many travelers arrive with some deep-rooted idea of what India is, previously held expectations of what India can offer—emotionally, physically, or spiritually—and a hardened determination to realize that imagined experience: "The trip to India begins early, with the idea that we have made, conveyed by our culture, its cliches, its legends, its myths, but also by our childhood fed by marvelous tales and stories." He included dozens of examples of foreign travelers he observed or treated: one had burned his passport shortly after arriving and spent two months in prison suffering from anxiety attacks; one had been wandering around India, in good health and spirits, for five years even as his parents had presumed him dead; and another had traveled to the holy city of Varanasi and believed that the goddess Kali could hear his dreams and was speaking to him. Many of the cases were more benign: travelers arriving with an emotional or traumatic history that was suddenly brought to the surface and confronted, which resulted in a breakdown.

Though India Syndrome, like many of its cousins, is not universally recognized or officially accepted as a psychological diagnosis, the symptoms have become enough of a concern that insurance companies selling travel packages to India-bound tourists have been known to include clauses that void the coverage if the traveler has a psychiatric history or if he or she takes drugs. Several embassies and consulates in India have permanent psychiatrists on staff to address and treat their nationals in distress. If they don't, they contact a psychiatrist such as Sunil Mittal, who has built a career in part on diagnosing and treating the conditions that arise from India Syndrome. As the senior psychiatrist at the Cosmos Institute of Mental Health & Behavioural Sciences, Mittal sees approximately one foreign tourist every week in his office in New Delhi who would fall under the umbrella of India Syndrome. The tourists arrive at the clinic through the recommendation of an embassy, in response to the concerned pleas of a family member, or as the result of an arrest made by police.

Mittal breaks down cases of India Syndrome into two categories. The first occurs among those who arrive as simple tourists but bring with them some emotional or psychological issue or trauma relating to their family, their job, their relationships, or their past.

"They come with a turmoil, and they have a breakdown here," Mittal explains. At the core of the person, he says, lies a vulnerability, a deep-rooted issue that he or she hopes to resolve. The second group is made up of those who come to India determined to embark on some form of spiritual journey to seek higher meaning or realization. They visit holy centers and sites and immerse themselves in training and study of meditation or yoga. They often become enamored by yogis or gurus and seek an extreme break from their conventional life. "On the path of a spiritual quest, all the values that have been ingrained in someone are questioned," Mittal says. "This can lead to a state of emptiness, a state of loss of direction, or a sudden feeling of exaltation—and then not knowing how to handle a situation."

Though drug use is rarely the only spark, it is often an accelerant. Cannabis has been consumed in India for centuries in three forms. The most common is *bhang*, prepared with ground-up leaves and seeds that are mixed into a drink like a yogurt-based *lassi*. *Ganga* is the flowering buds of the cannabis plant, most often consumed by smoking. And *charas*, or hash, is produced by rubbing the sticky resin off the leaves and buds of the plant until it forms balls that are smoked in a straight clay pipe called a chillum. Records of cannabis use in Ayurvedic medicine date back a millennium. But the plant most famously appears in Hindu mythology as a favorite of Shiva, who, according to legend, bore the plant from his body to purify *amrita*, elixir of life. Another tale is that the god took *bhang* to heal himself after consuming a great poison that had been unleashed on the world. In 1961, pro-legalization advocates in India successfully petitioned to have *bhang* removed from the definition of cannabis in the international Single Convention on Narcotic Drugs, arguing that it played an important ceremonial and religious role in festivals. But in 1986, India made the cultivation, consumption, and sale of all forms of cannabis illegal, despite its continued use by sadhus and international tourists alike. The convoluted gray area that cannabis occupies—semi-illegal, openly used ceremonially—has tempted many foreign tourists to experiment. The results can be overwhelming. "It's like a bomb," Mittal says.

The new lens that the traveler begins to see through can distort even the surest of convictions, replacing hesitation with complete openness, skepticism with blind trust. For a 2007 paper on the forces that push international tourists in India to renounce their lives, the Indian anthropologist Meena Khandelwal interviewed three foreigners who had moved permanently to India to pursue a spiritual journey and noted that a US consulate official in New Delhi had told her that "his office may see about twenty-five Americans each year who have exhausted financial resources and alienated family members in the United States." Changes can manifest themselves subtly at first, as strong culture shock. Some begin to wear a *lungi* or a dhoti, a saronglike garment, or one of the many forms of Indian sari. They carry walking sticks like the staff of Shiva, wear red threads tied around their wrists denoting blessings, and sport long necklaces of *rudraksha* seeds—Hindu prayer beads—around their necks. Travelers who are not Hindu or Muslim or Buddhist or Jain before arriving become, at least in appearance, a model example of a convert. They stay in ashrams or monasteries, where they study and learn, reform their lifestyle or system of belief, or preach asceticism.

Over his career, Mittal has treated hundreds of cases across a spectrum of severity. There was the American man found wandering near the Taj Majal, disoriented and confused. After noticing the man behaving bizarrely, the owner of a *dhaba*, a roadside eatery, called the police. The US Embassy was contacted and then Mittal's clinic. He determined that the man had arrived in the city of Agra like any other tourist; he had not been on a spiritual journey but simply wanted to see the iconic mausoleum. There, he had tried cannabis, something he had smoked back home with no adverse effects, but this time it had proved overwhelming. He arrived at the clinic unable to answer more than basic questions. "He left everything—his backpack, passport, everything—and just ran away," Mittal says. Within a month of his return to the United States, he had returned to his normal self. Then there was the British woman who had been living alone for a year in a small cottage in the mountains of the

state of Uttarakhand. Locals had become concerned after she had begun behaving and talking strangely and stopped paying her rent.
When police arrived, she claimed she had been captured by spirits.
Her family contacted Mittal, who saw that she was on a path to a
complete renunciation of her previous life. And there was the American woman in her twenties who had been traveling in India before
withdrawing from contact with home—one of the more severe cases
Mittal has seen. After months of searching, she was found living in
an ashram in Rishikesh and performing erotic, half-naked dances
each night. When confronted by Mittal's team, she was adamant that
she was an *apsara*, a female mythological spirit who tempts yogis
and priests to test their resolve in celibacy. She assured Mittal that
she was fine and that this was her path, but she appeared to be in a
trancelike state.

For both Airault and Mittal, in most cases, the treatment is simple: a plane ticket home—back to family and familiarity. But in
other, more severe cases, the experiences of some individuals in India
can leave permanent marks on their behavior even after they return
home. In one case, a Japanese tourist had been reported missing and
was tracked to Varanasi, where he had had a psychotic episode and
been detained by police after trying to board a train without a ticket.
When he was brought to the clinic, Mittal found him to be suffering
from schizophrenia and sent him home to Japan. Four years later, he
reappeared at the clinic, asking to be hospitalized. "He felt he was
going to be safe in India," Mittal says.

"At one end, it could be a true pursuit," Mittal explains, "and for
somebody else it could result in a psychotic state." At this darker
end, some travelers come to believe that they are inhabited by spirits or are a god reincarnate, India's version of a "Messiah complex."
Others place themselves in dangerous situations by pushing themselves to increasingly greater extremes in their search for spiritual
fulfillment—believing that India, above all other countries, will
offer the transformation and enlightenment they seek. As Airault
concluded in *Fous de l'Inde*, there are some "who wander aimlessly,

in another world and without desire, sheltered from emptiness, suffering and life. . . . At the end of the road, the limit may be death."

My first trip to the subcontinent lasted ten months. I traveled to nearly every state in India, from the glimmering salt plains of Gujarat in the west to the plunging valleys of Meghalaya in the east, from the serene and lush backwater canals of Kerala in the south to the romantic valleys of Himachal Pradesh in the north. Along the way I encountered dozens of international tourists who had arrived in Delhi or Mumbai or Kolkata and shed their cargo pants, quick-dry shirts, and sneakers in favor of linen wraps, beaded necklaces, and bindi dots on their foreheads. There were others, too, who went beyond superficial appreciation of a culture: some who had begun as tourists hoping to see the world but had become so enchanted by the country that they ended up returning year after year to spend six months in the country, others who had given up everything to live there permanently.

My trip culminated, as many pilgrimages and journeys to India do, in the Himalayas. I boarded a train from Delhi north to the foothills and then a bus to reach the town of Rishikesh. There, I found a simple guesthouse with a view over the river, watched pilgrims stroll across the prayer flag–draped bridges, and got lost wandering the condemned and overgrown ashram complex where the Beatles had stayed. One day, a chance encounter with a German tourist who had been living in a local ashram led to an invitation to visit a riverside cave in which, the man told me, lived a group of Hindu priests. I curiously went along. We walked out of town along a tree-lined road until we came to a faint trail through the forest heading down toward the Ganges River. Only a strand of red ribbon tied to an overhanging branch marked the path. At the riverside, I saw wafts of smoke rise from a campfire. To my surprise, the Hindu priests weren't Indian.

Near the fire sat a man with a shaved head with a red slash between his eyes, wearing only a white dhoti around his waist. He said he was originally from Sweden. When the man wasn't packing a chillum, he was fingering a string of bumpy *rudraksha*, moving each one between his thumb and forefinger. I recall him speaking about the dissatisfaction of his previous life and the "simple life" that he had found in India, in his cave overlooking the Ganges. A tall American man wearing similar garb was at the water's edge, filling a metal container with water. He tipped the contents into a pot over the fire and added tea leaves and sugar to prepare chai. Another disciple, a woman I estimated to be in her early twenties, emerged from the cave singing and walked down to the Ganges River to bathe. I asked the Swedish man how long he had been in India. He told me that seven years earlier, he had realized India was his future and had burned his passport. He had been living in India, predominantly in his riverside cave in Rishikesh, ever since. He had no intention of returning to Sweden.

I never arrived at such a clear realization about my future while in India. After the moment that I had long sought with my father hadn't materialized, I found myself sitting on the banks of the Ganges River, speaking to a man who hadn't given up his search for answers but rather had devoted his life to it. He was one of the latest generation who were arriving in India at a crossroads in their life, convinced that India would place them on a true course. They felt that India, above all other countries, would lead them toward a word with countless meanings: enlightenment. To the pious, it is an elusive, exalted state of spiritual achievement; to laypeople, even those who might call themselves secular, it is a moment of higher understanding about a fraught or muddled aspect of their lives—of finally seeing the light. For some, their moment of enlightenment may lie at the end of a hash-packed chillum or in the long shadow of a Himalayan mountain. It may arise from quiet contemplation in a monastery or an ashram, flow out of the mouth of a holy mountain spring, or spark from the intimate company of a holy man promising wisdom.

7
SOLITUDE

The Ganges River flows languidly past Varanasi. Over millennia the city has gone by many names—Kashi, Banaras—but throughout it has remained the spiritual epicenter of India as the permanent home of Shiva. Varanasi is often called the oldest living city in the world, though it is no historical relic but rather a pulsing artery of the spiritually devout who come to navigate the warren of stone alleyways and bathe in the Ganges River along its holiest bank.

Day and night, pilgrims descend the concrete steps, called ghats, that fringe one side of the river, and dunk their bodies into the water, believing that the Ganges will purify, cleanse, renew them. Men and women perform ablutions and pray or make offerings to Mother Ganga; pilgrims light candles nestled in cups made of leaves and float them out to be carried downstream. Varanasi is a city of purification but also a city of dying. Every hour, day and night, bodies are burned at designated ghats, where fires consume flesh in round-the-clock cremations. To have your body burned at Varanasi and your ashes carried downstream by the Ganges is to achieve what some call *moksha* and others call nirvana—the point when your soul is freed from *samsara*, the endless and torturous cycle of reincarnation. Members of an untouchable caste known as *dom*s carry the bodies through the alleys on their shoulders down to the burning ghats, stoke the pyres, and spread the ashes into the river.

"Yesterday was the full moon and summer solstice. My first day in India," Justin posted on June 21. He had arrived in the city after leaving Kathmandu by bus and crossing the border from Nepal into India. "I'm in Varanasi, one of the holiest sites for Hindus. No photographs are allowed at the burning ghats, but I was shown around by a man who explained the history of this place in an accent I could barely understand. I was shown an ancient Shiva fire, which has allegedly burned for 3500 years. A Hindu man there put some ash from that fire on my third eye as a blessing. I watched the bodies burn from up close but felt out of place there, like everyone was watching me. It feels wrong to stand next to family while a loved one burns." Despite knowing the rules regarding photography of the burning ghats, late one night, he climbed a building high above the river and shot video of the pyres and a procession of attendees from afar. He took a tour of the city's riverside in a boat rowed slowly after sunset, taking in the scenes of faith, riotous and calm, public and private. The boat passed within a few feet of a floating corpse. Some people cannot be cremated at Varanasi: infants and young children, who have yet to lose their purity; people bitten by snakes, an animal associated with Shiva, who are considered to be already on their way to another world; and holy people, including sadhus, who have already achieved a higher place. Their bodies are instead weighted and submerged into the river. Justin disembarked and explored the narrow alleys that make up much of the city's old town. He walked the entire night, until the sun rose again over the glistening waters. "I talked to Sadhus, boatmen, untouchables," he wrote. "I sat in the shadows near the funeral pyres and meditated while smoke and ash washed over me."

As the sun rises and sets on Varanasi, life becomes death, which becomes life again. A body is burned and released into the river while a family bathes their newborn downstream. The bloated corpse of a cow bobs past a man brushing his teeth using the same river water. City sewage trickles down the ghats and into the river, where children splash with glee. Realities are ignored or overlooked because the waters are deemed beyond pure, capable of curing all manner of ailments with a single dip or drink. Varanasi is one of the ultimate destinations for pilgrims in India, and a pilgrimage was what Justin was embarking upon.

India has countless trails along which seekers can act out a quest with a guide and a process, whether living in a meditation center, a silent retreat, or an ashram or walking a more informal and meandering path. Some pilgrims set out to gain spiritual credit, to perform a ritual or make an offering, to find purification or forgiveness, or to reflect. Buddhists flock to Bodh Gaya to sit under a descendant of the tree under which the Buddha achieved enlightenment; Muslims perform their prayers en masse at the Jama Masjid, in the heart of Delhi's hectic old town; and Sikhs circumnavigate their glimmering Golden Temple in Amritsar. Jains have their white marble hilltop temples, Zoroastrians have their fire temples, and Christians have their churches. And Hindus travel to innumerable destinations in the stories of their gods, to the Trimurti, a triad of deities at the top of the Hindu pantheon: Brahma the creator, Vishnu the preserver, and Shiva the destroyer and transformer of the world.

Several of Hinduism's ancient texts, including the Puranas and the Mahabharata, mention a series of pilgrimage destinations around South Asia called *tirtha*s, translated as either a "place of crossing over" or a "ford in a river." A *tirtha* can sometimes be a person who guides in the crossing over, the transition, but is most commonly a site of great sanctity and power or a place of healing and transformation, where the earthly and spiritual planes approach. India is dotted with *tirtha*s that attract pilgrims in droves. Some are built locations, such as a temple or a lingam or a tomb; the hilltop Venkateswara Temple in the south sees between 50,000 and 100,000 visitors every single day. But many *tirtha*s are natural formations: a cave where a saint appeared or a mountain that is home to a god. There are springs and glaciers that are holy, entire forests and individual trees that are sacred, and lakes and hot pools and above all rivers whose waters are a panacea. The Chota Char Dham, a series of pilgrimages to the sources of four holy rivers, including the Ganges, lures intrepid pilgrims to seek out the remote temples deep in the Himalayas. And India's Kumbh Mela festivals, held in Allahabad, Haridwar, Nashik, and Ujjain on twelve-year rotations, have been called the "world's largest human gatherings," where many millions make the pilgrimage to one of the four sites to bathe in the holy river waters; in 2013, an estimated 100 million pilgrims attended a particularly rare mela held in Allahabad to mark a Maha Kumbh Mela, held once every 144 years.

While in Varanasi, Justin stayed at a branch of goSTOPS, a chain of vibrantly painted hostels found around India with the motto "Live social. Experience more." On the hostel's rooftop, he met Brianna Welsh, a Canadian backpacker who had quit a job in finance in New York City and set out for India. "It was a combination of quitting my job, breaking up with my boyfriend, rebelling against my family's expectations of me. That whole 'find yourself' purpose," she says. In her bag, she carried a copy of Elizabeth Gilbert's 2006 bestselling memoir, *Eat Pray Love: One Woman's Search for Everything Across Italy, India, and Indonesia*, which chronicled the thirty-four-year-old American's journey of self-discovery in the wake of quitting her job and divorcing her husband; the "pray" details her spiritual quest in India. The book was the latest in a deep well of spiritual memoirs with titles from *Sleeping in Caves: A Sixties Himalayan Memoir* to *Holy Cow: An Indian Adventure*, each one depicting India as a place of transformation or salvation. When *Eat Pray Love* was adapted to film, Gilbert was played by Julia Roberts, who, like Steve Jobs and many other Western celebrities, had become captivated by Neem Karoli Baba, even long after the guru's death. Roberts converted to Hinduism the year the film was released, in 2010. Inspired by Gilbert's story, a new cohort of international travelers flocked to India; Welsh completed a ten-day silent Vipassana retreat in Bodhgaya hoping to have a journey similar to the author's. "The way she describes the retreat in the book was more along the lines of what I was expecting," Welsh remembers. Instead, it was sweltering and uncomfortable, not a profoundly enlightening experience but a useful one nonetheless.

"I was more unlearning all of the things that I had been taught rather than going too deep into myself. It was more of a healing than it was an elevating experience."

In Varanasi, she and Justin spent the majority of a week together, walking through the narrow alleyways to Dashashwamedh Ghat, where they watched the fire *puja*, a nightly ceremony held along the banks of the Ganges, marked by flickering flames and a cacophony of cymbals and chanting. "I have this view that when you have a lesson to learn, or need some guidance, you tend to gravitate to certain people who can help you learn that lesson faster," Welsh says. Justin was one of those people. "Meeting somebody who came from the kind of world that I was familiar with, but who was now in this new environment was very reassuring." Other travelers she had met on the trip flitted around the country casually and aimlessly, but Justin was deliberate in and confident about what he wanted. In a journal entry at the time, she noted that Justin had told her about his plans: to head north into the Himalayas and "go radio-silent and live amongst nature tech free for as long as he could survive, solo, hiding out in the caves of the mountains."

One evening when Justin was exploring the alleys alone, he met a skinny old man with rosaries around his neck, a gray beard, and thinning hair matted into dreadlocks. As thunder boomed and monsoon rain drenched the city, Justin listened to the man play a flute called a *bansuri*. Crafted from a single piece of hollowed-out bamboo, with either six or seven holes, the instrument—along with tabla drums and the sitar—is a staple of Indian classical music and a favorite of the Hindu god Krishna. "We practiced the Bansuri-bamboo Indian flute, and sat near the balcony as a monsoon blew in," Justin wrote about the encounter, posting a black-and-white picture of the man. The man wasn't Indian; rather he spoke with a strong German accent and said he had been living in India for the past two decades. "20 years in India," Justin wrote in admiration. "Never to return home. He lives a simple life, with few possessions." Justin's chance meeting with the German man—undoubtedly his first meeting of a foreign national living long term in India—left a mark on him, enough that he purchased a *bansuri* from a hole-in-the-wall music shop in Varanasi. To one end of the flute, he attached a foot-long piece of bamboo to create what he called a "musical instrument, walking stick, and self defense weapon against Indian street dogs."

After just over a week in Varanasi, Justin headed west across the Indo-Gangetic Plain to the bustling capital, New Delhi, where he checked in to Madpackers Delhi, a popular guesthouse in the south part of the city. On July 4, while his friends and family were celebrating Independence Day back home in the United States, Justin was celebrating what he called his ten-year travel anniversary. "I just boarded a flight from San Francisco to Kathmandu!" he posted, quoting a journal passage he had written during his 2006 trip. "It's happening. A group of us are spending the next month shooting a doc in the Nepali Himalayas and this might be the happiest I've ever been about anything. It just so happens to be the 4th of July, and that somehow seems significant. Freedom?" He included a photograph from that first trip to Nepal, in which he had knelt before a Buddhist shrine in the Annapurna Mountains. Ten years after that first summer in Nepal, Justin had come full circle. The freedom that he had then tasted had become his way of life.

At Madpackers, he ran into Alexander Gurov, a twenty-one-year-old Ukrainian man he had previously met in Kathmandu, outside the Alobar1000 guesthouse. The pair had explored the streets of the Nepali capital together and had returned to the cremation fires at Pashupatinath. Gurov had a knack for wandering into a crowd and disappearing, a trait that Justin called a "superpower," Gurov remembers. Justin was fascinated by Gurov's story. From a young age, the Ukrainian man had been curious about esoteric religious teachings, and at eighteen, he had left home for Nepal. By chance, he had found himself at a Hare Krishna temple in Kathmandu. The movement, now known as the International Society for Krishna Consciousness, had been founded in New York City in 1966 based on ancient Hindu scriptures including the Bhagavad Gita; it had become popular in Europe and North America during the counterculture wave. Gurov's introduction to Hare Krishna had sparked a spiritual journey that had led him to spend the majority of the following two years in India. He had abstained from alcohol, had been vegetarian and celibate, and had given up material possessions. He had spent six months touring holy places related to Krishna, the often blue-skinned Hindu god, who, in the Bhagavad Gita, counsels Prince Arjuna away from war and conflict and toward a life of peace and freedom. He had received an invitation to study in India but needed to return to Ukraine to secure a student visa. "My last night before my flight home, I had a realization that I wanted to stay forever," he recalls. He had returned to India as soon as he could, to be based in a temple in Vrindivan, one of the main centers of the Hare Krishna movement in India, for a year. As part of his initiation, he had shaved his head and donned white robes, and then walked barefoot from town to town across two states on streets so hot the asphalt would feel soggy underfoot, distributing copies of the Bhagavad Gita.

When he had met Justin in Kathmandu, he had been starting to question his own path: "I could feel the religious fanatic starting to rise, and I didn't like it." But Justin had been enthralled with what Gurov had done, the transformation he had gone through. It had been clear to the Ukrainian man that Justin was taking steps along his own spiritual journey, and he had felt that he could guide Justin toward what he felt was real spirituality, in a community rather than alone in the mountains. But when they reconnected in New Delhi, Gurov could see that Justin had hardened, become more serious and determined and, in a way, desperate. "He was looking for something higher—in taste, in life, in love," he says.

And Justin had a plan: he intended to stay in India's crowded capital only as long as it took to purchase a motorcycle to ride north into the mountains, to find the kind of independence that he had relished in the United States. He messaged Parakram Hazarika, who worked for a PR company whose largest client was Royal Enfield. The two men had connected through Instagram, where Hazarika had spotted a photo of Justin riding his green Royal Enfield across the United States. Hazarika was an avid rider himself, and was building a presence in India's online motorcycle community.

Hazarika took Justin to Karol Bagh, the largest market for used motorcycles in the country. "On Instagram, he looked unapproachable and intimidating, but in person he was the opposite," Hazarika recalls of their first meeting. Justin didn't want just any motorcycle or just any Royal Enfield. He had a specific look in mind—elegant, sleek—and wanted the bike painted and kitted out just so. A Royal Enfield was a smart purchase, Hazarika told him. Practically every mechanic in the country, particularly in the mountains, was trained to turn them inside out, fix them, and rebuild them in service of the horde of riders, both domestic and international, who plied India's northern Himalayan roads on the iconic motorcycles.

Justin found one he liked, a used Classic 500, but it needed work. Detained for close to a week by a bout of "Delhi belly" and a public holiday that delayed the purchase, he finally made the payment of just over 100,000 rupees, or around $1,500. The motorcycle was exactly as he had dreamed, revitalized with a fresh coat of matte black paint and primed for navigating rutted mountain roads. He purchased a "Ladakh carrier," a metal structure bolted to the rear frame to carry metal panniers and luggage, named after the northern region so popular with long-distance riders. He opted for straight handlebars and a chrome visor for the headlight, both of which accentuated the desired sleek look. Justin christened his motorcycle "Shadow" and rode through the waterlogged streets of Delhi, letting the monsoon rain baptize his new ride.

On July 10, he loaded the panniers, strapped his backpack across the metal carrier, and drove north out of the capital along the Grand Trunk Road. The country's principal thoroughfare has been built and rebuilt for two millennia, with sections dating to the third century BCE. "It is to me as a river from which I am withdrawn like a log after a flood," remarked a character about the road in Rudyard Kipling's novel *Kim*. "And truly," continued Kipling, "the Grand Trunk Road is a wonderful spectacle. It runs straight, bearing without crowding India's traffic for fifteen hundred miles—such a river of life as nowhere else exists in the world." But Justin was tired of the buzzing roadways that connect the subcontinent's metropolises and chose to ride into the foothills of the Himalayas, to Dharamshala and the quaint hillside enclave of McLeod Ganj, where the Dalai Lama resides, a place that perennially hums with the soft rumble of Buddhist chanting. Justin took a music lesson from a Buddhist flute player from Nepal and hiked to nearby waterfalls. He posted a photo of himself squatting shirtless by a river, practicing his flute. "Nature is my temple. This is where I worship. I finally found a quiet place in India."

He continued over twisting mountain roads, posting videos and photos as he moved east, then turned north just past the town of Mandi, joining the main north-south thoroughfare that bisects the state of Himachal Pradesh. He entered the Kullu Valley, once known as Kullant Peeth or Kulanthapitha, which translates into "the end of the habitable world." The road was skirted by apple orchards and thick conifer forests. Mountains began to rise up before him. If he had continued north, he would have come to the great range that separates Himachal Pradesh from the region of Ladakh and would have fulfilled his dream of riding one of the most famous motorcycle trips in the world.

Instead, Justin detoured. When he had been in Nepal, he had met a man originally from a remote valley in Himachal Pradesh that boasted holy hot springs, secluded temples, and mountain hamlets with intimate views of the Himalayas. Justin was looking for solitude and quiet, posting that he was "feeling the need for some alone time with mother Himalaya." On July 19, he rode across the Beas River over a bridge draped in multicolored prayer flags and into the Parvati Valley.

Some Tibetan Buddhists believe that across the Himalayas lie hidden sacred valleys, called *beyul*, where the planes of the physical world overlap with those of the sacred world. Scrolls unearthed by a Tibetan yogi after meditating in a mountain cave in the fourteenth century claimed that these valleys are paradises on Earth that can be discovered only after an arduous journey of trials and obstacles undertaken by the most intrepid and worthy of seekers. Tenzin Gyatso, the current Dalai Lama, called *beyul*s "sacred environments . . . [that]

are not places to escape the world, but to enter it more deeply. The qualities inherent in such places reveal the interconnectedness of all life and deepen awareness of hidden regions of the mind and spirit." According to legend, Padmasambhava, also known as Guru Rinpoche, an eighth-century Buddhist monk who is often referred to as "the second Buddha," consecrated several valleys of immense beauty and power, where illumination and healing can be found. The search for a secret valley paradise in the Himalayas, the ultimate sanctum sanctorum, has remained in the minds of lamas and monks, travelers and explorers, believers and questers for centuries.

The mythical kingdom of Shambhala, thought to exist somewhere in the Central Asian mountain massif, likely originated as one such *beyul*. The French explorer and writer Alexandra David-Néel thought the kingdom might reside in Afghanistan's Balkh region, noting that the Persian phrase *sham-i-bala* meant "elevated candle." In Sanskrit, the phrase is translated as "place of peace or silence" but the Persian phrase brings forth the notion that Shambhala might be not a place but rather a state of being—of illumination. During a speech in Bodhgaya in 1985, the Dalai Lama alluded to such a broad definition of Shambhala: "We can only say that it is a pure land, a pure land in the human realm. And unless one has the merit and the actual karmic association, one cannot actually arrive there." The notion of Shambhala being a lost, utopian realm endured for centuries and might have been the inspiration for James Hilton's fictional valley Shangri-La in his 1933 novel *Lost Horizon*, inspired largely by an earlier account, *Om: The Secret of the Abor Valley* by Talbot Mundy. The idea of a lost civilization or mystical utopia deep in the Himalayas spurred countless expeditions of explorers, writers, and spiritual seekers to follow cryptic clues in ancient texts to scour the mountains. Legends emerged of people finding these lost valleys, shedding their belongings, and entering naked through the gates, passing from one world into the next, never to be seen again.

Entering the Parvati Valley feels like stepping into a bucolic Himalayan sanctuary a world away from the din and bustle of cosmopolitan India. Trails spiderweb throughout the valley, terminating at temples and mountaintops, hidden glens and secret alpine meadows filled with wildflowers, waterfalls, and glacial lakes. Snow leopards appear out of clouds, Himalayan black bears with white moons on their chests lurk in the forests, and tusked musk deer and crescent-horned ibex roam. Tigers have even been seen skulking through the deep vales, padding through a land of medicinal plants and aromatic trees that perfume the air and through ancient forests of rhododen-dron that bloom in a blush of red or white. The valley is remote, isolated, and dramatically picturesque. Surrounded by such natural beauty and peace, it is easy to imagine that if one follows the bumpy road that follows the holy river, some fragment of higher under-standing or meaning will emerge within reach.

Justin was one of thousands of visitors drawn to the valley that year. In a country where summer temperatures can spike to 120 de-grees Fahrenheit, the tourists follow the rains to escape the heat, as-cending to higher locales—to a handful of hill stations, relics of the British Raj dotted around the country, and to hamlets and villages in the cooler Himalayas. He rode past a series of small villages wedged between road and river where passersby stop for turmeric-spiced sa-mosas and creamy chai. He rode past shrines to Shiva and Parvati built around a sacred tree or a holy spring where pilgrims murmur a quick prayer out the window of a car or bus as they flit past. The air was thick and humid, scented with pine and deodar, as Justin arrived in Kasol, the largest town in the valley, centered around a square flanked by backpacker cafés and markets.

The moment tourists step down from a bus in India, they are often accosted by touts offering a tip on a cheap guesthouse, a tour, or a trinket. But in the Parvati Valley, the assumption is that every tour-ist arrives seeking one thing. It is offered by clean-cut young men in broad daylight or red-eyed sadhus who sidle up to a newcomer and whisper in their ear, *"Charas?"* They open their hands or pockets to reveal marble-sized balls or deck of cards–sized bricks of potent black hash.

And for those who see the Parvati Valley as a destination for drugs, all paths lead to Malana, a remote village in a steep-sided glen that forks off the principal valley. Situated just below a ridge at 8,700 feet in elevation, the village consists of a cluster of multicolored buildings almost constantly hidden from sight in the clouds. Legend holds that the village was founded by deserters from the army of Alexander the Great after he invaded northern India. Alexander's soldiers had grown weary of the hostile land, and after an eight-year campaign and with the threat of another conflict approaching, they mutinied and retreated for home. But some soldiers, the story goes, are said to have defected and hidden out in a remote valley, where they intermarried with locals.

Since its inception, the village has maintained a form of independence from the country at large, in part due to its geographical isolation. Until 2003, when a dam was built across the Malana Glen, the village was accessible only by foot, via a full-day trek. The Malanese speak Kanashi, an autochthonous language that those in neighboring villages can't understand; govern themselves with their own laws under the epithet "the oldest surviving democracy in the world"; and view themselves as a caste above everyone else, exchanging goods with outsiders by dropping an item in the dirt to ensure that there will be no physical contact. Malana's location on an alpine slope makes it challenging to produce food crops. In the mid-twentieth century, noted Colin Rosser, a Welsh anthropologist who visited in the 1950s, the Malanese practiced pastoralism and modest agriculture in terraced plots. One crop, however, thrived; the abundance of rain and sun that graced the high-altitude meadows made the region an ideal location to cultivate cannabis. Villagers grew the plant to produce hemp and wove the fibrous stalks into baskets, mats, rope, and sandals. But the plants also produced sticky buds of marijuana that were initially consumed for ceremonial and recreational purposes. Over time, cannabis production replaced other sources of revenue.

As foreign tourists began visiting the Parvati Valley en masse during the Hippie Trail years, the region's hash, grown and produced on clandestine plantations or rubbed from plants that grow wild along river and road, turned commercial and then gained an international reputation. In 1994, Amsterdam's Cannabis Cup opened up its categories to include not only marijuana but also hash. In the first three years, products from the Parvati Valley, including a variety called Malana Cream, were ranked among the world's top three; they won first place in the category's inaugural year. European tourists put Malana, as well as several other villages scattered up glens throughout the valley, onto the global drug tourist map. Some hashish, such as that manufactured in Morocco, is golden in color, like the North African desert; that produced in the hills of Afghanistan is a deep, coffee-colored brown; and that rubbed in the Parvati Valley is much darker still, a deep forest green two shades from black.

The Parvati Valley's reputation as a tourist destination has been marked by waves: first Italians in the 1970s, which sparked a flood of other curious Europeans looking for an offbeat destination in India; then Japanese tourists, who started arriving in the 1980s; and then in the 1990s the valley was put on the map for travelers from Israel, who saw it as a must-visit destination for any trip to the subcontinent. Kasol became a hub where you could buy a djembe drum or a beaded purse, a handmade dream catcher or a cheap plastic bong. It became a place where a shepherd would steer his flock of sheep along the rutted main drag through town while mellow Buddhist hymns floated out of backpacker cafés serving banana pancakes and lasagna. And the rest of the valley followed suit. Once remote mountain hamlets became villages with homestays and guesthouses, cafés and shops catering to backpackers. The official estimate is that 10,000 foreign tourists visit the Parvati Valley each year, but there are likely many thousands more. In 1992, the government of India launched a program to track foreign tourists around the country in which any hotel, guesthouse, or paid lodging was required to electronically file a record, called a C-Form, for every guest staying at the establishment. It required each tourist's passport and visa numbers, his or her previously visited location, and his or her next destination. In larger urban centers and more popular tourist destinations, the C-Form process was straightforward, initially submitted on paper and then entered into an online database run by the tourism department. That way, if someone went missing, there would be a digital trail. In more rural areas, however, C-Forms were often ignored. For decades, travelers entered and exited the Parvati Valley without being recorded.

The rest of India attracts a gamut of tourists from wealthy celebrities to recent university graduates on round-the-world trips, from students of yoga looking to hone their postures to New Age hippies looking to relive the old days. Some tour the Golden Triangle, blitzing past the Taj Mahal and a series of desert forts, while others spend languid months along the southern beaches of Goa. The tourists who are attracted to the Parvati Valley, by contrast, come for an escape— from the bustle and noise, from the heat of the Indo-Gangetic Plain, from the pollution and the haze. They come not to check off lists or visit must-see sites but to experience the epitome of *shanti*—peace and tranquility.

Many tourists undoubtedly come to consume copious amounts of hash and marijuana, but others gravitate to the region's remote villages, where law enforcement, regulation, and oversight are effectively nonexistent. They trek and camp under the shadow of the great Himalayas. And many seek a spiritual experience: to make a pilgrimage to the valley's riverside temples, to bathe in hot springs that spill as if from the mouths of gods, to congregate with wandering sadhus and saintlike mystics, or to find their own path onward and upward. Most who visit the valley's backpacker towns and hillside hamlets quickly settle into a pace of life common in this remote corner of India: days that turn into weeks and weeks that blur into months.

In Kasol, Justin found Wi-Fi and messaged Christofer-Lee Humphreys, a Frenchman who had been following Justin's travels after connecting on Facebook as like-minded travelers. He had suggested that the American join him "in a village called Kalga in the Parvati Valley" so he could offer "a few tips to avoid the swell of tourists." They met at a local café before setting off up valley, with Humphreys hitching a ride in a car and Justin following on his motorbike. They passed the temple town of Manikaran, whose hot springs were said to have been created by a mythical snake who had returned the goddess Parvati's earring, or *mani*, that had been lost in the river. Busloads of pilgrims arrive throughout the year to soak in water that bubbles up from the ground so hot that it can cook rice and has to be diluted with cool river water to make it tolerable for bathing. Sikh pilgrims, who believe that Guru Nanak, the founder of Sikhism, visited the site, rub shoulders with Hindu pilgrims, who come to visit sites connected to Shiva and Parvati. But it can be a dangerous road. In 2002, a bus filled with pilgrims plunged into the river near Manikaran. Thirty-nine people died. Neither their bodies nor the bus was ever found. The summer before Justin arrived, a tourist bus filled with pilgrims heading to Manikaran had skidded off the road and tumbled into the river. The final death count was hard to determine, but estimates were as high as thirty. "The bus is still untraceable," then Kullu deputy commissioner Rakesh Kanwar had told media in the days after the accident. "Most of the bodies might be still stuck in the bus or washed away."

Justin zigzagged up along the rutted road and parked where a dam, slated to be the largest in the valley, was under construction below the village of Kalga. Before industrialists and developers had recognized its hydroelectric potential, the flow of the Parvati River had been controlled solely by natural fluctuations: unusual snowfall one winter would yield a fury of meltwater; a bountiful monsoon summer, so welcomed in the fertile plains elsewhere in India, would violently swell its banks. As more dams were introduced into the valley over the years, the energy of the river, often attributed to the fickle whims of a goddess, was tamed and regulated. Except where it could not be. Above Kalga lies territory that is inaccessible to industrialists. It is too remote, too rugged, and too dangerous to exploit. There, however, the power of the river is at its most fierce. It is where the monsoon clouds slam into the mountain wall and disgorge rain in relentless, pounding sheets. It is where the snowpack releases its icy water into the thousands of tributaries that feed the Parvati River.

Justin left his motorcycle by the dam, slung his backpack over his shoulder, and joined Humphreys on the steep dirt trail to the village. Situated at the edge of a hill, Kalga offered a handful of wooden guesthouses and homestays with basic rooms that featured views of the sun setting over the head of the valley. The two men walked past establishments with names such as Snow Line, Apple Cottage, and Mantra until they reached Om Shanti, a simple two-story guesthouse with mud walls painted in bright colors. Like every other building on the hillside, it was surrounded by apple trees; Kalga had long been an orchard village, with dirt trails dipping under leafy branches laden with white and pink blossoms in the spring, red and green apples in the fall. Farmers sold them by the plastic crate, shipping them out of the valley to be distributed throughout the state and beyond, helping earn Himachal Pradesh a reputation for producing some of the best apples in India.

Justin checked into a simple room at Om Shanti with roughly painted walls, a hard mattress on a wooden bed, and a window that overlooked the valley. That night he and Humphreys ate dinner together and swapped stories. Humphreys was heartened to see that Justin matched his Instagram persona: charismatic, adventurous, pensive, kindhearted. That wasn't always the case.

Over the following few days, the pair bonded quickly after realizing they had visited some of the same places around the world. One evening on a rooftop, Humphreys led Justin through some yoga; the French man had been practicing for years and demonstrated a few asanas as the sun dipped lower toward the mountains. They talked about the near impossibility of maintaining stable relationships while on the road. And Justin opened up about a fear that had been troubling him for years, something he felt Humphreys might understand: he was concerned that he was pawning off his adventures—posting photographs and stories for an audience online—without fully living and appreciating them. He had previously written online that he worried that Instagram was removing him from his experiences: "It takes a lot of time, and sometimes I struggle with the vanity in telling a story about myself. But I do love to share my love and myself with people." He and Humphreys spoke about how a search for authenticity fit into the ethos of their travels, about the benefits of being connected to the natural world, and about "trying to stay true to their spirit without selling it off onto the web," Humphreys recalls. It was something Justin had contended with for some time, once writing online that he felt pressure to keep amplifying his adventures to keep his audience engaged.

It appeared to Humphreys, however, that what had long been a niggling concern had come to a head for the American man. Justin was trying to understand where his ego lay. "I think he was at a time in his life when he was asking himself some questions and didn't know exactly what direction he wanted to go," Humphreys says. Still, it struck him that Justin had an immediate plan. "He was just getting ready to do his thing," he remembers, to cut himself off from the guesthouse culture and traveler society. Humphreys had been in the Parvati Valley for three months and more or less on the road continuously for the previous decade. He had come to the valley that spring to attend a Rainbow Gathering, a counterculture congregation held in different locations around the world since the early 1970s that promotes anticonsumerism, peace, and mutual respect. Over a month that spring—from the new moon on May 5 until the new moon on June 6—a gathering had been held in a meadow near Kheerganga, a temporary camp around a holy hot spring a half day's walk higher up the valley, where Shiva had fallen in love with the valley and named it after his wife, Parvati. Apart from the travelers who had slept in tents, Humphreys told Justin, a couple dozen had opted to sleep in boulder caves in the surrounding forest. Humphreys had spent the occasional night there himself.

Justin once described the ethos behind his travel as "not moving to something but moving towards something"—living with vague and changeable plans rather than a fixed goal. But in India his actions were deliberate. What might have started as a nebulous idea of visiting a remote, mountainous holy valley took shape as a clear image in his mind—not to smoke away the days in some grubby guesthouse, musing with fellow travelers about boilerplate Buddhism until his visa ran out but to head into the mountains on his own. "I suppose he wanted something a bit more authentic," Humphreys says. On July 22, Justin posted to Instagram a photograph of him riding his motorcycle along the valley's narrow main road with a quote from Ted Simon's motorcycle memoir *Jupiter's Travels: Four Years Around the World on a Triumph*: "I began to remember who I was, and what I have already done, and the strength came pouring back into me."

Justin's plan was crystallizing: he wanted to leave the relative comforts of a guesthouse to live in a cave.

In villages such as Kalga—and its neighbors Tosh and Pulga—days and weeks tick by slowly as the pilgrims and spiritual tourists wait for the mist to break, for the mountain peaks to be revealed, for things to become clear. But the obscuring fog can make some anxious and impatient. And so they head higher. Humphreys directed Justin farther up the valley, noting that what he sought could be found at Kheerganga. He mentioned the hot springs and the mountain views, the quiet forests and sunlit meadows.

Justin didn't waste time. On July 23, he wrote a long post outlining his plan: embarking on a "solo trek into the upper Parvati Valley in the Indian Himalaya, to live in a cave." He noted that he would carry "some oats, nuts and raisins, a metal cup, knife, rain poncho, journal, candle, sleeping bag, camera, and my flute–walking stick," and that the landscape and ecology appeared familiar enough to recognize edible plants and that "this high in the Himalayas, streams are pure enough to drink." He had heard that the area around Kheerganga was pocked with caves, and home to bears and snow leopards, he added.

Some caves are inhabited by Sadhus, eccentric—mostly naked—Indian men living in the wild, who follow an ancient, mystical yogic tradition. They meditate in caves for months or years at a time; smoking chillums (Indian pipes) of the world's finest Hashish—ganga grows everywhere—and renouncing the world in search of enlightenment. I plan on doing my own version of that and it's something I've been called to do for years now. Not to renounce the world or become enlightened, but to wander alone in these majestic Himalayas, eat from the land, drink straight from the rivers, sleep in caves, meditate, and play my flute to the mountains. To be human. I should be back soon. I'm exited [*sic*] to get on with my motorcycle trip to Ladakh.

P.s. If I get into trouble or begin to starve, I can hike down to a village and get help or eat. I won't die.

THE VALLEY 8 OF DEATH

In the summer of 2015, exactly a year before Justin entered the Parvati Valley, a recent university graduate from Poland named Bruno Muschalik visited India. Muschalik had been offered a coveted job in Krakow with the international consulting and accounting firm Ernst & Young, but he wanted to take a three-week holiday before he started work. He traveled from Delhi north to Kashmir and then to the town of Manali in Himachal Pradesh, where he messaged his girlfriend that he was leaving for the Parvati Valley. It was August 9. He said that he planned on staying a few nights there and might go on a trek in the surrounding mountains. He left some of his belongings at a guesthouse in Manali and boarded a bus. Several days went by, and Muschalik didn't contact his girlfriend or his family. They waited until his scheduled return flight date passed in case he had simply lost his phone. When Muschalik failed to show at Krakow's airport on August 22, his father flew to India to launch a multiyear search for his missing son.

One of the Parvati Valley's first recorded disappearances of an international traveler had taken place nearly twenty-five years earlier, in the summer of 1991. Twenty-four-year-old Odette Houghton, an Australian backpacker, was last seen at a temple commune in the mountains. Her parents grew worried when parcels and letters they had posted to her were returned and approached the Australian Department of Foreign Affairs and Trade. "They seemed to think Odette didn't want to be contacted and advised us not to go looking," her father recalled in an Australian magazine. Her parents flew to India to search the valley, plastering posters everywhere they could, but found no leads. The following year it was Marianne Heer, a thirty-year-old woman from Switzerland, who vanished after having last been seen at a temple in the town of Manikaran. In October 1995, an Australian, Gregory John Powell, disappeared from either the Manikaran area or near Malana; where was never officially determined. The year 1996 saw one of the more high-profile cases, the disappearance of Ian Mogford, a twenty-year-old British backpacker who had been traveling in India with his girlfriend, who was there on a study grant. Mogford struck out on his own into the Parvati Valley, where, after calling his girlfriend and his parents, he vanished. Mogford's father traveled to India to search for him, remembering that days before his son had disappeared, he had called his father and told him that he had befriended a sadhu. Mogford had shown an interest in India's holy men, but his mother doubted that he would have been tempted to adopt their lifestyle. His father suspected the worst: "It is not beyond the realms of possibility that my son went into the mountains with someone and for some reason my son got attacked and is lying on the bottom of a gorge and his body hasn't been found," he told the *Telegraph*. Still, for years, Mogford's parents held out hope that their son was alive.

The year after Mogford disappeared, twenty-six-year-old Ardavan Taherzadeh traveled to India after completing a year of law school in Vancouver, Canada. He made his way from Chennai, a city in the south, to the mountains, where he placed his last call home, on May 21, 1997, from a phone booth in Kasol. He asked his parents to buy him tickets to a Canadian jazz festival later that summer. He never called again. His mother, Homa Boustani, traveled to the valley and throughout India several times to search for him, once with a small film crew, producing a short documentary called *Missing in Kullu*, in which she appears always sporting a T-shirt with her son's face and the words MISSING IN INDIA printed on the front. She never found a trace of her son. Years later, a close friend of Taherzadeh wrote a post reflecting on what might have happened: "Did Ard see something he wasn't supposed to see? If the motive was money, then why weren't his credit card or traveller's cheques cashed? Why haven't any of his personal belongings turned up? Is Ard wandering around drugged, as one traveller did for eighteen months having sampled an extremely potent hallucinogenic plant. Is he dead or alive?"

In September 1997, four months after Taherzadeh disappeared, Nadav Mintzer, a twenty-seven-year-old tourist from Israel, went missing in the valley, possibly on his way to Malana. His passport was later offered for sale, and travelers' checks were cashed using a signature that wasn't his. Rumors circulated that he had been murdered and robbed by a migrant worker who owed money to the local drug mafia. During a search for Mintzer, a corpse was found in a river, but before it could be repatriated or any analysis could be performed, it disappeared. Three years later, Mintzer's skeleton was found near the village of Malana. It was one of the few bodies ever recovered and confirmed to be one of the Parvati Valley missing. The body of Maarten de Bruijn, a twenty-one-year-old man from the Netherlands who disappeared in the spring of 1999, was never found. He was last seen in the Manikaran area, possibly heading up higher into the valley toward Kheerganga. While backpacking in India, he phoned home every two weeks, but a call on his father's birthday was the last time his parents heard from him. His father retraced his son's footsteps, questioning locals and village elders, but was met with indifference.

By the end of the 1990s, the number of vanished foreign travelers in the Parvati Valley had begun to draw international attention. Through the turn of the decade, the string of mysterious disappearances continued. In the summer of 2000, Alexei Ivanov, a thirty-three-year-old economist from Russia, vanished while hiking above Manikaran. In 2004, it was a thirty-year-old Italian backpacker named Francesco Gatti, who sent his last email back home on

June 26, a day after he had said he wanted to go to "a village where you can't touch people," hinting that he was interested in visiting Malana. After weeks without word, his girlfriend launched a blog to provide updates on the search. "They found his things," the final update, posted in the beginning of August, read. The police had discovered a kangaroo-style pouch off a tributary path near Kheerganga, and inside were Gatti's travel documents, return plane ticket, and journal with a final entry dated June 28. "The pouch is broken as if somebody tried to wrench it away from him," Gatti's girlfriend wrote.

The following summer, in early August 2005, Daniel Mountwitten had been in the valley for only a few days when he went missing. The twenty-three-year-old dual citizen of Israel and Australia had finished his military service in Israel and was in the middle of a long international trip. He had been traveling with a friend and staying at a guesthouse in a small village across the river from Kasol. One morning, he woke up early and went for a walk. Come nightfall, the friend grew worried and, after looking for him along the banks of the Parvati River, raised the alarm with district police. Despite comprehensive searches of the surrounding trails and gorges, Mountwitten was never seen again. A private investigator's report concluded with a suspicion of foul play.

On July 21, 2009, Amichai Steinmetz, who held citizenship of both Israel and the United States, set out on a trek from Kheerganga toward the mountain meadow of Bunbuni. He was with a friend, but they took different routes. Steinmetz never reached Bunbuni or returned to Kheerganga. Three months of searching were conducted along the trails and in the forests around the camp, but no clues were uncovered relating to his disappearance. "But I still believe that my son is alive and stuck in the high mountain passes," Steinmetz's father told Indian media during the search. "He is strong enough to survive even in difficult climate conditions."

In the spring of 2011, a Russian backpacker named Vladislav Kesternov went missing after embarking on a hike in the mountains around Kasol. Similarly, Petr Slanina of the Czech Republic disappeared while hiking in the Kasol area in August 2013. Both of their bodies were eventually located and identified, recovered from the bottom of gorges. But most of the cases resulted in no such closure.

It's not the deaths that make the Parvati Valley unusual, it's the disappearances into forest or mountain or valley with little trace. And there are more accounts than those noted in police registries and written into headlines that make the news, shared as stories and desperate pleas from family members posted on online message boards and travel forums with scattered details. Communication with loved ones and friends ends abruptly, with a final letter, phone call, or email before blinking out, leaving faint trails for heartsick families to follow.

Some blame the mountains. As in any range, there are gorges and cliffs that can trouble inexperienced, and even some seasoned, hikers who push themselves too high and too far beyond their capabilities and lose themselves to a wild animal, down an errant turn on the trail, or to starvation. Yet nearly all paths, within a day or two's walk, lead to a village. Unless a trekker ventures into one of the tributary glens that fork off the main valley, it is hard to lose sight of the Parvati River. It is an orienting landmark, yet its banks are treacherous and its waters swift. Many tourists, both international and domestic, have died after stepping too close to it and losing their footing.

Some people believe that the disappearances are the result of the valley's isolation. Far from help, tourists are prime targets of opportunistic robbery and murder. In 2000, two hikers from Germany were shot while camping, and one lost his life. In another attack that year, a couple and the woman's fourteen-year-old son were attacked while camping between Kheerganga and Mantalai Lake. Their bodies were thrown into a gorge. The woman, María Ángeles Girones from Spain, and the boy died, but the man, Martin Young from the United Kingdom, miraculously survived. "I think it was completely random," Young told the BBC while recovering in a hospital in

Delhi. "I don't think they picked on us in particular. But it was premeditated, certainly premeditated because the attack and our pleas for mercy as they were beating us just increased the assault. And the motive was simple robbery." In 2007, an Israeli backpacker, Dror Sheck, was hiking with a group of friends around Kheerganga when they noticed he had lagged behind the group and was out of sight. When they went looking for him, they "found him bleeding, lying on a small path. Next to him was a knife stained with blood and the leaves next to him had blood on them too," one of the friends told the *Jerusalem Post* shortly after Sheck's death. He died before help could arrive. "Tourists from all over the world come to this magical place that's also known for its dangerous history," David Danieli, Israel's ambassador to India, told the *Post* at the time. "Gangs of criminals and drug dealers wander around in this isolated area and can commit a crime and disappear." In 2012, a fifty-two-year-old Italian tourist named Alessandro Tesi was found dead in the hall of his guesthouse in Kasol.

The majority of disappearances have involved men in their twenties and early thirties who fit a profile of adventurous travelers seeking to push themselves physically or spiritually. This profile has led to a theory that a single serial killer has been lurking in the forested hills for decades, preying on a particular kind of traveler carrying valuables such as cameras and passports, drugs, and cash. Some speculate that the killer is a Hindu holy man, while others believe it is a foreigner who blends in with tourists to hide in plain sight. According to one foreign national who has been living near the Parvati Valley for decades, in the late 1980s and early 1990s, an Indian man was charged with and jailed for the murder of a foreign tourist; it was rumored that he had killed a total of thirteen foreign travelers in the region before his arrest. "If you slip anywhere along that river, then no one will ever find a body. You'll be pulverized into microscopic pieces. Who would know what had happened?" the foreign national points out.

The theory harkened back to the 1970s, when the Hippie Trail was haunted by a string of mysterious murders of international travelers in Thailand, Nepal, and India. Some were eventually linked to Charles Sobhraj, a French national born in Saigon to a Vietnamese mother and Indian father, who was open about his disgust of the beatniks and hippies who were arriving from around the world en masse throughout South and Southeast Asia. Sobhraj followed a set pattern: befriending tourists, robbing them of passports and money, often traveling under their identities, and, in some cases, murdering them. He was eventually arrested in 1976 after drugging a tour group of French university students in New Delhi. Sobhraj became known in the media as "The Bikini Killer," for some of his more high-profile victims in Thailand, and "The Serpent," for his ability to evade authorities and his escape, in 1986, from Tihar Prison, India's most notorious penitentiary. He was arrested again in Kathmandu in 2003 and imprisoned on a life sentence for the 1975 murder of two tourists in Nepal.

Police are understandably hesitant to entertain the theory that a serial killer has been preying on foreign tourists in the Parvati Valley. They are adamant that some of the disappearances are undoubtedly, if tragically, linked to the valley's drug trade. Nishchint Singh Negi, who served as additional superintendent of police for the district that includes the Parvati Valley from 2015 to 2018, saw the case files of several missing international tourists fall onto his wide wooden desk at the main police station in the city of Kullu. Inside his green-walled office, he listened to pleas for assistance from worried families and concerned friends searching for lost loved ones. In his mind, the valley's hash is a powerful lure. "Most of the tourists that come here are coming for the hash—the quality is one of the best in the world," he says, rubbing his forefinger and thumb together as if rolling a marble. "The Malana hash—it's sticky." Regional and national police forces are fully aware of the hidden plantations throughout the Parvati Valley, but they have done little to curb the steady black ooze from the valley. Every year, small cohorts of officers occasionally descend on villages in the early fall with machetes and electric weed whackers to cut down plants. But these actions are mainly for show. They may destroy thousands of hectares of cannabis plants in the valley, but the larger plantations, where the majority of the valley's cannabis is grown, are tucked up mountains on high-altitude meadows accessible by steep trails, with names such as Magic Valley or Valley of Devils.

The police do what they can, but either they fear the power of the organized drug traders or they are reluctant to shut down one of the region's primary tourism draws. Negi has seen many foreigners engage in both cultivation and trafficking. A couple months' work can produce hash worth thousands of dollars, after all. Or, when purchased in bulk at its source in the valley, it can be sold at marked-up prices elsewhere in the country—and fund a traveler for months.

The families of some of the valley's missing believe that their loved ones succumbed not to the drug trade but to the drugs themselves. Hash isn't the only drug of concern; there is another, much more powerful one found in the region, from a plant with trumpet-shaped, purple-white flowers that can be toxic in large quantities and hallucinogenic in small doses. Known as devil's snare, thorn apple, or nightshade, it can be found around the world, but its most common name, datura, traces its origins to India. There it is a holy plant, a flower that in one of Shiva's depictions appears tucked into his matted locks. Once used in Ayurvedic medicine as a treatment for various common ailments including headaches, inflammation, ulcers, and asthma, its potency is so difficult to control that its distribution has been banned.

Datura seeds, which hold the plant's most toxic element, are sometimes mixed with marijuana or hash and smoked in a chillum as a powerful hallucinogen. But the side effects can include delirium, confusion, and psychosis that can last for several weeks—reactions known to be so severe that the plant has been used to poison people, mixed into their food in order to rob them. A 2015 report in the *Indian Journal of Forensic and Community Medicine* noted, "Suicide and homicidal cases have been reported. Most commonly used as stupe-fying agent and road side poison. Seeds are mixed with sweets and given to the unsuspecting victim. The drowsy or stupefied victim is robbed off [sic] his money or valuable articles." The same article recounted that in 2014, a thirty-five-year-old tourist traveling on a train was offered *prasad*—a piece of food typically consumed during religious ceremonies—by a sadhu. Within an hour, he became giddy and delirious, then drowsy; next he began vomiting. While in a stupor, he was robbed by the man who had given him the food. It was later determined that the tourist had been fed datura.

Datura has even been found to produce amnesia. In the documentary *Missing in Kullu*, a man from South Africa named Sacha Beattie, who had intentionally taken datura while in India, described how he had "disappeared—from my own mind and from reality." His daze lasted eighteen months. "I forgot about everything. I never thought about my parents, I never thought any myself, I never thought about God, I never thought about a cup of tea. I had no thoughts." His family heard that he had been involved in a motorcycle accident. "I was a missing person," Beattie said in the interview. "I was found the minute I walked into an embassy on my own will."

Beyond drugs, another form of illegal activity has long flourished in the valley: providing cover for people wishing to disappear. Locals can rattle off names of foreigners who have lived illegally in the forests and hills for years, sometimes decades. They have come from the United Kingdom, Germany, Italy, Israel, France, and the United States and have found remote cottages, homestays, and even caves in which to make a new home. Some have engaged in the drug trade, while others sought a peaceful existence away from distraction or regulation, growing vegetables and living off the land in a beautiful and spiritual corner of remote India. Many point to Malana when asked where the valley's intentionally disappeared might be found. "In the days of the Rajas," the anthropologist Colin Rosser wrote in 1956 after spending two years studying the village, referring to India's precolonial period, "Malana provided a sanctuary for absconding offenders and criminals bent on escaping from punishment by the Rajas' courts. . . . This custom continued throughout the period of British rule and still continues." Malana's independence as well as its legendary inaccessibility have drawn curious outsiders to try to glimpse behind the veil.

There is one man, the valley's most legendary long-term international resident, whose name is still uttered in hushed tones. It is often written as "Glenu." He arrived in the late 1970s and was often credited with igniting the region's commercial hash production by teaching locals how to make "cream," a more refined version of *charas*. In the fall of 2009, two filmmakers from a cannabis travel show called *Strain Hunters* went to the Parvati Valley to film an episode about India's world-renowned Himalayan hash plantations and to seek out "Glenu." An Italian man named Franco Casalone, a cannabis activist and the author of several books on cultivation, led them through the valley. Casalone had visited India several times in the late 1980s and early '90s, and then, in 1996, had come to the Malana region, where he lived in a shelter built into the lee of a giant boulder. He stayed for a decade—where he became, as he's been called, "perhaps the greatest European expert in traditional charas production techniques."

Casalone led the filmmakers to a wooden house tucked away up a mountainside across the glen from the village of Malana. There lived an old Italian man named Galeno Orazi, the renowned "Glenu." Orazi had a long gray beard and wore the woolen vest and cap common to locals in Himachal Pradesh. "He decided to come here," Casalone said in the documentary, "and to forget this fucking new world." Orazi cooked over a firepit, grew his own food and cannabis, and remained largely disconnected from the outside world. In the early 1980s, he was reportedly arrested twice, for drug possession and for overstaying his visa—which only inflated his legend.

The attention, however, has had its downside. After one amateur documentary was posted to YouTube, showing close-up shots of production and kilograms of black hash, police arrived in full force, cutting down plants and making arrests. Orazi himself was apprehended by authorities in November 2010, a month after the episode of *Strain Hunters* aired. Local police conducted a raid in the Malana glen and arrested the Italian man, then sixty-five, for an expired travel visa. "He had been living in this village for two years. To our surprise, he could speak fluent Hindi as well as the local Malani dialect," a police officer told the *Indian Express*. The newspaper called him a "self-styled baba." In fact, Orazi had been living in the Parvati Valley on and off for more than twenty-five years.

The story of Orazi is not unique. Some foreigners have passed entire travel visas in the valley, returning year after year to spend six months at a time; others have ignored the exit date on their visa entirely and stayed for long beyond. Tales of these long-termers have quietly floated around the Parvati Valley's deepest corners for decades. A report published in the *Guardian* in 2002 identified several foreigners who had been living in the valley for years. One man from the United Kingdom had been living near Malana for six years until he was arrested, upon which he claimed to be a reincarnation of Shiva and therefore, he maintained, required neither passport nor visa. There was also a former British Airways stewardess who, in 1998, requested a new passport after having lived near Malana for fifteen years; a German woman who had been in the valley since the early 1990s, who earned income by buying and selling hash; and a man who had given up his life in Italy to live in the Parvati Valley and who claimed to be named on a missing-tourists list that was maintained by local police. "Maybe it's been ten years now, you lose track of time up here. Don't even know if my passport's valid," Paolo, an Italian, told the *Guardian*. "The missing don't go looking for the missing. We don't want trouble with the police. There are lots of us here, and we keep ourselves to ourselves." A source in the article mentioned that in the early years of the 2000s, thousands of foreign nationals had been living illegally in the mountains around the Parvati Valley.

The local authorities were well aware of the situation. "In the older cases, like Ian Mogford and Ardavan Taherzadeh, I don't think I'll ever be able to tell the parents what happened because of the lack of support from the foreigners living here and previous police failings," Venu Gopal, superintendent of police for the Kullu district during the early 2000s, told the *Guardian*. "This solitary, secret life, of the deliberately missing, the selfish life of those who would rather protect themselves than help others, is going to come to an end. I am slowly pulling in everyone who has no visa or passport. I know for certain that a couple of the people on my missing list are living in the mountains. But soon it will no longer be possible to just vanish in Himachal Pradesh—whether deliberately or by accident." Yet in the decade and a half after the district superintendent of police made that bold pledge, the trend continued, and every year the department makes arrests of foreigners living illegally in the valley. In 2010, a new district superintendent of police, K. K. Indoria, told the Indo-Asian News Service, "We have information that a large number of foreigners who disappeared mysteriously are illegally staying in various tribal areas." In the early 2000s, an Austrian national reportedly reappeared in the Parvati Valley after having been missing for a dozen years. He allegedly stated that he had simply wanted to disappear and live on his own in the mountains.

The families of many of the valley's missing and disappeared have clung to stories like these. Years after Ian Mogford's 1996 disappearance, rumors persisted that the British backpacker was still alive and still in India. According to a now-defunct investigation company, posters with Mogford's picture were pasted around the Parvati Valley, as well as in Delhi's popular backpacker quarter, Paharganj. In Delhi, someone immediately removed the posters; when they were replaced, they were torn down once again. "Around Christmas 2001," read an article in the *Guardian*, "the investigators say that one of their agents picked up Mogford's trail, traced his movements for three or four days, and approached him. He ran."

As Homa Boustani, the mother of Canadian tourist Ardavan Taherzadeh, continued to search for her son, year after year, she began to question if he had simply decided to step back—"To stay away, cut off for a year, two years," as she said in the documentary *Missing in Kullu*. In a handwritten letter to a friend, Taherzadeh had written about how he had been questioning his life's direction: "It doesn't have to be that way. I think life is supposed to be much easier. Do I have a place to sleep? Do I have food? A place to sit?" He wrote "a shirt" before crossing it out, as if to suggest that clothing was too trivial to even mention. During her first trip to the valley, Boustani spoke with a group of sadhus, who suggested that Taherzadeh had disappeared intentionally.

Each addition to missing-persons lists has begged the question: Of all the travelers who disappeared without a trace, who were lost or murdered—and who simply did not want to be found?

When Piotr Muschalik arrived in the Parvati Valley in August 2015 to search for his son, he met with Chhape Ram Negi, a longtime local mountain guide whom he had found online and who for decades had provided his services, knowledge, and skill to attempt to rescue missing tourists in the Parvati Valley. In 1983, Negi had founded Negi's Himalayan Adventure, one of the valley's first trekking outfits offering guiding services, after destinations such as Malana and Kheerganga began drawing tourists. Over two decades, Negi says, he has conducted hundreds of search-and-rescues: trekkers stuck in the mountains after a change in weather; backpackers lost while under the influence of drugs; and travelers who had vanished without a trace. "When somebody has gone missing, the parents focus on the *charas*," Negi explains. "But they don't think that there is more than *charas*. It's a mountain area, and the mountain area is difficult, especially if you are going alone." He points out that many who come to the valley are looking for more than trekking or drugs. "There are natural powers in the mountains," he says. "They are powers that sometimes help us and sometimes hurt us."

As Negi's reputation grew, he became known in the area as "Mountain Man" and has been featured on the TV series *Toughest Men in India*. He parlayed his contacts with local police into becoming the go-to hire for search-and-rescue contracts. It was a natural fit: by day he offered trekking services and mountain guiding; by night, he applied the same skills to search-and-rescue for the valley's missing and disappeared. His wasn't the only outfit. So many travelers went missing or ran into trouble that a microeconomy of sorts emerged.

Shiv Ram Thakur once worked for Negi as a mountain guide, but the search-and-rescue wing of the company always troubled him, especially the competition for contracts from bereaved families. Born in the Parvati Valley, Thakur was in elementary school when he began noticing the foreign tourists trekking past his house into the mountains. When he was a teenager, he went fishing with his father in the Parvati River; in the winter, when the waters receded and ran low, he remembers seeing bodies, which he came to suspect were either casualties of the valley's rave and party years or the tragic conclusions of something more nefarious. He eventually found work as a trekking guide, before completing a mountaineering course. With his new skills, he was hired by Negi but never saw eye to eye with him and soon split off to form his own mountain guiding business, Little Rebel Adventures. Thakur volunteered to carry out several recoveries of bodies of tourists in the valley, only asking the police to cover food and lodging for his guides and porters; he paid their wages out of pocket. Friends told him that he should charge the police or family members, as there was good money to be made, but Thakur demurred. To him the goal of the rescue work was good karma, not profits. But not everyone shared his point of view. Within the first year of launching Little Rebel Adventures, another person appeared on the scene, who went to the superintendent of police and claimed that the company had folded and was rebranding under a new name. This person even provided documents with a photoshop of Thakur's logo. But it was all a lie, an attempt to divert police contracts toward a new outfit.

When Piotr Muschalik contacted Negi, the man offered his search-and-rescue services for a fee of $150 per day. Upon arriving in the valley shortly after his son had disappeared, Piotr asked to see what work had been done—anything that might show where he or his team had searched—but Negi couldn't offer documentation. In a remote area, he said, it didn't work that way: he searched on foot and worked his sources and contacts in the valley. Piotr decided to take on the search himself, distributing hundreds of posters and leaflets throughout the region. There were several false leads from people who came forward claiming to have seen Muschalik within the past few days or weeks. In Manali, Piotr convinced the police to use its canine unit to try to trace one lead; the dog caught a scent off an article of Muschalik's clothing and followed the trail through town until the scent ran out. In Kasol, Piotr spoke with a bus conductor who was certain he had seen Muschalik traveling between Bhuntar, at the head of the valley, and Kasol. Piotr eventually returned to Poland empty-handed.

The following March, six months after his son had disappeared, Piotr hired an outfit based in Israel that had experience searching for missing tourists in the Parvati Valley. Yechiel "Hilik" Magnus, the chief rescue officer of Magnus International Search & Rescue, has conducted numerous searches in the valley, predominantly for missing citizens of Israel, since the late 1980s. Born in Sweden and raised in Israel, Magnus built a career on searching for missing people around the world: in Sri Lanka after the 2004 tsunami; after the 2011 earthquake in New Zealand; and in the wake of the earthquake that struck Nepal in 2015. But the Parvati Valley has offered his company the most contracts, "dozens and dozens of search-and-rescue missions," Magnus claims, if not hundreds. Most of the cases he investigated were, in the end, often the result of a miscommunication between a tourist extending a stay in a remote, disconnected area without informing his or her family. But many remain unsolved. Magnus has files on thirty-nine cases of international travelers who have vanished into thin air since he began working in the valley.

Piotr hired Magnus International to search for his son—at a cost of around $30,000 for a ten-day effort. He felt that little concrete came of it; Piotr later learned that Magnus International subcontracts much of the on-the-ground search to Chhape Ram Negi. The family did find a clue on their son's computer, which he had left behind in Poland: Facebook and WhatsApp messages that had synced with the phone he carried in India, including a conversation with an Indian man in Delhi that had begun before Muschalik had left for India. The man had encouraged him to visit the Parvati Valley and offered contacts for when he arrived. It was later determined that the man was from Malana, the region's legendary hash destination, and was a dealer. On the ground, the Kullu police were of little help, Piotr recalls. He didn't learn that Muschalik was the latest in a long history of disappearances in the valley until he came across old news reports; the police had never told him. Instead of pursuing leads, they had sent him photos of random items found in the forest—a piece of clothing, a pair of women's sandals—that clearly did not belong to his son.

Piotr continued to travel to India after his son disappeared in the hope that he was still alive. He made fliers and posters with a picture of his son altered so that he appeared older, with long hair and a shaggy beard. During his second trip to India, he heard that his son had been sighted at a temple in the Parvati Valley, but it turned out to be a Ukrainian tourist who bore a passing resemblance to Bruno. Piotr never believed that his son had been seeking a spiritual experience in the Parvati Valley, but he recognized the impact India might have had on him. "India is a country that can change your thinking. You can change 180 degrees in your mind," he says. "I would be happy if he was found in an ashram."

In the version of Lonely Planet's *India* guidebook that back-packers carried in 2016, the section on the Parvati Valley included a warning: "If you plan to head into the hills, we recommend going with a guide who can steer you away from natural—and human—hazards. It's a good idea to let your guesthouse know where you are going and when you plan to return. Avoid walking alone, and be cautious about befriending sadhus (holy people) or others wandering in the woods." *The Rough Guide to India* also advised caution: "Several theories have been put forward to explain these disappearances, from drug-related accidents on the treacherous mountain trails, to attacks by bears or wolves or foul play by the numerous cannabis cultivators in the region; some even claim that the disappeared may have joined secret cults deep in the mountains. Most likely, however, they were victims of bandit attacks, motivated solely by money, with the wild waters of the River Parvati conveniently placed for disposing of bodies." Even before Justin arrived in the Parvati Valley, he was aware of its history. After he posted about his plan to live in a cave near Kheerganga, someone commented about the valley's reputation for missing people. "Yes I've heard of many people disappearing out here," Justin replied. "I'll be careful."

Certainly unbeknownst to him, just one month before he parked his motorcycle below the village of Kalga, another foreign tourist had gone missing in the valley, to little fanfare or news coverage. Shota Sakai, a twenty-seven-year-old backpacker from Japan, had spent a couple of months in India. On Facebook, he posted photographs from Varanasi and then connected with a backpacker from Israel in Rishikesh and again later in Manali. In one of Sakai's final updates to Facebook, he posted a black-and-white photograph of an Indian man with dreadlocks wrapped around his head whom he had met on a previous trip. "My Guru. His name is Manoj Giri. He is Indian holy man 'sadhu,'" Sakai wrote under the picture. "I met him 4 years ago. Then I got Indian name from him. And this time I met him again on the street in India. Amazing connection!" Under Sakai's name on Facebook, in parentheses, was the name his guru had given him: Sati Giri. One friend of Sakai's says that he was interested in attending a psytrance music festival, which was likely the Parvati Peaking Festival, scheduled to take place at the end of May; on Facebook, Sakai mentioned that he would be returning to Japan in July. He was last heard from in the middle of June. Curiously, shortly thereafter, someone using his debit card withdrew money from an ATM in Pushkar in the desert of Rajasthan, more than five hundred miles away. Official records kept by the district police who oversee the Parvati Valley note that Sakai disappeared in the Kasol area on June 24 or 25, 2016.

That summer, Piotr Muschalik returned for the third time to the valley, marking one year since he had last heard from Bruno. He continued to pressure police officers and locals for information and to paste missing-persons fliers on signs, windows, and power poles anywhere he could. He hiked to Kheerganga to continue to ask questions and investigate leads. He didn't know it, but an American backpacker had ridden his black Royal Enfield motorcycle into the Parvati Valley. Piotr may have even passed the younger man somewhere on the trail—a desperate father descending empty-handed, stepping off a narrow trail for a young man heading deeper and higher into the mountains.

THE CAVE

"Tomorrow. Into the Wild," Justin wrote online on July 23, referencing Christopher McCandless once again. He posted two pictures to Instagram that day: in one he is sitting in a forest meadow overlooking the slate-roofed homes and guesthouses of Kalga, and in another he is surrounded by a cloud of smoke as he puffs on a chillum. Justin left his main backpack, filled with the majority of his belongings, in storage at the Om Shanti guesthouse, packed his day pack with a few essentials, and began hiking farther up the valley. Within a hundred feet, he passed a sign that had been nailed to a tree. It read WHAT GOES IN MUST COME OUT. It was referring to garbage, a subtle effort to keep one forest path clean in a country with a notorious plastic refuse problem. An hour later, he passed another sign, white metal with hand-printed words, affixed to the trunk of a tree. It was located at a point in the route where the trail runs high and steep above a gorge that spills into the Parvati River. "Amihay Cohen R.I.P. (1975–1999) Here fell & died a dear man & a good friend. Young, full of joy at the prime of his life. Who wasn't careful enough taking this road . . ." Someone had hand painted WALK CAREFULLY across the sign.

The trail cut through the forested hillside above the Parvati River, past waterfalls and under canopies where troops of gray langur monkeys jumped from tree to tree. After hiking just over six miles, Justin arrived at Kheerganga, the Parvati Valley's last base camp before the high mountain wilderness. Its mythical stature notwithstanding, Kheerganga is a ramshackle cluster of tarpaulin, corrugated aluminum, and wood-pole structures. Each summer high season, the camp is erected to accommodate the thousands of tourists looking for an escape a half-day's moderate hike beyond cell phone range. When temperatures drop and snows threaten, the camp is dismantled as the tourists descend for warmer climes. Located on a north-facing meadow at nearly 10,000 feet above sea level, Kheerganga lies in full view of a panorama of mountain peaks and dramatic cliffs seemingly close enough across the valley to touch. Above the camp an iron pipe protruding from the hillside spews steaming geothermic water into a concrete pool. The water runs milky—like that of rice pudding, or *kheer*, after which the site is named—as it swirls around soaking pilgrims. A thin trickle of steaming water bubbles its way down the hill through the heart of the camp and eventually joins the glacial Parvati River far below. The hot spring is said to have arisen when Parvati was cooking *kheer* for Shiva and their son, Kartikeya, while they were out hunting and spilled some onto the ground.

The pilgrims who are drawn here come to practice yoga and meditate, to camp on an alpine meadow as Himalayan condors soar overhead. But most of the spiritual tourists come to venerate Shiva, who is said to have meditated there for thousands of years. There is no god in the Hindu pantheon who holds such exalted and popular status as Shiva or carries so much familiar symbolism: the master of meditation and yoga, the supreme ascetic who has renounced possessions, the world's transformer. From his dreadlocked hair flows the holy Ganges River. His ash-covered body represents human impermanence. The cobra around his neck and the bull at his feet symbolize his mastery of animals and nature. His three-pointed trident staff is a weapon to relieve the three states of suffering: physical, spiritual, and ethereal. Many sadhus worship and emulate the god, and many foreign tourists follow suit.

Justin Alexander Shetler was born on March 11, 1981, to parents Terry and Susanne, who goes by Suzie. While he was an independent child, he desperately wanted a connection with a sibling. *(Courtesy of Suzie Reeb)*

Justin grew up in Sarasota, Florida, where he adored the water and being in nature. He was an introspective boy who would climb trees and onto the roof of their house to clear his head and find calm. *(Courtesy of Suzie Reeb)*

From an early age, Justin idolized heroes and superheroes. He was also drawn to the works of contemporary mythologist Joseph Campbell, who popularized the concept of the hero's journey. *(Courtesy of Suzie Reeb)*

After Justin's parents divorced, his mother moved from Florida across the United States to Oregon, living in Montana along the way—a place Justin adored and where he first experienced the big wild of the American West, which he had read about in survivalist and naturalist books. *(Courtesy of Suzie Reeb)*

The octagonal pavilion formed the heart of the Wilderness Awareness School in Washington State, where Justin discovered his love of the natural world, and survivalism. "I dropped out of high school to study naturalist, wilderness survival, and ninja skills. I helped build this place. It had a dirt floor and a firepit where we started a fire each winter morning by rubbing sticks together," he would later recall. *(@adventuresofjustin/ adventuresofjustin.com)*

Justin (*farthest right in the white T-shirt*) with a group of youth students in front of a leaf shelter at the Tracker School, in the Pine Barrens of New Jersey. In the summer of 2000, he nearly died in a truck accident while driving west across the country. (© *Jahnis Wish, 2000*)

Building a wildlife-viewing platform at the Tracker School, where Justin honed his survival skills. Students and fellow instructors were in awe of the eighteen-year-old, who could start a fire with a bow drill in fifteen seconds. (© *Tom McElroy, 1999*)

Justin's first international trip was to Nepal in 2006, a country he returned to several times, including in 2014, pictured here. That first trip set in motion a lifelong love of travel, which he took pains to distinguish from casual tourism. "I don't describe myself as a tourist," Justin wrote. "I mostly live outside, am homeless, close to penniless most of the time, never stay in resorts, don't hang with foreigners, and make every attempt to make my own way in the world. Adventuring is not a vacation, it's a lifestyle." (*@adventuresofjustin*)

In Thailand, Justin studied to become a Buddhist monk, memorizing 222 rules in Pali, the sacred language of Theravada Buddhism. When he passed the initiation process on January 1, 2007, around 800 people from a village outside Lampang attended the ceremony. (*@adventuresofjustin*)

Justin embraced his role as the lead singer and songwriter of the San Francisco–based punk rock band Punchface. The group seemed poised to break out on the heels of a successful Japanese tour in 2009 but broke up by the end of the year. (© *Margaret Jow, 2009*)

When after three years Justin abruptly quit his job at the Miami-based tech startup iProof and hit the road, he was unequivocal about his decision: "I am running from a life that isn't authentic; that isn't me. From the numbness that accompanies a sterile life of luxury. I'm running away from monotony and towards novelty; towards wonder, awe, and the things that make me feel vibrantly alive." (*@adventuresofjustin*)

At the Wilderness
Awareness School,
Justin had been trained
in finding a "sit spot"—
a place to return to day
after day, month after
month, until you become
so acutely attuned to
your surroundings
that you notice the
minute fluctuations and
connections in nature.
(*@adventuresofjustin*)

In 2015, Justin attended a gathering of Indigenous shamans in Brazil, where he partook in fourteen ayahuasca ceremonies. "Ayahuasca is a powerful hallucinogen that triggers an emotional/spiritual/somatic detox and cleanse," he wrote, "removing baggage that has been built up over years and providing its user with clarity and a fresh start." (@*adventuresofjustin*)

Justin was quick to push his body and his mind as far as each could go—scaling bridges and buildings, cliff diving, living in the wild with minimal supplies—to see what could be found at the extremes. His proclivity for taking risks, which increased as the years passed, was a source of deep concern for some friends. (@*adventuresofjustin*)

Before departing the United States in early 2016 on an indefinite international trip, Justin brushed up on his survival skills at a course on the Caribbean island of Saint Croix. (© *Tom McElroy, 2015*)

Justin surprised many people when he had an outline of an eagle tattooed across his chest during his last visit with his father before departing the United States. Initially he worried that it "looked more like a pigeon than an eagle" but soon came to regard it as a "talisman on his skin." (*@adventuresofjustin*)

In the Philippines, Justin reached a remote Tao't Batu village by hiking through the jungle around Mount Mantalingajan, risking exposure to malaria, dengue fever, and Islamist terrorists. "If it were safe," he wrote, "it wouldn't be much of an adventure would it?" (*@adventuresofjustin*)

As he had on every trip to Thailand since his first a decade before, Justin returned to visit his "adoptive" family in a village near the city of Lampang. In 2016, he arrived in time to attend the monk initiation ceremony for a member of the family. (*@adventuresofjustin*)

In the spring of 2016, Justin volunteered to help build a school in Bhachek, Nepal, located six miles from the epicenter of a devastating 2015 earthquake. He was often deeply affected and impacted by the places he visited, leading him to financially support people he met, raise money, and donate to causes. (*© JacquelineWoo, 2016/@adventuresofjustin*)

"I was shown an ancient Shiva fire, which has allegedly burned for 3500 years," Justin wrote from Varanasi, his first stop in India. He found the Hindu ritual of cremating bodies along the banks of the Ganges River captivating but unsettling. "It feels wrong to stand next to family while a loved one burns." (*@adventuresofjustin*)

Music was always a part of Justin's life; in addition to the guitar, he played the mandolin and harp. In Varanasi, he purchased a bansuri (flute) that he converted into a walking stick and took a lesson from a Buddhist flute player in McLeod Ganj. (*@adventuresofjustin*)

When Justin decided to buy a motorcycle in New Delhi, there was no question it would be a Royal Enfield— India's iconic bike. He navigated "Shadow" north along potholed roads into the foothills of the Himalayas, and on July 19, 2016, he entered the Parvati Valley. (*@adventuresofjustin*)

The camp of Kheerganga, at 9,700 feet in elevation, is a ramshackle cluster of tarpaulin and canvas tents serving trekkers and pilgrims who come to bathe in the holy hot springs. It is the Parvati Valley's last base camp before the high valley. (© *Harley Rustad, 2019*)

Justin was fascinated by the places caves held—in literature, in history, and in myth—as sites of transformation and realization. He spent at least three weeks in this cave, a twenty-minute walk from the Kheerganga camp into the forest. (*@adventuresofjustin*)

"I've heard stories about the magical powers of these Babas," Justin wrote—prophetically, perhaps—about Satnarayan Rawat, a sadhu he befriended while living in the Parvati Valley. "They can see into your soul and know your past and future. They can bless or curse. They are holy men but wild, and are even above the law in India. Police won't arrest them; even for murder, which happens I'm told." *(@adventuresofjustin)*

In the forest outside Kheerganga, Justin helped Andrey Gapon, a Russian man on a self-made spiritual retreat in the Parvati Valley, establish himself in a nearby cave. "If I didn't see a living example of a man staying there," Gapon says about Justin, "I wouldn't think it was possible." *(Courtesy of Andrey Gapon)*

In late August 2016, Justin embarked on a "spiritual journey" to Mantalai Lake, a glacier-fed pool at 13,500 feet in elevation, in the company of the sadhu Satnarayan Rawat. Justin disappeared shortly after arriving at the lake. *(© Sanjay Singh Rawal, 2020)*

"My back is in bad shape, (broken when I was 19) and even with daily soaks in hot springs, this cave/mountain life has recently put me in a state of constant discomfort," Justin wrote in his final blog post. "I'm sadly inflexible, and I can't even sit still for a few minutes without pain. Maybe Baba Life will be good for me. I should return mid September or so. If I'm not back by then, don't look for me ;)" (*@adventuresofjustin*)

The Parvati Valley branches off to a region known as the Valley of Gods, but it has earned other nicknames: the Valley of Shadows, the Valley of Death. Since the early 1990s, dozens of international tourists have mysteriously vanished in and around the area, contributing to its dark reputation as India's "backpacker Bermuda Triangle." (© *Harley Rustad, 2019*)

On Suzie Reeb's second day in India searching for her son, she found herself in the middle of the interrogation of sadhu Satnarayan Rawat, forced to face a man Justin had trusted—and who had possibly betrayed him.
(© *Jonathan Skeels, 2016*)

Views from the helicopter the search team hired to trace the route to Mantalai Lake and circle above the camp of Kheerganga from the air. A few days later, a small search team would land on foot and comb the trail for evidence of Justin.
(© Jonathan Skeels, 2016)

The hut at Tunda Bhuj is home to a sadhu who offers tea and a roof for pilgrims and trekkers on their way to and from Mantalai Lake. It is the only permanent dwelling in the high valley above Kheerganga and acts as a relay point for news and gossip. In one of Satnarayan Rawat's stories, it was here where he last saw Justin—who was turning to head back up the valley.
(© Harley Rustad, 2019)

The path to Mantalai Lake is frequented by shepherds and pilgrims, and follows a single path along the bottom of the valley. It is a straightforward trek, except for one section that requires careful scrambling in parts through a narrow gorge known as Stone Valley, where searchers made an unwelcome discovery along the banks of the Parvati River. (© *Harley Rustad, 2019*)

When Sunny Panchal *(blue jacket)* and Nirmal Patel *(red jacket)* ran into Justin on September 3 near the lake, they had no way of knowing these would be the last photos taken of their new American friend. They sensed he was loath to leave the high mountains and so they asked him to join their trekking group. Justin declined, telling them that he was now on a journey of his own. (© *Sunny Panchal, 2016*)

Riding Shadow across a mountain pass into Ladakh, part of India's northernmost region, Jonathan Skeels strikes one of Justin's favorite poses. Skeels had met him only once, but felt compelled to quit his job in London and fly to India to head the on-the-ground search. "Justin led a life that people wanted to lead," Skeels says.
(© *Tom McElroy, 2016*)

It was midday when word floated up the hill and reached Roy Roberts, who was working in one of Kheerganga's informal open-air cafés, that an American traveler was asking for him. Over six feet tall, with a shaved head and a bright smile, the Indian man was well known in the camp and easy to spot. When Justin found him, they sat down and introduced themselves over chai. "He had a pure American spirit, laughing, fun-loving, talking," Roberts recalls about their first meeting. He noticed that Justin had packed light, was wearing khaki-colored hiking pants and black military-style boots, and was carrying his flute–staff. The handle of a black machete poked out of his day pack. Of all of Justin's distinct characteristics—his height and appearance, his eagle chest tattoo, the flute–staff he carried— there was one trait that stood out to Roberts: "I remember his eyes; they were very inquisitive, absorbing."

Roberts was originally from Delhi but had been living in the south Indian city of Bangalore working as a music teacher before he had arrived in the Parvati Valley that spring. He had been looking for a break after going through a trying divorce and had heard from his sister, who was already living in the valley, that the area was hosting a Rainbow Gathering. The concept of a self-supportive pop-up community in the mountains had intrigued him, so he bought a bus ticket north.

What he had found was an eclectic gathering of around two hundred people socializing, singing, playing music, and cooking at a makeshift open-air kitchen. Some of the community had pitched tents or erected lean-to shelters in a meadow around a central fire; others, who sought more isolation and more of a challenge, had found caves in the surrounding forest in which to sleep. Just above the meadow was a large cave formed beneath a cluster of car-sized granite boulders. It had been named Garam Gufa, or Hot Cave, because the sun heated the rocks during the day and kept the interior space warm even when outside temperatures dropped. It was a spacious refuge from the elements.

Justin lamented that he had missed the festival but lit up when Roberts spoke of the mountain caves. Roberts remembers that Justin was "doe-eyed" about Indian spirituality, like an "inquisitive little child," curious about aspects of Hinduism, including reincarnation and asceticism. He wanted to know why people embark on pilgrimages or do penance in order to climb higher. He asked about the sadhus who come to the Parvati Valley, and how they often seek out caves in which to live. "He was there for a specific reason," Roberts says. "He was there to go inside himself, not specifically to just come have an adventure." In the middle of their conversation, Justin opened a small leather satchel to reveal a brick of black hash, wrapped tightly in plastic. Roberts was alarmed that he would be so open with a stranger. He knew that people would be drawn to what the American was carrying, sadhus perhaps more than anyone. "They don't need any food. They'll eat half a roti, and the whole day they'll just keep smoking." He told Justin to watch out, to be more circumspect with others.

Several travelers who met Justin in Nepal and in India confirmed that he had purchased a kilogram of hash in or around Kathmandu after he had failed to procure some while trekking in the Annapurna Mountains. He had told one person that he had bought "the best hash in Nepal." He had dipped into it for personal use as well as casually selling it to tourists he met on the road. One fellow traveler in Kathmandu had to discourage Justin strongly from flying from Kathmandu to Delhi, knowing the high likelihood that he would be caught smuggling drugs and face a lengthy prison sentence, suggesting instead that he go by bus across one of the more permeable land border crossings, where backpacks are rarely checked.

In that fellow traveler's estimation, for Justin carrying hash was not about dealing drugs but rather a means of creating a challenging and intriguing personal narrative: the act itself was the high. It's possible that he was trying to emulate the romantic stories he had read. Several people who encountered him along the way, however, believed that it was merely a means to an end, a way to make small amounts of money while on the road; that the only way he could have afforded the purchase of his black Royal Enfield motorcycle in New Delhi was to sell a portion of the kilogram. "He told me that was how he paid for his travel, at least partially," one backpacker recalls. Justin even passed on some tips: find "the greenest, newest tourists first" and "give them a decent price so they come back to you."

Justin often hinted that the success of his work in Miami had provided him with a "passive income" to fund his travels, claiming that he remained with the company in an advisory capacity and still held shares long after he quit. But there was an inconsistency in the way he presented himself on social media and in podcast interviews: at times he was a former entrepreneur successful enough to fund a life of adventure, while at others he was a "close to penniless" vagabond. "I 'practice poverty' (in the stoic sense) by both necessity and philosophy," he once wrote on his blog. Several people who connected with him in Asia that year noted that he was running low on cash. When Linda Borini arrived in Kathmandu, one of the first things they did was find an ATM, where he asked if he could borrow $300. She assumed he would pay her back when he returned to the United States.

Were the funds he had saved running out? According to Robert Gutierrez, Justin's former boss at iProof in Miami, when Justin had quit, he had in fact severed all ties with the company. He had no longer owned shares, and there had been no formal agreement or passive income. Instead, Gutierrez had occasionally helped Justin out financially, as a friend who had been there for him and his business for years. After he had left the United States, Justin hadn't asked for help. "I wouldn't say he was hurting, but I wouldn't say he was flush," Gutierrez says. It is likely, even when Justin had money, that he posed as an impecunious world traveler because he enjoyed the image it produced. In that version, he wasn't a fortunate American who had the means to choose this life but one who walked the path—sleeping on the streets in the United States and in caves in India—almost out of necessity.

Justin's tenuous financial situation was also, at least in part, self-made. After the 2015 earthquake in Nepal, Bishal Kapali, who had met Justin in Kathmandu almost a decade earlier, began a fundraising campaign to help supply food and medical supplies to people in need and raised around $20,000. More than a quarter of that, he says, came from Justin. Then, a month before he arrived in Nepal in the spring of 2016, Justin launched a GoFundMe page to encourage his followers to donate to the Nepal Survivors Fund, which had been building schools since the earthquake. He later told Stefano Vergari, the friend he had met on a business trip to Milan, that he had donated much of his savings to various development organizations in Nepal. Vergari thinks that Justin's fundraising and personal donations were in part altruistic acts on behalf of the country that had initially ignited his international travel spark, but that they were also designed to absolve himself of his acquired affluence, to create a situation in which he felt more challenged. "I think he gave the money to Nepal so that he could go back to the purest way of adventure," Vergari says.

In 1963, the American actor and sailor Sterling Hayden published his autobiography, *Wanderer*, in which he waxed enthusiastic about the nature of penurious travel:

> To be truly challenging, a voyage, like a life, must rest on a firm foundation of financial unrest. Otherwise you are doomed to a routine traverse, the kind known to yachtsmen who play with their boats at sea—"Cruising," it is called. Voyaging belongs to seamen, and to the wanderers of the world who cannot, or will not, fit in. If you are contemplating a voyage and you have the means, abandon the venture until your fortunes change. Only then will you know what the sea is all about. . . .
>
> What does a man need—really need? A few pounds of food each day, heat and shelter, six feet to lie down in—and some form of working activity that will yield a sense of accomplishment. That's all—in the material sense. And we know it. But we are brainwashed by our economic system until we end up in a tomb beneath a pyramid of time payments, mortgages, preposterous gadgetry, playthings that divert our attention for the sheer idiocy of the charade.
>
> The years thunder by. The dreams of youth grow dim where

they lie caked in dust on the shelves of patience. Before we know it, the tomb is sealed.

Where, then, lies the answer? In choice. Which shall it be: bankruptcy of purse or bankruptcy of life?

Shortly after arriving in India, Justin shared this passage from *Wanderer* on Facebook, calling it "the most inspiring and true thing I've read about the spirit of the Adventurer." In India, he had enough money to travel cheaply, staying in guesthouses for at most $10 per night; the room he rented at Om Shanti in Kalga was less than half that. When he reached Kheerganga, he could have rented a space in a communal canvas tent for a few dollars a night. Regardless of his financial situation, he wanted to live in a cave—and not just for a few days but for weeks.

Roberts felt that Justin held slightly unrealistic expectations for the experience he had envisioned. "He wanted to have a cave where he could stand, where he didn't feel restricted with his flute," Roberts recalls. "Bro, this is not apartments," he told Justin. "You just have to see what is there and fit into it." He directed Justin to walk over a grassy hill, cross a small stream, and head into the forest to find the cluster of boulder caves beyond the meadow that had once hosted the Rainbow Gathering. Roberts said that if he needed help, to find the large "hot cave" above the meadow known as Garam Gufa; his sister was still living inside. Justin left the busy Kheerganga camp, walking past a blue-painted plywood wall of one of the temporary guesthouses upon which someone had scrawled an oft-quoted travel maxim, "ADVENTURE BEGINS WHERE THE ROAD ENDS." He followed the tree line over a hill strewn with boulders where shepherds often brought their goats down from the higher mountains to graze. He walked for around half an hour before crossing a creek and ascending a forested hillside to enter the clearing where the Rainbow Gathering had been held months prior. In the surrounding forest of pine and deodar trees, he found his Himalayan cave.

The cave was raised slightly off the ground, with an opening that required carefully scrambling up two boulders sandwiched together. Justin slid between the granite slabs and into a spacious cavern. He arranged the few belongings he had brought with him. He lit a fire near the entrance to keep him warm at night and provide a sense of security—a warning to animals that might be looking for shelter from the rain. He lay down, looked up at his rock ceiling, and went to sleep.

Caves had fascinated Justin since he had been young. One of his favorite childhood books had been *Way of the Peaceful Warriors* by Dan Millman, a semiautobiographical story about the author's tutelage by a wise man he called Socrates. Millman had experienced a rebirth and an awakening while in a cave: "I awoke to reality, free of any meaning or any search." When Justin had motorcycled around the United States, he had carried with him a copy of Don Miguel Ruiz's *The Four Agreements: A Practical Guide to Personal Freedom*, a self-help book that traces the parable of a man who "was studying to become a medicine man, to learn the knowledge of his ancestors, but [who] didn't completely agree with everything he was learning. In his heart, he felt there must be something more." In a cave, the man had a realization about life—that the world is an illusion and we are just a tiny fragment of "one living being."

Caves feature as sites of transformation in nearly every religion. In Christianity, Jesus Christ, after the crucifixion, is said to have resurrected from within a cavelike tomb cut into rock. In Islam, the prophet Muhammad meditated in a cave called Hira on Jabal an-Nour, or Mountain of Light, near Mecca, before receiving his first revelation from the angel Gabriel. Buddhism's Guru Rinpoche achieved a form of immortality after meditating in Maratika Cave in eastern Nepal. India is pockmarked with thousands of caves that hold historical and spiritual resonance, from Bhimbetka, which holds the earliest traces of humans on the subcontinent, to the mythical cave in which King Muchukunda is said to have slept for generations and, upon waking and feeling trapped between the world of mortals and the world of gods, renounced his life and became a hermit. Some caves hold centuries-old frescoes and carvings, while others are tied to historical figures. Before Siddhartha Gautama became the Buddha, the legend says, he spent years fasting in a cave before achieving nirvana. Caves have been featured in myth, folklore, and fiction. E. M. Forster, in his 1924 novel *A Passage to India*, set the most dramatic and pivotal scene—an alleged assault—within the Malabar Caves, a fictionalized site inspired by the Barabar Caves in the state of Bihar, using the bewildering darkness as a literary mechanism to create confusion and ambiguity. For millennia, countless lamas, mystics, and pilgrims of all creeds have wandered India in search of their own mountain cave. The image of the remote Himalayan cave became an emblem of the seclusion that some pilgrims seek, to sit within a physical representation of the process of boring into hard rock until answers hidden far within are illuminated.

In wilderness survival, a cave is a gift—a ready-made shelter. But in the teachings of Justin's former mentors, caves can be much more. As Tom Brown, Jr., recounted in *The Vision*, Stalking Wolf told him that caves hold "the answers to many questions, even to those not yet formed." Stalking Wolf claimed to have reached one of his greatest realizations after meditating and sleeping in a cave, where he was met by a warrior spirit who revealed four warning signs—each one darker and more ominous than the last—that hailed four possible futures for himself and for the earth. Brown had a similar experience himself. "The journey [there] was part of the quest," Brown wrote, "like an ancient rite of passage that tested the searcher to see if he was worthy to receive the wisdom of the cave." Inside his cave, he faded into and out of sleep, following tunnels to glimpse visions of the past. Brown's cave provided not only answers but, upon his emerging, a clear way forward.

Justin had spent his entire life consuming those foundational stories. And for years throughout his travels, he sought out locations known for their caves or hermitic people. In the summer of 2014, during his second trip to Nepal, he trekked to the Upper Mustang Valley, an arid corner of the country near the border with Tibet, to the village of Tsarang—which translates to "eagle rips the flesh" because of a practice of sky burials. Justin was most intrigued by how the ancient people who had once inhabited the valley had carved caves out of the sandstone cliffs. Some were intricate networks up to five stories tall, with rooms and staircases and tunnels deep within the mountain. He posted a picture of a tourist placard that noted how the tradition has continued and some families from Tsarang still live in caves. Justin hiked up a mountainside above Tsarang, found a cave, and crawled inside. Without a sleeping bag to keep warm, he covered his body with handfuls of dried grass, an age-old technique to combat temperatures dropping during the night.

The year after, while in South America, he explored the caves of the Temple of the Moon near Macchu Picchu in Peru. The complex is said to represent the three planes of existence: those of the earth, the heavens, and the underworld. Then, six months before going to India, he visited the Singnapan Valley in the Philippines, where the Tau't Bato, meaning "people of the stone," take refuge in caves during the rainy season. "Most caves are high on cliff walls and before each rainy season (peaking in August) the people build massive rattan and bamboo vine ladders to reach them," he wrote online. Alongside a photo taken deep inside one cave filled with mosquitoes and bats, he wrote that there was something about being inside a "giant pitch black space that feels so primal and powerful. Good place to meditate or vision quest." In between stints building the primary school in Nepal, Justin visited Mahendra cave near the lakeside city of Pokhara and afterward proclaimed online, "I want to live this free life for a while I think; there is just too much beauty in the world to stay in one place." So he continued on—as if he was searching for the ideal cave in the perfect location. In the Parvati Valley, in the ancient forest near the holy hot springs of Kheerganga, he found his ultimate refuge.

Swapnashree Bhasi swirled a pot filled with milk, tea leaves, and sugar over a small fire. It was nearing the end of July, and she was taking shelter from a downpour inside Garam Gufa. When the chai was ready, she poured a cup and handed it to an American man named Justin who was sitting cross-legged inside her cave. In many ways, she recalled, the two were unlike each other, yet looking back she feels that they had both been driven to the Parvati Valley by similar motivations. Bhasi, like her brother Roy Roberts, was musical: she carried and played a bansuri flute similar to the one Justin was never seen without.

After the Rainbow Gathering had ended, Bhasi had continued living in the cave on her own for two more months. She had initially come to the valley in February after quitting her job as a choreographer and dancer in Bangalore, giving up her apartment, selling her belongings, and setting out on a pilgrimage. "I started to question a lot of things: I was not married, I didn't have a family, I was solo," she recalls. She looks back on 2016, nearly the entirety of which she spent in the Parvati Valley, as "the year it all transformed." As she had entered her midthirties, she had grown increasingly depressed at the way her life, both onstage as a performer and offstage, circled around "me" and "I." She wanted to marry and start a family but felt that it could be too late. She also felt as though she were in a toxic bubble—an artistic community in which alcohol and drugs were readily available. When the bubble burst, she traveled to Bodhgaya near the end of 2015, the first steps of a "spiritual path" to figure out her life.

After spending a month in a monastery, where she realized the life of a nun would not give her fulfillment, she heard a story about a woman named Jetsuma Tenzin Palmo. Born Diane Perry, the spiritually curious young woman had moved from England to India in 1964, at the age of twenty. Before the end of her first month there, she had become a Buddhist nun. She was given a new name and spent the following thirteen years serving in Himalayan monasteries. In 1976, she sought a greater test of isolation, moving into a cave at 13,200 feet in elevation deep in the Spiti Valley, which neighbors the Parvati Valley. Meaning the "middle land" between Tibet and India, Spiti is a high-altitude desert surrounded by peaks that block

the majority of the life-giving monsoon. Initially, Palmo occasionally visited the surrounding monasteries, or received curious visitors
at her cave, where they would sit with her, drink tea, and meditate.
But then she pushed further: she retreated into complete solitude,
speaking to nobody for three years until a policeman appeared and
told her she had been living in Spiti illegally.

Upon arriving in the Parvati Valley, Bhasi found a copy of Palmo's 1998 biography, *Cave in the Snow: Tenzin Palmo's Quest for Enlightenment*, and after reading the details of the woman's life became
determined to follow in Palmo's footsteps. She found a new home in
the Parvati Valley connected to nature and far from the distractions
of her old life, while working for three months as a cook at a guesthouse in Kalga. "The moment I got to the mountains, I decided I
didn't want to go back," she says. In April, she packed up the few
belongings she had brought and hiked up the trail to Kheerganga to
live in a cave during the Rainbow Gathering. A month later, after
the crowds departed for other locations elsewhere in India, Bhasi
stayed in Garam Gufa. She collected firewood from the forest to keep
warm at night and lived off the food left over from the gathering
and what she could collect in the forest: mushrooms, nettles, and, if
she looked hard enough, wild strawberries. As the weeks of solitude
at Kheerganga ticked by, she started to feel as if a weight were being
lifted off her. "It was like a hundred layers of makeup on your face
falling away," she recalls. She woke up every morning and asked
herself, "Where do I belong?" And by nightfall she knew it was
exactly there, in that cave, in that valley, in those mountains. "The
beauty of the Himalaya drowns you," she says. "You think you are
already enlightened."

Justin lived in a cave a few minutes' walk farther into the forest,
and Bhasi would see him reading, taking pictures, or sitting quietly by himself. They shared several conversations over the weeks.
During one, he confided his plans to ride his motorcycle to Ladakh
but said that he was conflicted about the plan and frustrated with
his compulsion to complete grand journeys. "Why should I go?"
she remembers him asking her rhetorically. "Why go anywhere else?

Where does it end? To be a tourist, to be a traveler, or to live in nature?" Can one live in solitude for your entire life? seemed to be the gist of his wondering aloud, Or am I rather in a phase that's simply a means to an end? "I remember we were discussing do we go back," Bhasi says, "or do we go further." They talked about Palmo and her dedication to live in solitude in a cave for years.

In the first few days after Justin arrived, Roberts met often with him in Kheerganga. They soaked in the hot springs and chatted over tea at one of the open-air cafés in the camp. Roberts remembers that initially the American man had been so excited to be in the Himalayas, surrounded by peaks, established in a mountain cave. Justin had found a source of clean drinking water and was collecting berries and wild edibles from the forest. But Roberts began noticing a shift in him, felt him pulling away. "Three or four days pass, and then I could see him go deeper within himself. He became more concentrated," Roberts recalls, and that then he had "switched off from us." The Indian man recognized the path that Justin was on and figured it was best to leave him be.

Still, he spotted the American man strolling each morning to the hot springs at the top of the grassy slope. What had started as morning ablutions became a ritual, one that included a daily visit to a hut just down from the baths. The hut was one of the few permanent structures in the camp, built of stone and wood rather than metal pipes and tarpaulin. Attached to a long wooden pole near the door was a faded saffron-colored pennant that whipped back and forth whenever a strong enough breeze coursed down the valley. The color of the flag signaled that a sadhu lived inside. On one of Justin's first mornings in Kheerganga, after beginning his day with a bath in the hot springs, he had been beckoned inside by the man who called the hut home, a man named Satnarayan Rawat.

Originally from Nepal and approximately forty years of age, Rawat had come to Kheerganga when the weather had warmed. The man wore little—just an orange dhoti, a single piece of cloth wrapped around the waist and tied at the front, and an orange head wrap around his matted dreadlocks. Though the holy site drew many sadhus in the warmer months, Rawat stood out because of an obvious health issue: large swellings or growths, some as large as lemons, on his elbows, knees, and ankles. The summer season also brought an influx of tourists and pilgrims to bathe in the holy hot springs, to sit where Shiva meditated, or to receive a blessing from a resident sadhu. Inside his hut, Rawat would host those who were curious enough to enter on grass mats dyed blue and yellow, positioned around a small clay-rimmed pit where a fire burned day and night. A pair of tablas, Indian drums, lay behind Rawat.

Every day, Justin left his cave in the forest, crossed the meadow to soak in the hot springs, and then strolled down the slope to spend hours inside Rawat's hut. "Every time, Justin was going from his cave to the baba's house and back," Roberts says. "That's it. He never went anywhere else."

The annual summer monsoon had kept the skies cloudy and the mountain rivers swollen with rain for much of the summer. It was one of the first sunny days in weeks when Andrey Gapon met Justin in Kheerganga. The Russian man had been drawn to that stretch of the Himalayas like others in a lineage of Russian spiritual thinkers in India, in particular the painter and philosopher Nicholas Roerich, who had settled in Naggar, just north of the Parvati Valley, where he died in 1947. Gapon had begun his own spiritual retreat in the Parvati Valley earlier that spring by isolating himself in a hut in the mountains above Kasol for forty days before moving higher up the valley to Kalga for another couple of weeks. Gapon had been planning to move on from the region, but as he had trekked to Kheerganga, he says, he had been struck with the feeling that his journey in the Parvati Valley was just beginning. "Kheerganga has a very special energy. Every time I went there something special happened." The first time, one day in late July, as he passed by the stone hut below the hot springs, he saw an American man with an eagle tattoo across his chest sitting outside. Next to the man lay a long bamboo flute. Gapon introduced himself and asked the man where he was staying.

"In a cave," Justin replied, nodding in the direction of the forest beyond the hill.

Gapon's pulse quickened. He had been contemplating spending time in a cave himself, but the only time he had tried to, he had struggled even to light a fire. "And then I see Justin, in his matter-of-fact way, says that he has been living in a cave for days," Gapon recalls. "I asked if he could show me."

Justin led the Russian man to his forest cave. Inside, Gapon felt an initial rush of fear as he thought about sleeping in the dark each night, far from others, with little food and only a fire for warmth and safety. There were animals that could appear in the forests, snow leopards and bears, not to mention snakes and insects that might be drawn to a warm cave at night. But as his eyes adjusted to the light, his mood softened.

Justin kept his cave tidy—"Forest clean," Gapon calls it—with a dirt floor swept with a tree branch in one part and piled with tree needles where he slept. He had neatly organized the few items he had brought: a handful of drooping candles waxed to rock ledges, a book and a metal mug, clothing hanging to dry across his flute–staff, which he had wedged near the opening. There was a stack of firewood that Justin had collected to keep his pit fire rolling each night. The shelter was comfortable, Gapon thought, for a cave—cozy, even. He was impressed. "If I didn't see a living example of a man staying there," he says, "I wouldn't think it was possible."

He asked Justin if he could join him for a couple of nights, but Justin instead pointed him to another cave just around a bend on the hillside. It was smaller and not as dry, with several cracks in the ceiling leaking dribbling water down the walls, so Gapon suggested attaching a tarp to the ceiling, an idea Justin rebuffed as not "authentic." Yet within a couple hours of meeting Justin, Gapon was inspired to follow his direction. He felt drawn to Justin—a magnetic pull. "When I was speaking, he was listening to me," the

Russian man recalls. "It was not just polite talk. He asked questions." Gapon was lacking some supplies, including a sleeping bag, so he asked his new friend if it would be possible to borrow Shadow to drive down valley to see what he could find. He offered his passport as collateral, but Justin shook his head and simply flipped him the keys.

Justin's only reading material in his cave was a worn paperback titled *The Geography of Bliss: One Grump's Search for the Happiest Places in the World* that Linda Borini had given him before leaving Kathmandu, telling him, "You're going to need this more than I will." The book's author, Eric Weiner, had traveled to countries widely considered to be the happiest in the world. One of his stops was India, which he approached "with a question I desperately needed to answer: Why do so many presumably sane westerners leave their wealthy, functional nations behind and travel to a poor and dysfunctional nation in search of bliss? Are they romanticizing the east, falling for charlatans with flowing beards? Or did the nineteenth-century scholar Max Mueller get it right when he said that, by going to India, we are returning to our 'old home,' full of memories, if only we can read them?" What stood out most in the book to Justin, Gapon remembers, was the section on the correlation between happiness and trust. "Trust is a prerequisite for happiness," Weiner wrote. "Trust not only of your government, of institutions, but trust of your neighbors. Several studies, in fact, have found that trust—more than income or even health—is the biggest factor in determining our happiness." Even though Justin told him stories about having been cheated and robbed in the past, "He said he still prefers to trust people," Gapon remembers. "It was in his nature."

Gapon returned three days later with a sleeping bag and some food. The sun that they had met under had disappeared behind silvery clouds once again, replaced with torrential monsoon rain the entire time he was away. He was starting to dread the thought of a night in the damp, isolated cave. But at the least, he had to return the motorcycle keys. When Gapon poked his head into his cave, tears filled his eyes. In the corner was a tidy stack of firewood that Justin had collected and piled inside to dry. He had swept the dirt floor. And he had left Gapon a couple of candles to light his stay.

When he met up with Justin, Gapon noticed that the outgoing man who had showed him the caves had become quieter, more reserved. Justin told him that he had been visiting Rawat in his stone hut, learning yoga and spirituality from him. Gapon felt that Justin was "messy" with his ideas, trying to sort through what made sense for him. But in one way he was clear. "For him, spirituality was to become completely ascetic," Gapon recalls. "He was thinking that only if he renounced all the pleasures and the material, mundane world, only then can he find what he is looking for. . . . Maybe he felt that he was weak because he couldn't push aside all this."

Justin told Gapon that he was struggling to find a balance between a life of solitude and a life of connection, that there was a part of him that wanted to renounce everything and to keep living simply in his cave. "He was looking for the way to be free, independent of whether you have money or no money, whether you have comfort or no comfort." In Gapon's view Justin was "torn apart" by the tension between the side of him that appreciated material pleasure and reputation and the side of him that desired trials and hardships. "I think he came to a point where he realized that just being able to survive in tough conditions is not enough to really be free," Gapon says. It was a notion that Gapon would think about long after their conversations.

After several nights in the cave Justin had set up for him, Gapon packed up his belongings and set off on a trek to the glacial source of the Parvati River, Mantalai Lake, then over the Pin Parvati Pass and into the Spiti Valley. He departed worried about his new friend but was thankful for their time together. He felt as if he had met a long-lost brother in the mountains.

Justin would later post online about his first meeting with Rawat and his curiosity about Indian sadhus, providing a window into what he was thinking during his weeks in Kheerganga. He called sadhus "wild holy men who wander naked and alone in the Himalayas, live in caves, smoke chillums of powerful hashish, and meditate. A lot. They are living their lives in the image of Lord Shiva, who spent much of his life doing the same. Some of them are reported to go months without food, living on pure life energy. And hash."

Inside the hut, Justin would sit around Rawat's fire and the sadhu would offer food: tea and chapatis, Indian flatbread, or *kheer*. It was often Justin's only meal of the day. "Being unsure of customs, I was careful to be observant, and not do anything silly like: pass anything over the fire, point my feet at the fire, or touch his fire," Justin wrote. Rawat would also demonstrate his prowess at yoga, bending and contorting his body into complicated asanas before anyone who gathered in his hut. They would offer cigarettes, hash to pack his chillum, or a hundred rupees in exchange for a blessing from the holy man. To those donations of money to a man who should have little need for money, Justin chose to turn a blind eye. "He has renounced the trappings of the world: both money and women," he wrote online. "He says most babas are fake, that they enjoy money, women, and posing for tourist photos for cash; basically fake-holy-man bums. But he assures me that he is the real thing."

"Justin was enthralled," Roberts says. A part of Roberts understood what Justin admired in the Hindu holy men: "They go to extremes, start pushing the body to see how much they can take. And when the body has no food or anything, the thought processes begin to change, they enter a different state of mind." Roberts has had experiences with sadhus that have left him in awe. During the Rainbow Gathering, a baba from the western Indian state of Rajasthan kept a fire crackling in the meadow around which visitors would sit and receive a blessing. Roberts recalls watching him closely: as the sadhu stood up, his fire would dwindle, and as he sat down, it would surge again. But Roberts wasn't moved by anything emanating from Rawat's smoky hut. "He likely ran away from certain things in his life and ended up there," Roberts says. "Many criminals murder someone, go up to the mountains, grow a beard, dress like a sadhu, and assume a new identity." He was intensely skeptical of what Rawat could be offering Justin or anyone else, yet saw many foreign backpackers taken in by his mystique.

Some who worked in Kheerganga said that Rawat was new to the valley, but others claimed he had been coming to the camp for years. Few, however, believed that he was a genuine holy man. Many referred to him as a "business baba," a holy man who looks and dresses the part but who wanders the country searching not for enlightenment but for cash. Such babas preach spirituality in vague, loose terms and take advantage of the naivete of tourists. Of all the sadhus who flock to the Parvati Valley, locals estimate that only one in ten is on an authentic path of pilgrimage; the vast majority are drawn to the *charas*, the valley's black hash, and the possibilities of earning a modest income by playing the role of a wise man.

Yet Justin was drawn to Rawat, and the sadhu was drawn to Justin. Whenever an Indian pilgrim joined them inside his hut who could translate, Rawat asked Justin simple questions about his life and Justin asked him questions about the life of a sadhu. On one occasion, Justin showed Rawat pictures of his cave, which particularly interested the holy man. In exchange for what Justin saw as teachings, he would wash the dishes after a meal or sweep the sadhu's dirt-floored hut. The relationship developed into a subservient one, a classic bond between a guru who holds wisdom and a *chela*, a disciple or student, who seeks to learn. But Justin saw their connection as equal. "Over the next two weeks we became friends," he wrote. "I think."

Justin appeared to recognize a harder edge to his new friend, writing that sadhus "are not notoriously kind and loving, or particularly happy, like the Buddhist monks I'm used to. They are mountain warriors. Sometimes [Rawat] would get very aggravated with a visitor for some reason I couldn't understand. But he seemed to enjoy my polite, quiet company, and invited me inside every time I passed." The first time Swapnashree Bhasi visited the sadhu's abode, Justin was sitting cross-legged across the fire from Rawat. The sadhu turned to her, knowing she spoke Hindi. "Tell him to give me five hundred rupees," Rawat told her. "I'm his baba. I teach him. Tell him to give me money." Bhasi had witnessed the way Rawat sat behind his fire preparing tea for curious tourists who paid to be in his presence. She translated Rawat's demand for Justin but cautioned him that the man might be using him. Justin ignored her and passed a crumpled bill into the man's outstretched fingers. "I want to be a good friend of him," Rawat told her, motioning to Justin. "I want him to be my student, I want to teach him. But he needs to give me gifts." It's possible that Justin saw no issue with paying to be in the company of a sadhu.

Justin posted that "it was an honor to spend some time with this holy man" and that he was learning "some things about the world through his eyes." Justin may not have called himself a "guru worshiper," as he clarified once, but it was clear that he had become enamored of the sadhu. "I've heard stories about the magical powers of these Babas," he wrote. "They can see into your soul and know your past and future. They can bless or curse. They are holy men but wild, and are even above the law in India. Police won't arrest them; even for murder, which happens I'm told."

Like many of his generation, Justin was searching for spiritual expressions that resonated with him personally, cobbling together morals, teachings, and elements of various faiths to form his own. In many ways, he fit into the twenty-first-century surge of believers who consider themselves spiritual rather than religious. He once said that he didn't like the adjective "spiritual" but that it was the closest to how he would describe himself. "It's the only word I can find that I think has the feeling that I'm going for," he said. But at times he pushed back against the platitudes often preached by this community. "If you miss the bus," he once wrote, "it wasn't 'meant to be' it was because you got up late. It's this kind of hands in the air 'oh well' kind of optimism that is really annoying about spiritual people. I want to know why. I want to understand exactly why, and I want to learn a lesson from a tragedy. Otherwise what's the point?"

Justin repudiated the Big Three religions, Christianity, Judaism, and Islam. In grade six, he had attended a Christian school in Florida but hated it, often coming home after school in tears, his mother remembers. But he had remained fascinated with religious traditions, sharing articles and videos online and engaging in debates with friends and on social media. Traveling became his conduit for exploring other traditions and spiritual persuasions around the world—from the animistic traditions of remote tribes in Southeast Asia to the sun-worshipping faiths in South America, from the multifaceted pantheon of deities in South Asia to the shamanistic traditions in North America. "Religion is a very very attractive, alluring, sparkly arrow," he once said in a podcast interview, "and everyone gets focused on what kind of arrow or what it's made of or what kinds of jewels are on it or what kinds of feathers—and no one's looking where the arrow is pointing, which is at truth." "Truth" is the one word that many who knew him used to describe the goal of Justin's longtime quest. He often spoke of his "path to truth" when describing what he sought in life. He acknowledged that at the base of religion there was a kernel of "real truth" but in his view, spirituality was simple: it was seeing the connection that existed between people and with the world around us. As his mother had often told him, all he had to do was to "find his own truth."

Justin told Kishwor Sedhai, his Nepali friend, that he believed in some kind of higher connection among all things that only few of us come to see and understand. His curiosity to uncover it fueled his actions. But many saw the quest as one without end. "If he was having these deep spiritual experiences," says Brittany Ceres, who taught alongside Justin at the Tracker School, "it's got to be deeply frustrating to know that something exists and not be able to catch it. I can imagine him in his reckoning with being so talented in all these ways of the earth: 'Why can I not catch this thing that I know exists, that I glimpse in every moment of every day?'" In his mother's mind, her son was constantly searching for what she calls "the divine"—the connections that might flow between himself and something bigger. "He wasn't one of these stark, what-you-see-is-what-you-get, nothing-happens-when-you-die kind of people," says

Layla Brooklyn Allman. He didn't want quick, shoestring spirituality. "He wanted the Siddhartha Gautama, fasting for forty-nine days and meditating kind of enlightenment, where you push your body to its physical limits and you remove yourself from the grid and you unlock some layer of the human mind that's capable of perceiving a spiritually that you can't in mundane life. Every incarnation of Justin that I saw had to do with not wanting to be ordinary." And each one was an attempt to try to tap into something greater.

He came close in the early months of 2015, a year before he embarked on his final international trip, while traveling in South America with his girlfriend Indhi Korth. They had met on a dating app the previous summer and had ended up seeing each other for around seven months, with Justin using her artist's loft in Los Angeles as a base while he traveled around California. Originally from Canada, Korth had spent the previous seventeen years on the road; she had lived in Bali for a year and Australia for just over a year but had principally traveled nonstop around the world without ever returning home. When she met Justin, however, she was hitting pause on that life. "I was attempting to ground out," she remembers, "while Justin was on the opposite schedule. He had a passive income, and he never planned for two. I don't think he ever saw a big picture of someone in his life that he deeply cared for." That was one of their central conflicts in the relationship; the other was spirituality.

A few years earlier, Korth had begun dipping her toe into the world of mediumship, a side of her that Justin struggled to understand or connect with. "It was really hard for him to digest things that I believed in, and it caused confrontation," Korth says. "He just couldn't foresee a future together because we didn't meet in those places." She felt he had been rebelling from his spiritual side, pushing back against what was unknown in his mind, and searching for what he could tangibly sense and understand. "He was terrified of losing his freedom," she says. "The only picture he painted for himself was to travel the world for the rest of his life." Even though their relationship was turning unsteady, Korth suggested that Justin accompany her to the Condor Eagle Festival in Brazil, a gathering of Indigenous shamans and medicine men from around Latin America that is held every two years on a forested plateau called Chapada dos Veadeiros.

Korth had attended two years before and found the experience powerful. "Justin had shadows, traumas that he needed to work through, and I was providing a solution. In hindsight, I probably should've never convinced someone to do a trip like that because you can't force people into that world, they have to feel the call." Still, Justin built up his expectations for what the ceremonies might offer or reveal to him. He knew that Stalking Wolf had achieved a great realization in the jungles of the Amazon, where he had met an old Indigenous man who had "truly found the final path to spiritual enlightenment," Tom Brown, Jr., wrote in *Grandfather*. "It was challenging for him because I was very open," Korth recalls. "I think he was expecting to have the same experience."

Justin spent three weeks at the festival, participating in daylong ayahuasca ceremonies. His experiences with hallucinogenic drugs, including ayahuasca, magic mushrooms, and peyote, had provided him with what he once said had been some of his strongest spiritual experiences. One summer when Justin was fourteen, his father had taken him to a cabin in Tennessee for two weeks and introduced him to beer, wine, and hard alcohol, as well as marijuana and magic mushrooms. It was meant to be educational, dabbling in a safe environment. Justin told one friend that his most significant spiritual side had begun when he had taken hallucinogenic drugs with his father when he was a teenager. "Ayahuasca is a powerful hallucinogen that triggers an emotional/spiritual/somatic detox and cleanse," Justin later wrote in a Q and A for a travel website about his experience in South America, "removing baggage that has been built up over years and providing its user with clarity and a fresh start." Justin had tried ayahuasca several times before but prior to going to Brazil had never completed a guided ceremony.

At Condor Eagle, he participated in fourteen ceremonies, each one running from sunset to sunrise, and each one brought him new "realizations," he said in a podcast interview shortly after returning from South America. He said the experiences hadn't been about conquering fears but about confronting the limits of self-belief and working through feelings of guilt and shame. In one ceremony, he had caught a glimpse of his future: he and Korth were together, happy, and traveling with their kids. But that future, full of joy and connection and freedom, quickly evaporated. He and Korth broke up shortly thereafter. "I think things started going a little differently in his life when he was in South America," his mother, Suzie, remembers. And many point to Condor Eagle as the inspiration for his chest tattoo, a permanent reminder of the difficulty of realizing a dream, of mapping a future.

Justin had experienced something at the Condor Eagle ceremony, perhaps the closest he had come to what he was looking for: a revelatory moment that opened his eyes to a higher power that he had doubted and questioned his entire life. He had found a glimpse of that higher power in South America, one that he had begun to chase. "He wasn't ready for that world, and it opened up a curiosity in him," Korth says, "which is why he ended up in India in search of truth." Perhaps he was looking for a kind of epiphany, like those in the stories of Tom Brown, Jr., one of his teachers, and the legends of Stalking Wolf, one of his heroes. "There is a world beyond that of our everyday physical, mental, and emotional experiences," Brown wrote in *The Vision*. "It is a world beyond the five senses, and different than the realm of the imagination. It is the world of the unseen and eternal. The world of spirit and vision. It is a dimension of life that very few people of today seek, to perhaps care to know." Justin sought to know, to understand. For Stalking Wolf, so the story goes, it was a skill long honed—an ability to see connections and patterns and to bring nature's every movement and choice and moment together into a unified totality—but for someone like Justin it could have felt nearly impossible, a layer that he could see in his mind's eye yet in the tangible world always remained in the just-beyond. It was a layer the Native American shamans, he knew, could interact with;

it was what he sought to experience with ayahuasca and hash; and it was what he hoped an Indian sadhu might be able to provide him.

His mother believes without a doubt that her son had gone to the Parvati Valley to search for a deeper meaning behind his life, that it had unquestionably been the culmination of a long spiritual quest. "I mean," Suzie says, "he ended up in a cave in India."

Toward the end of Justin's three weeks living in the forests around Kheerganga, Rawat began talking about embarking on a pilgrimage. Every year in late August or early September, depending on the Indian calendar, pilgrims flock to the Parvati Valley to bathe in the area's hot springs. One night is particularly significant, when fires are lit and songs are sung and *puja*s—prayers—are offered, leading up to ritual bathing at the most auspicious moment at dawn. It is believed that submersing oneself in the holy waters can cure all manner of ills and ailments. Some pilgrims drive to Manikaran, park in the multistory concrete lot, and take a quick dip in the temple hot springs. The more intrepid head farther up the valley and hike to Kheerganga, where they soak in steaming baths at the top of the hill. Perhaps the most devout spend days trekking to the source of the Parvati River, where they briefly dunk themselves in the frigid glacial waters, considered to be the most pure.

A new moon was approaching, scheduled to appear on September 1, and Rawat wanted to make offerings to Shiva, the god he revered above all others, at the most holy site in the valley: Mantalai Lake. He turned to his new disciple, the young American man who was living in a nearby cave, and asked if he would like to join him.

FINDING 10 FREEDOM

The three weeks Justin had spent in his cave had left him weak and sore; his back ached from sleeping on the ground, his old accident injury was flaring up. His meager diet had turned his typically muscular frame lean. But he emerged with a heightened determination to take a greater step on his Indian journey. He gathered his few belongings, stuffed them into his day pack, and descended along the forest trail, returning to the village of Kalga. He had a new goal and he needed to prepare.

On August 13, after three weeks of inactivity online, Adventures of Justin blinked back to life with new posts and photos. "I've been living in some caves in the Indian Himalayas for the last couple weeks," Justin wrote under the self-portrait he had taken while reclining inside his cave, together with a series of hashtags including #caveman, #nomadiclife, and #freedom. He outlined his new plan: "I just came down from the mountain and will soon head back. A Sadhu has invited me on a pilgrimage high in the Himalayas to meditate. . . . He invited me along on his pilgrimage: three days hard trek to a lake at 13,000ft (4000m), and then ten days meditating in spiritual retreat, living amongst the rocks, in a place without vegetation or wood to burn. Then three days back to a small village." On Instagram he wrote that his next journey "might be the hardest thing I've ever done."

He also posted a picture of the sadhu he had befriended, a black-and-white photograph of Rawat sitting cross-legged in his stone hut and drawing on a chillum. Tendrils of smoke snake from the end of his clay pipe. Behind him, the faces of three Hindu gods look down from posters that had been affixed to the wall of his hut. The large swellings on Rawat's wrists and elbows are in full view. A long post introducing Satnarayan Rawat to his followers accompanied the photo. Justin wrote that the sadhu had told him that he had cut off his penis as an extreme renunciation of lust, mentioning that he had found the act "both upsetting and impressively dedicated." Rawat had asked Justin if he liked women. When Justin had answered affirmatively, the sadhu had shaken his head: "Nai baba!" he had told him. "I am not a baba he says. Confirming that I'm unwilling to truly renounce the world," Justin quipped.

After picking up his motorcycle by the half-built hydroelectric dam near Kalga, Justin rode down the bumpy road to purchase supplies for the trek to Mantalai Lake, passing buses of tourists and pilgrims heading up the valley, until the steam from the hot springs at Manikaran and the prayer flag–draped bridges that cross the Parvati River came into view. When he reached Kasol, while he wandered the town's market streets purchasing food and a blue tarpaulin, he met Nirmal Patel and Sunny Panchal, two friends from the western Indian city of Ahmedabad, who were on holiday in the Parvati Valley. They were picking up supplies as well, for a trek along the same route to Mantalai Lake and then across the mountain pass into the Spiti Valley, the route Andrey Gapon was at the time navigating. Patel, a bansuri flute player himself, commented on the instrument Justin was carrying. After finding what they needed in the market, the three went to a café and chatted about their respective forthcoming hikes. Over tea, Patel taught Justin a couple of simple classical Indian tunes, as well as the theme of *Malgudi Days*, an Indian TV series that's based on a book of parable-like short stories by R. K. Narayan. Patel and Panchal, who were both working in film and cinematography, recall bonding with Justin over photography and following one another's Instagram accounts.

A woman named Archana Singh, who struck up a conversation with the group at the café, remembers Justin talking about his "baba trek" and how a sadhu was going to teach him yoga on a pilgrimage to Mantalai Lake. Singh told him that she understood his desire to embark on such a journey, away from civilization. Justin then told her that he was very soon going to cut himself off entirely from the modern world—and that he was excited. To Singh, one word he used that stood out above all others: "disappear."

Before Justin departed, Patel took out his camera and snapped a portrait of Justin, one he would later send to the American's iPhone. The group shook hands and parted, wishing one another well on their journeys farther into the mountains. Maybe, Panchal recalls thinking, they would see each other again.

After Andrey Gapon completed his trek, he felt pulled to return to the Parvati Valley. When he had found cell service again, he saw Justin's posts about Rawat the sadhu and the plan to trek to the lake. On the midafternoon of August 21, he met up with Justin at the Om Shanti guesthouse, along with Christofer-Lee Humphreys and Villas Bambroo. Bambroo recognized Justin as the man he'd previously seen sitting on the grassy hill at Kheerganga playing his flute. Bambroo, who was originally from Kashmir but who was living in the central Indian city of Indore, had visited the Parvati Valley many times before, but this year he had arrived with a plan to make a pilgrimage to the holy lake.

Justin listened attentively as Gapon and Bambroo recounted their separate treks. "Mantalai Lake is a very special place," Gapon told him. "It has energy that is transforming. It makes karma work very fast." But Justin leaned in when Bambroo told his story—of how, two weeks earlier, he had completed the journey entirely solo. He had carried little food, he told the group sitting on red plastic chairs in Om Shanti's courtyard, just some *paneer*, a kind of fresh cheese, and a bag of potatoes that he had preboiled—food that would be easier to prepare in the absence of firewood. He had also packed nothing in terms of shelter, as he had heard that there were boulder caves along the route and a blanket would suffice. Despite the muddy trail, he had moved quickly, reaching his destination within three days. He had settled into a shelter built of stones in the lee of a boulder near the lakeshore. For two days, nobody else had arrived. Then, over the next few days, a group of trekkers or a solitary pilgrim had approached the holy lake in the evening, camped for the night, and departed in the morning. During the nights he had kept warm by making a small fire out of wood shavings that he had collected among the rocks and some trekkers' discarded kerosene.

Bambroo had spent eight nights at the lake relishing the quiet and the solitude. As time passed, he told Justin, he had experienced a transformation: he had come to feel total fear in the light of day and complete comfort and calm in the dead of night, until, he says, his existence became clearer. "When you are up in the mountains," he says, "this idea of one mind and individual selves and bodies leaves you, and you become connected to a bigger self, which is the nature, which is the mountains, which is the flowing river, which is something more than you." In this state it is easier to approach a greater force, whether it goes by the name of God or Shiva or the universe or nature, whether it appears externally or arises within. You are forced to reconcile how you relate to the mountain or the river, the glacier or the star. "It's also asking you if you want to stop here or move, and if you're keen on going ahead to see what's in store for you— your way forward." Each day Bambroo confronted those forces, those questions. After his food ran out on the ninth day, he packed his blanket and made his way back down the trail to Kalga.

Justin asked him to outline the main stages of the route, how far someone could walk in a day, and the approximate location of the boulder cave shelters. Bambroo said there were a few, located around Pandu Pul, Thakur Kuan, and Mantalai Lake, but he also mentioned that there was another cave off the main trail, much larger than any along the route. Justin then asked Bambroo to take a look at his provisions in his guesthouse room. Most of Justin's belongings were packed in a large green backpack, except for the few items he was planning on taking to Mantalai Lake. Bambroo examined the food Justin had bought and figured that it was enough but not a lot, especially since Justin said he was planning a journey of around a month. It was then that Justin revealed that he was in fact not going on the trek alone, but with a sadhu he hoped could teach him his ways. Bambroo remembers feeling concern. "I haven't met any holy man who could really teach me who would be different from a schoolteacher," he says. "It's not that they're fake, but they're not as learned or as holy as they claim. They are also travelers, and in order to get by and in order to live their journey, they have to hold to this image of a baba that serves their purpose."

Gapon and Humphreys had both briefly interacted with Rawat in Kheerganga and had found the experience uncomfortable. Gapon had seen the sadhu demand money and hash from those who sat before him in exchange for a blessing. Humphreys, who had spent weeks in Kheerganga during the Rainbow Festival, had always been wary of Rawat, who had been banned from some cafés in Kheerganga because he was known to pick tourists' pockets. "Some babas are very charming and outgoing, but this baba was rough and crude," he says, noting that "there was something that was very hard and very aggressive with his spirit." Humphreys once warned Justin to be cautious with the sadhu, but the American seemed to shrug off his concerns.

Bambroo had seen other foreigners succumb to the pressure to experience profound moments of realization during their Indian travels. In his estimation, Justin's motivation was flawed, as he was embarking on the journey to prove something rather than to find peace. And as competent as he appeared in the outdoors, he didn't know the terrain. "When I met Justin," Bambroo says, "I felt that his journey was more of a challenge. And when you challenge the mighty mountains, especially the Himalayas, which have their own spirit and their own energy that resonates, however you challenge them, they give you your own challenge. And sometimes you don't get through."

As Justin detailed his plan, Bambroo remained largely quiet. Justin picked up on the Indian man's unease, clarifying that he wasn't planning on spending the whole time at the lake with the sadhu. His idea was to have the man guide him along the trail, spend a few days together at the lake, and then tell the sadhu to leave and return to Kheerganga. Justin hoped to remain at Mantalai Lake alone, as Bambroo had done.

As the sun sank lower toward the hills, the four men left the guesthouse and weaved through the buildings and apple trees and up the hill overlooking the village. They wanted to find a view of the sunset and of the whole valley before them. Perched on a large boulder, the group watched the sun dip toward the mountains. It set directly over the mouth of the valley, casting a vibrant orange glow, one last flare of light and color before the sky went dark.

Before Justin departed, while he still had cell service, he made a series of phone calls to people he cared deeply for: friends, at least two former girlfriends, and family back home in the United States. Linda Borini remembers seeing his pixilated face appear on her phone and noticing how gaunt it was. "That's when I got worried," she recalls. "He was so skinny, he was so frail." She remembered that they had both lost some weight during their hike in Nepal, but his new state was alarming. Still, she trusted him to know the limitations of his body. Justin told her that because of doing this trek, he wouldn't have enough time to ride his motorcycle to Ladakh, the journey they had both dreamed of one day completing, as the nearly 13,000-foot Rohtang La mountain pass would be impassable with snow by the time he returned. She told him that many people ride motorcycles along that renowned highway but that this journey, a pilgrimage to a remote holy lake in the company of a sadhu, was an opportunity for a unique experience that the vast majority of people who travel to India would never be fortunate enough to have. "You owe it to all the people who want to have this kind of adventure but can't," she said to him, words that have weighed heavily on her ever since. Justin said that he was falling in love with India and that even though he was only a third of the way though his six-month tourist visa, he felt he needed more time in the country. He told her that he had met someone in India who could help him extend his visa by another six months and lamented that his visa wasn't the kind that lasted ten years. Borini asked when he planned on returning to the United States. Justin was frank: "I don't think I'm going to come back."

Justin called his mother and walked her through his plan. Every time her son mentioned the word sadhu, Suzie had a "visceral reaction" that she couldn't explain. She never wanted to project anxiety onto her son, but she couldn't hold back from telling him that she was worried about this journey. "If you get up there and it's not right, what can you do?" she asked him. He told her that he felt compelled to go but reassured her, as he had done many times before, that everything would be fine.

Then Justin called his father. In the two years prior, they had largely reconciled and reconnected, but Justin had seen Terry only once; he had arranged a stopover in Florida while flying back to California after attending Tom McElroy's survival class in the Caribbean. So when Terry picked up the phone and listened to his son describe a plan to embark on a possibly monthlong hike to Mantalai Lake with a sadhu, Terry didn't feel in a position to offer cautionary fatherly advice. As he had told his son when he was a boy, he wanted to support him in his search for contentment. Still, Terry couldn't help but flash back to his own trip to India in the late 1970s and the warning the tour group had received about sadhus. "Whatever you do, don't go and look them in the eyes," he remembers someone saying, "because they'll hypnotize you and you'll end up mindlessly following them around." In Delhi, Terry had seen a young European man doggedly following a sadhu "like in a trance," he says. He realized that the man had likely been stoned.

But he didn't share that memory with his son. He didn't want to dissuade him. In the moment, he felt that Justin was about to find what he was looking for, as Terry had on his own journey in India. "I couldn't ask him not to do it. The light is hard to refuse."

On the morning of August 22, Justin packed his day pack with some rice and oats, nuts and raisins, tea and sugar, and flour to make chapatis—very little for someone hoping to subsist for nearly a month trekking in the Himalayas. Rawat had told him that "he doesn't need to eat," Justin had written. He carried no tent or stove, just a thin sleeping bag, his metal cup, and his machete. He packed a large tan-colored woolen shawl that he could wrap around his shoulders or use as a blanket, and wore his khaki hiking pants, a white long-sleeved Tibetan-style shirt that buttoned at the side, and a black lightweight down jacket. He also brought dental floss, less for oral hygiene than for its manifold backcountry uses: as rope or thread, clothesline or makeshift shoelace, fishing line or snare. There was confidence in what little he packed, as well as what he left behind. Still, something was weighing on him. "He had a feeling that something was going to go down up there, a premonition or something," recalls Christofer-Lee Humphreys, who saw Justin off at the Om Shanti guesthouse. Before Justin left, he joked to Humphreys, "If I die, write something nice about me on Facebook."

Humphreys shot him a look. "Don't talk like that," he told him. "Come back down safe."

Justin's heart was in the journey to Mantalai Lake, but he worried that his body would hold him back. "I've been cold, damp, and hungry a lot recently, and feeling a bit malnourished and weak already. I think this is going to be a challenge on every level and I'm nervous," he wrote as a conclusion to the final post he uploaded to his blog. He noted that the area around Mantalai Lake was completely "uninhabited" and that the trail was "notorious and it's landslide season." He expressed concern that because he and Rawat didn't share a common language, communicating any "ancient doctrine" would be a challenge.

"But from what I understand," Justin continued,

he wants to mentor me in the ways of the Sadhu; of Shiva—The First Yogi. He follows a strict spiritual routine that I know nothing about, and I am intensely curious. These Babas are said to have magical powers from decades of an ancient yoga practice. But. I really don't know what to expect. I've never done yoga, and his style is extreme—based on the grotesque swellings on his joints. But I want to see the world through his eyes, which are essentially 5000 years old, an ancient spiritual path. I'm going to put my heart into it and see what happens.

My back is in bad shape, (broken when I was 19) and even with daily soaks in hot springs, this cave/mountain life has recently put me in a state of constant discomfort. I'm sadly inflexible, and I can't even sit still for a few minutes without pain.

Maybe Baba Life will be good for me. I should return mid September or so.

If I'm not back by then, don't look for me ;)

PART III

THE PATH

There is no stopping place in this pilgrimage; it is one continuous journey, through day and night; through valley and desert; through tears and smiles, through death and birth, through tomb and womb. When the road ends, and the Goal is gained, the pilgrim finds that he has traveled only from himself to himself. . . .

—Sri Sathya Sai Baba, Indian guru

The last part of life's road has to be walked in single file.

—Sri Ramakrishna, nineteenth-century Indian mystic

PART III

THE PATH

11
SEARCHING

Justin knew the trail. It began in the forest of deodar and walnut where gray langur monkeys chattered and barked above. It continued gradually, crossing rickety pole bridges that spanned mountain creeks. Within half an hour of leaving Kalga, all service bars on his cell phone winked out. He saw no more comments or notifications, no likes or words of admiration. He walked on, passing a handful of spots along the trail that sold bottled drinks, chai, and instant noodles under a tarp strung up between trees. The trail followed stairs cut directly into the stone until finally, after one more push, Justin emerged into a meadow and the camp of Kheerganga. Rawat was awaiting him in his stone hut near the hot springs.

Justin passed nearly a week back at the camp, possibly renting a canvas tent in which to sleep or perhaps returning to his familiar cave in the forest. When it was time, he gathered his belongings and met Rawat, and together the two men made their way to the trailhead to the higher valley. The path began near a boulder cave, one that was often occupied by another sadhu and marked with Shiva's trident painted in red on the rock. The summer cicadas in the forest were deafening, but it was the roar of the Parvati River that was the constant sound, a reminder of their destination that lay many days' walking ahead. Occasionally, a break in the trees offered a view across the river to bright green cannabis plantations being cultivated in seclusion. Harvest time was nearing, and growers would soon trek along mountain paths before vanishing into seven-foot-tall bushes to rub black *charas* between their palms.

Justin and Rawat crossed wooden bridges over glacial streams and through leas full of shoulder-tall purple thistles and creeping wild strawberry, the air perfumed with wildflowers and medicinal plants. They entered one meadow across from an amber cliff face, where Himalayan condors soared overhead, catching the valley's updrafts and leaving winged shadows on the ground.

They climbed through a forest of yew and pine up to Tunda Bhuj, an alpine meadow where a lone sadhu has been living for years on his own. In his stone house on the ridge, the only permanent dwelling in the high valley, he cooks instant noodles and boils tea for trekkers, pilgrims, and shepherds seeking a respite. He is a gatekeeper of sorts to the upper reaches of the Parvati Valley, and everyone who passes by stops in for refreshment, for gossip, or just to take a curious look inside the house. On one side of the main room is an open-air kitchen with a firepit that has blackened the side wall with soot; on the other is an elaborate shrine to Shiva with golden statues and stone lingams. A curtain conceals a back room where dozens can sleep on mats on the floor, if the weather turns, around a small wood stove.

The trail continued in the shade of rhododendron trees that had bloomed red in the spring, scrubby juniper bushes, and the skinny, white-barked birch that now replaced the larger trees of the lower valley. Eventually, the pair passed beyond the tree line and into the higher alpine slopes, leaving behind the stubby groves of Himalayan silver fir with branches of stiff needles and blue cones that stood upright like eggs in a nest. The mountainsides here were marked with great scars, evidence of landslides that had torn through grass and scrub and stream. The men descended slightly through a narrow section of gorge where the river runs fast and violent. Five years before, a fierce river surge had destroyed the bridge that crossed the gorge, leaving disconnected stone platforms on either bank and fragments of timbers reaching out to one another like outstretched arms.

Rawat led Justin along a narrow track that followed the cliff along the river's southern bank. At a couple points, they used their hands to scramble along the trail until it flattened at Thakur Kuan, an expansive meadow filled with blue wildflowers. A keen eye would have spotted the abandoned ruins of one of the earliest hydroelectric projects in the valley. Nearby, one of the tributaries feeding into the Parvati River leads to a natural spring and the spot where, in the 1990s, a group of British gem hunters went looking for fortune. They had hired local porters—keeping mum about their search—and established a base camp near Thakur Kuan, launching expeditions to scour the mountain slopes for sapphires. After the true reason for their expedition was found out months later, the guides and porters abandoned the amateur prospectors to their quest, leaving them to survive on their own in the high mountains.

The trail kept close to the river before descending sharply toward the rushing waters. To cross to the northern bank, Justin and Rawat navigated the giant boulders at Pandu Pul, said to have been dropped by the Pandava brothers, great warriors of legend. They climbed up the first boulder using some well-placed stones, then descended by following a quartz seam in the rock that led them to the next boulder. From there, they found a larger stone ramp to return to a sure footing on the trail.

As the peaks grew closer, the shrubs and grasses grew smaller, as if pressed by the weight of the mountains. The trail wended past a series of grassy meadows, called *thach*es, where shepherds rest and graze their flocks and pilgrims find shelter in the lees of great pieces of stone broken off the mountainside. Above Odi Thach, Justin followed the sadhu as they picked their way across the flat valley bottom. Here the Parvati River began to change. What had been churning whitewater lower down the valley mellowed closer to its source. As the two men trekked slowly higher, a wall of scree spanning nearly the entire breadth of the valley came into view, a remnant of the gargantuan glaciers that long ago formed an impenetrable barrier of ice and crevasses. As the glacier had retreated, it had left behind this barrier that acted like a natural dam, holding back the waters that formed Mantalai Lake. More of a sprawling gray-blue pool, the lake is filled, drip by drip, by the seasonal snowpack and the melting glaciers. Here the noise of the Parvati River dissipates, and the water is calm and serene. By day, the glacial melt fills the basin, swelling the lake; by night, the waters spill out into the river and the lake recedes—a daily cycle, as if the lake itself is breathing.

At the water's edge, pilgrims have marked the spot with stone cairns and a *mandir*, a shrine to Shiva. Those who came before plunged tridents, replicas of Shiva's weapon, upright into the earth and tied prayer flags and red and gold pennants to flutter in the wind. The heart of the open-air shrine is marked by a stone lingam around which devotees light incense and lay offerings, ring a large brass bell, and prostrate themselves before the lake. They leave offerings at the shore and fill containers of water to bring blessings home.

Justin had reached the source of the holy river.

Many of Justin's friends were quietly concerned by what they had been reading online since he had arrived in India. Amanda Sansoucie had been following his posts after last seeing him in Nevada around Christmas, weeks before he had departed the United States, and had grown increasingly alarmed by his more recent posts. "They started to seem more depressing," she recalls. "The longer he was there, it just felt more grim." They felt darker, the words of someone at the end of his rope. Everything he messaged her privately felt odd to her, too, and she worried that his barometer for reading people was off—especially after he had messaged her saying how strange it was that a sadhu had approached him, of all people in the valley, and had singled him out, as if he had been chosen.

Since leaving Nepal, Linda Borini, too, had sensed a darkness developing. She was excited that he was living his dream but felt it was clear that Justin was pushing himself farther than he ever had. "He was trying to make this perfect, ideal hero image of himself, to carve it out of himself—and choose what to let go of and what to hold on to," she says. "And India made him let go of it all." What worried her most of all was Justin's fascination with the sadhu and his extremism and what pushing himself so far and so high might stir up in his psyche.

Justin bore scars from the shards of glass that had worked their way to the surface of his skin for years after his truck accident. His back, broken in that accident, gave him chronic pain. But he also had invisible scars that lay much deeper. When he was eight and the family was living in Florida, his father had worked shifts in construction and his mother had taught dance classes at a boys' and girls' club. On Saturdays, their schedules had overlapped. Suzie was usually home by lunchtime, but someone was needed to supervise Justin on those mornings. One day, she came home to find her son distraught. "I knew something was wrong when I went into his room and he was crying, and saying 'I'm so bad, Mom. I'm really bad.'" The man who had been entrusted to care for Justin had been sexually abusing him. It was devastating for Suzie, and she struggled to find words of comfort; she held him tightly and told him that nothing was his fault.

Terry and Suzie went to the police, but she remembers them as ineffective. Instead, the family moved to another area in Florida. But the man, Suzie recalls, followed them, sometimes sitting on a motorcycle outside their home. They moved again, onto the gated property of a family that had hired Suzie as a childcare worker, but the man returned, trying several times to break into the complex. Suzie didn't know what exactly had happened to her son; she didn't want to pressure him to speak about it. Then one day she came home from work to find him watching *The Oprah Winfrey Show*. A guest was talking about abuse he had experienced as a child. "Justin looked at me really funny and said, 'That's what happened to me. That's what happened when that man came over,'" Suzie remembers. He opened up and told his mother that he had been scared to tell her about it because the man had threatened that if Justin ever told anyone, the man would kill his mother.

Justin was eleven when his parents divorced, and two years later he and his mother began the cross-country move that ended in Oregon. When he was fifteen, the year before he began his studies at the Wilderness Awareness School, he found a summer job working as a farmhand in a rural part of Washington for a man who had experience in tracking and wilderness survival. Justin had just begun dipping his toes into that world and was keen to learn. Their agreement was that the man would teach Justin in exchange for work. Partway through the summer, a family friend visited the farm and returned to tell Suzie that she needed "to get him out of there." The man had sexually assaulted Justin.

That was a history that Justin carried with him and one that he occasionally hinted at publicly. The lyrics of "Let It Go," a song he wrote for Punchface while in San Francisco, include the stanza:

> *There is a stone in my hand, and it is all that I am*
> *The harder I hold the more it hurts*
> *And I begin to believe this form I'm holding is me*
> *The tighter I go, the more I am assured*
> *And I am dying to see how I can finally be*
> *Free from incessant suffering*
> *And now I open my hand. I find a fistful of sand*
> *The world comes pouring in.*

The inspiration had arisen from a conversation with a Buddhist monk during Justin's first trip to Thailand in late 2006. Justin had asked, "How do you let things go?" The monk had poured some sand into Justin's open hand and told him that all the grains in his hand made up his life. Then he had instructed Justin to close his hand tightly; the sand had leaked out from between his fingers, falling onto the ground. "If you are too hard with your life," the monk had said, "you won't see that your life is falling apart." Then the monk had placed a rock into Justin's palm. "Twist it, turn it around. Look at that rock," the monk had said. "That is pain in your life. Now squeeze it." The more tightly Justin had squeezed, the more it had hurt. "The same with your life as with your pain," the monk had said. "Treat both gently."

Justin shared aspects of his past with several people he was close to and felt safe with, revealing fragments of what he had gone through. Later, he opened up to a girlfriend about much of that history. "I just think that there was something so incredibly broken inside him," she says, "that psychologically there were things that he was never able to repair, to control, to get past." She noted that some of his favorite books explored various notions and theories of sexuality and psychology or were set in hypermasculine environments. He had confided in her that, after the first childhood assault, as he had grown older—taller, stronger, more confident—he'd assumed that what he saw as a vulnerability in himself would dissipate. He had thought that such abuse wouldn't, couldn't, happen again, she recalls him saying. He sought solitude in nature, she believes, as a way to work through his trauma after being assaulted the second time. Deep in a mountain forest, on his own, he had control over his life, a power over his surroundings and his existence. It was a reality he wanted to live in—a reality where he found meaning, strength, connection. "Everything from that moment on was about him trying to prove that he was stronger than that being done to him, that somebody couldn't take his power away like that ever again," the ex-girlfriend says. He worked out at the gym constantly and trained in several martial arts and self-defense techniques, including Muay Thai; he dreamed of joining the military. "That was his quest in life, to regain that power and to show people that he was not that person who was attacked, he was not that person who was abused, he was not that person who was belittled."

After they had ended their relationship, the woman had thought a lot about a shattering comment Justin had once made: "Shame is the most powerful human emotion you can feel." Much of what drove his searching, she believes, was an attempt to find a path away from that shame, to right those wrongs. In her mind, Justin donned various identities as a form of escapism. He was a greasy vagabond on a motorcycle and a slick front man for a punk-rock band, a suited businessman at a startup and a barefoot survivalist in the wilderness. "He created these personas that allowed him to escape those stressors or feel like he was worthy of certain things," she says. "Because really, inside, he felt very conflicted about who he was and how he wanted other people to see him." Travel can be a mask. A plane ticket can provide the opportunity to reinvent oneself: land in a different country, and nobody knows your past. Justin's constant movement and drive for independence offered him the opportunity to transform with every sunset and every sunrise. "You can be whoever you want when you're solo," he once said in an interview. You can remake yourself—more friendly, more outgoing, more charismatic—while simultaneously feeling that you're donning a suit of armor. The ex-girlfriend says she will never forget something else Justin said to her: "I wonder who I would've become if those horrible things hadn't happened to me."

Tracy Frey had been aware of his history since their days at the Tracker School. "He believed so much of his purpose was to be the protector, but really he was trying to protect himself. When you look at all those skills he acquired, I think it was him trying to tell that little boy inside him that he was going to be safe, that he was going to protect him." His dedication to mastering survival skills, she says, was a way to build a shield against what had happened to him. "It is core to what made him the person he was and is core to him being a person who was always seeking and always looking for . . . originally I was going to say 'answers,' but what I think is the better word is he was always looking for trust, and he was always looking for acceptance. I don't think he found it in most of the places he looked. Up until the end, I never saw him as somebody who gave up—I don't know if he was willing to let it in or if he was looking in the wrong places—but I think there were times when he got close to that."

There is a Hindu parable of a master who instructs his apprentice to fetch a handful of salt and pour it into a glass of water. The apprentice does so and takes a sip, then deems the water bitter and undrinkable. The master tells his apprentice to sprinkle another handful of salt into a lake and then take a drink from the lake. This time the water tastes clear and pleasant. "The pain of life is pure salt; no more, no less," the master says. "The amount of pain in life remains the same, exactly the same. But the amount of bitterness we taste depends on the container we put the pain in."

One wonders if a goal of Justin's searching was to try to shed his grains of pain one by one along the many roads that he traveled. But his journey was long, and those grains were sharp, lying just below the surface like jagged shards of glass.

As Justin made his way toward Mantalai Lake, many of his followers swooned over his stated journey, but many also wished him some version of a "safe return," a common response to his posts while he was in the Parvati Valley. The followers were also watching the latest video that Justin had filmed and uploaded to his social media accounts and above the final post to his blog. He had worked on it for weeks, editing together a series of clips he'd filmed on his iPhone over the previous month in and around his cave in Kheerganga. As in his previous videos, there is no dialogue or narration; instead, soft music—from *Baraka*, his favorite film—plays in the background.

The video opens with a shot of Justin sitting on a rock, draped in a gray shawl like a monk, surrounded by silhouettes of pine trees fading and reappearing like apparitions in the fog. Next he walks barefoot through a meadow, using his flute–staff as a walking stick; he washes his metal cup with water from a mountain stream and takes a drink; he pans the camera for a view through the forest. He is seen inside his cave, splitting wood with his machete. He lights a fire and lies down.

The next shot is a close-up of the Parvati River, foaming and spewing mist. The footage of the river is overlaid with one of Justin meditating, eyes closed and expression calm. The mist fades into smoke and a man appears through the haze: Satnarayan Rawat, sitting in his hut, his head wrapped in a saffron scarf, puffing on a hash-filled chillum.

The video fades to black.

12
ALARM

Whenever Justin had stepped off-grid before, he had always made contact quickly after his return to cell service. There were many friends who anticipated receiving a message when he was finished with his trek to Mantalai Lake. Linda Borini was among them. But she knew how important the journey was for Justin and from her own travels in India knew that people can easily become delayed or waylaid. Still, on September 12, she messaged him on Facebook, noting that he should be on his way down from the lake by now. A few days later, she received a parcel in the mail: a motorcycle part that he had bought in the New Delhi market for his green Royal Enfield and shipped to her address in Los Angeles. She messaged him again to tell him it had arrived.

No response.

Justin had written on his blog that he would return "mid September or so," but on Instagram he wrote "mid to late September"—an imprecision that worried few. Nevertheless, something twisted in Borini's gut. She messaged Christofer-Lee Humphreys, whom Justin had tagged in several photographs online and who was still in Kalga, asking if he had seen Justin return from his pilgrimage. Humphreys told her that Shadow was still parked near the dam below the village and that Justin's large green backpack remained uncollected in storage at the Om Shanti guesthouse. She should give him time, he told her, at least a few more days, before getting worried. He had also heard a rumor that Justin and the sadhu had recently been spotted together at a café in Kheerganga. "I'm sure everything is fine," he told Borini. "You know Justin."

But then Humphreys received a message from Andrey Gapon, who had returned to Russia. When mid-September passed and Justin didn't respond to messages, he reached out to Humphreys. Having two concerned friends express worry nearly simultaneously alarmed the Frenchman. It was time, he realized, to hike the three hours to Kheerganga to see what he could find—or at least try to find the one person he knew had last been with Justin.

To help, Humphreys needed to find someone who spoke Hindi. He asked Villas Bambroo, who was also still in Kalga, to join him, but Bambroo declined. "What kind of friend are you?" Bambroo remembers Humphreys castigating him. He had met Justin only once, for a couple hours, he explained, and, more important, he remembered what Justin had told him at Om Shanti before departing for Mantalai Lake. Justin wanted solitude; he wanted to stay at the lake for as long as possible; he was going to send the sadhu back and remain in isolation. "I did not want to take that trip because I felt that maybe Justin wanted to be left alone," Bambroo says. "If a person told me that he wanted to be alone in the Himalayas somewhere, why would I go and bother him?"

Humphreys then moved on to Swapnashree Bhasi, whom he knew from the Rainbow Gathering, and asked if she had seen Justin. Bhasi had lost track of the passage of time during the four months she had lived in her cave. "I started to feel that I don't need friends, I don't need family, I don't need my phone, I don't need anything," she recalls. She wondered if Justin had become similarly distracted and taken a break out of a deep desire for quiet and solitude. Even though she wasn't worried and tried to reassure Humphreys that Justin was likely safe and had simply extended his journey, she agreed to accompany him to Kheerganga to see what they could find.

In Kheerganga, Rawat had returned to his stone hut below the hot springs. He had returned to a new cohort of tourists camping on the hillside. He had returned to the sound of djembe drums and flutes and pilgrims bathing in the hot springs. Nobody had questioned his return; they had assumed that the American man who had embarked with him for Mantalai Lake had simply departed for elsewhere in the valley or the country. Several people living in the camp in the early weeks of September recall that nobody there had wondered about Justin's whereabouts at all. So many trekkers and pilgrims travel to and from Mantalai that a single person—even someone who had been living around Kheerganga for nearly a month and who sported several prominent identifying features, such as a flute–staff and an eagle tattoo—blended into the crowds.

When Bhasi and Humphreys reached the camp and began asking questions, the typically serene tone of Kheerganga changed. The pair was met with indifference at best and hostility at worst. Some shrugged at their questions about a missing person and turned their backs. "Nobody gives a shit," Humphreys says, thinking back on that fall in the Parvati Valley. "You get a little look of worry, and then life continues. People disappear all the time in the mountains." Finally, he and Bhasi walked up the hill to the home of Satnarayan Rawat. They found the sadhu in his habitual pose, sitting cross-legged in his stone hut near the hot springs, a saffron wrap around his waist, beaded necklaces over a bare chest.

As Humphreys and Bhasi entered the hut, the sadhu's eyes widened.

"Baba, where is Justin?" Bhasi asked in Hindi.

The sadhu laughed. "Oh, now you come," Bhasi recalls Rawat responding, "to ask me where is Justin. It's been a while, hasn't it?"

Bhasi and Humphreys quickly grew alarmed. "I left him long back," Rawat told them in Hindi. "We had a fight. He was going crazy in the valley." He told them that Justin had refused to descend to Kheerganga and had wanted to stay at Mantalai Lake for weeks. They had argued, Rawat said. Then the sadhu had left and started to descend, thinking that Justin would follow. They had had another argument farther down the trail near the hut at Tunda Bhuj, Rawat continued, and alluded to the fact that someone had been hurt. He claimed that the last time he had seen the American, Justin had turned around and was heading back up the valley, back toward Mantalai Lake. When Humphreys pushed harder for details, about who exactly had been hurt, the sadhu became angry, shouting in English, "Justin crazy! Justin crazy!"

Humphreys didn't believe the story.

"Yesterday I had a dream," Bhasi recalls the sadhu then said. "I had a vision of him playing his flute. He's no longer with us."

Chatter began to spread that yet another foreigner had gone missing in the Parvati Valley, creating a stir in Kheerganga and beyond. When Humphreys suggested to some locals that a police report should be filed, they became angry. A police presence would attract unwanted attention during the peak of cannabis harvest season.

Once he returned to cell service, Humphreys messaged Linda Borini. He said that he had spoken with the sadhu and that the rumor of Justin having returned to Kheerganga safe was false. Furthermore, the sadhu had been back in his stone hut since the first week of September. Nobody had seen Justin return. Humphreys relayed Rawat's story that he had last seen Justin turning back in the direction of Mantalai Lake. Borini and Humphreys concluded that it was time to do two things: alert the police and ring the alarm.

It was late afternoon in Oregon on September 30 when Suzie's cell phone rang. The woman on the end of the line introduced herself as a friend of her son. Suzie heard the concern in Borini's voice, concern that she herself had been feeling for weeks but had tried to push from her mind. Two weeks before, Suzie had been startled awake from a dream in the middle of the night. As she had done for decades, she had reached for a journal to write down what she remembered. "Tuesday, September 13, 2016," she had written at the top of the page. "Had horrific, terrifying dream. It was real—lucid—a person was being attacked and thrown into a river from a high hill or mountain. Sat up in bed, jumped out frantically screaming for Justin, heart pounding with fear." She had felt as if a bucket of water had been dumped over her. "I know with every fiber of my heart & being that the person was Justin," she had written. When her son traveled, she rarely felt nervous. She trusted his judgment, his instincts, and his capabilities—even when he had climbed the Brooklyn Bridge at night or gone off-grid for weeks. But his trip to India had been different. She worried. Still, in the weeks after the dream she had tried to remain calm and trust her son, reminding herself that he was still on track to meet his noted schedule.

After hanging up from the phone call with Borini, "the world tilted," Suzie remembers. "In that moment, it was the validation for my feeling."

Borini then quickly turned to social media, posting to Facebook that she was worried about her friend's whereabouts and tagging the post with Justin's name so it would appear on his personal page. She expected compassion and concern but was met with vitriol and cynicism. She recalls her post as benign: she noted concern that he hadn't returned and asked if anyone had seen him. But the response was instant and scathing. Justin's followers flooded the comments, dismissing her worry as unwarranted and exaggerated; they said to leave him alone, that he was achieving what he wanted, that he was barely late, that he didn't want to be found. And they told her to stay in her lane: Who are you to be so concerned? Borini was shaken, so much so that she eventually deleted the post.

Convinced, however, that something needed to be done, on October 1 she opened a GoFundMe account and titled it "FIND JUSTIN ALEXANDER." Whether it added gravity to the situation or simply acted as a centralized rallying point for a different kind of follower and friend, the GoFundMe pinged around social media, bouncing from platform to platform as it was shared. Friends, followers, and strangers began donating $10 or $25 or $100. Some contributed $500. In the first two days, the fund raised $4,000.

That weekend, the GoFundMe page appeared on the Facebook

feed of Tracy Frey, who immediately "went into a panic," she remembers. Her feelings of protectiveness roared to life again. As someone who knew Justin's history well, she had found herself reading between the lines of his social media posts. When he had mentioned that sleeping in a cave for three weeks had taken a toll on his back, she had surmised that the resurgence of that pain might have also been fueling unrest and reawakening some of the questions that had plagued him for years after his accident. Justin's last post about joining Rawat on a pilgrimage to Mantalai Lake had "screamed" at her, she recalls. "I was worried that he had gone too far."

Frey immediately called Tom McElroy, their old friend from the Tracker School, to ask if he shared her worry. He reminded her that travel plans often change and people can be easily delayed even in normal wilderness situations. Shortly thereafter McElroy sent a message to Frey: "His post on Facebook says he'll be back mid to late September so at this point he's only a few days late, which I imagine is normal when on a spiritual pilgrimage. I wouldn't tell anyone not to do what they feel is right but I wouldn't be surprised if he walks out of the hills feeling like people over reacted."

At a bar in London, Jonathan Skeels stared at his phone with the GoFundMe post and Justin's unmistakable big smile. The last time he had seen Justin had been over the Fourth of July long weekend at Big Sur the year before, when they had ridden their motorcycles along the coast. Something stirred in Skeels, a feeling he would later describe as an alarm ringing in his head and a call to action. Apart from the weekend they had spent together and a handful of subsequent Facebook messages, Skeels wasn't close with Justin. They were barely acquaintances who had crossed paths, bonded over motorcycles, and hung out for a single weekend. The September after Big Sur, they had messaged about possibly meeting up in Las Vegas, but it never happened; when Justin had been building the school in Nepal, Skeels had reached out to inquire about joining the project. He had been looking for a break—"Looking to hit the reset button," as he had messaged Justin. But the project had been winding down. "Nothing like showing up at the end and taking all the credit," Skeels had replied. It had been their last exchange. Five months later, when he saw the GoFundMe, he had been working in London at an unfulfilling job, was nursing a breakup, and, only a few days before, had had a US work visa denied. He reached out to Borini with an offer to help.

Within days, a disparate group coalesced online. For many, concern was mounting. Each person represented a particular point in Justin's life: McElroy, whose concern had grown after reading Justin's posts about Rawat, had known him as a teenager devoted to survivalism; Frey as a youth mentor and band front man; Robert Gutierrez, his former business partner, as a high-flying tech entrepreneur; and Linda Borini and Jonathan Skeels as a solo vagabond and world traveler. They shared information using the workplace communications app Slack and cast their net wide to uncover any information about Justin's days in the Parvati Valley. McElroy tapped his network of wilderness survivalists for advice; Gutierrez began searching for the identification numbers of Justin's iPhone, which was tied to his company; and Frey, who was working for Google in California after a stint in government in Washington, DC, used her contacts to petition California congresswoman Nancy Pelosi as well as a senior federal government official to help reach government counterparts in India. Skeels focused on Facebook and Instagram, scouring the sites for anyone who might be able to help, even reaching out to so-called influencers with massive social media followings who had either communicated with Justin or commented on his photos. He hoped that they could use their platforms to spread the word of his disappearance. Some, with hundreds of thousands of Instagram followers and the potential to signal-boost to millions, saw the plea but never wrote back.

Meanwhile, on the ground in the Parvati Valley, Christofer-Lee Humphreys left Kalga and caught a bus to Manikaran, where he entered the green-walled police station on the bank of the river and filed a missing-persons report. Upon his return to Kalga, he noticed a contingent of police officers hiking through town and onward to Kheerganga. He kept a low profile, fearful that his alerting the police would bring trouble.

In the first week after the GoFundMe was launched, Frey remembers a chaotic scene of people dumping information, some relevant and some not. Distractions arose, including a person on social media who flagged a fake profile on Facebook that was using Justin's photographs and harassing women. Skeels was also contacted by someone who had been in touch with a clairvoyant who claimed that Justin was alive, residing with a family of shepherds, and sitting near a fire nursing an injured leg. The psychic sent maps, pinpointing Justin's location to near a town called Chouki. Skeels was immediately skeptical: there are two towns in India spelled similarly to Chouki, one in the Kullu region, the other—the one the psychic had pointed to—in the state of Gujarat, nearly 1,500 kilometers from the Parvati Valley.

Over the furious first week of October, several people in the search group voiced the idea in back channels that Justin could simply walk out of the mountains; they were shocked that anyone had been concerned, let alone that a GoFundMe had been launched to raise money to find him. Dozens of theories as to what might have happened were floated. Some were benign: Justin had found another Himalayan cave to live in; he had lost his way along the trail; he had decided to remain at Mantalai Lake longer and had lost track of the days. The hopeful recalled accounts of people who had gone missing for weeks, only to reappear with barely a scratch and a good story. The more concerned pointed to news articles about foreign tourists who had been arrested for a variety of nebulous reasons and languished in Indian prisons for months without being able to get word out. Some speculated that Justin had been robbed and abducted and was being held for ransom.

Many of Justin's online followers felt that they knew him so well, even just from following him on Instagram for years, that they weren't shy about offering theories. They noted that they had seen this all before: six months prior to his India trip, Justin had announced that he would be going off the grid in the Philippines. He had posted about visiting the Palawan tribe for ten days, said that he would be out of contact and away from social media, and noted an estimated date of return. He had mentioned possible dangers, but concluded, "If it were safe, it wouldn't be much of an adventure would it?" Now his followers were saying that if anyone could make it through a struggle or a trial in the wild, it was Justin. He was just late. Others said Justin was overcoming deep-rooted pain, that he was on a spiritual journey, that he was clearly going deeper into himself. They insisted that he was in the middle of an important experience and to leave him alone. One woman who claimed to have been in near-daily contact with Justin said that he was safe somewhere in the mountains. Another claimed that the sadhu had led Justin to the mythical gates of Shambhala. One person shared a recent dream of an eagle flying over snowcapped mountains. Another shared a dream of Justin swimming underwater and emerging into a giant underground cave in which the only exit was the way he had come in. It was open to the sky, and the sun beamed down onto a meadow on an island. Somehow he had everything he needed there, and he was happy.

In public, the search was being coordinated by a team of friends, old and new. But in private, cracks were forming. "Everybody felt like they had a claim on him," remembers Borini with a touch of frustration. She had spent those first worried days messaging dozens of Facebook groups connected to the Parvati Valley and tourism in the state, asking for assistance. She was the one who had alerted Justin's family. Some in the search group claimed that she had posted accusations directed toward the Indian police and the US Embassy in India and that these had been counterproductive; she says that as others had materialized to help search, she had felt she was being ostracized. She began to step back.

During the first week of the coordinated search, Michael Yon, an American independent foreign correspondent, reached out to Skeels and Frey after reading posts about Justin's disappearance. He had been following a story that he felt might be relevant, about a particular sect of sadhus. While in India years before, he had heard about an American man named Gary Stevenson who had claimed to have been accepted into the Aghori sect, a sadhu group fiercely devoted to Shiva, whose intensely eremitic lives were associated with aspects of death. Its members often cover their bodies in the ashes of cremated bodies, collect human bones and skulls, and allegedly practice cannibalism. Born in Texas in 1950, Stevenson—who had often claimed to be a descendant of *Treasure Island* author Robert Louis Stevenson—had set his sights on India after reading *Autobiography of a Yogi* in his twenties.

Yon tracked him down in Varanasi, where Stevenson told Yon that he had been living in India for years. In a September 2006 profile for Vice titled "American Aghori," Yon wrote that Stevenson had "set off on a spiritual path that took him to San Francisco, Hawaii, and finally into India and Nepal in an ever-deeper slide into the extreme. Along the way he shed his identity, legally changing his name to Giridas Rama Sitanatha as he sought a magical path to immortality and enlightenment." In Varanasi, Stevenson had connected with a group of sadhus who had accepted him and gave him a new name, Kapal Nath. "We perform rituals using the human skull—drinking alcohol from it gives you power, enables you to speak with the spirit," Stevenson had said in an interview published in 2005. "The spirit comes into you when you eat the flesh of a dead person—it kind [of] speaks to you, gives you power and so much energy."

Frey had been wondering if what Justin had admired in the Indian sadhu he had met in Kheerganga was similar to what he had long respected in the Native American shaman: the ability to live a simple, sometimes solitary and untethered way of life. "You have this person who, on the surface, looks like somebody who spends his days in a form of meditation," Frey says, "who has dedicated his life so much so that he has eschewed all trappings of modern life; he lives entirely on donations and what he can find for himself. I understand how all of that is compelling, because it seems like an opportunity for an incredibly powerful experience." But upon hearing Yon tell the story of Aghori sadhus she was horrified: "It was so deeply upsetting to think that that's who Justin might've gone on this trek with." Yon was indeed insinuating that perhaps some member of the Aghori, a cannibal sadhu, might be to blame. But he was also relaying Stevenson's story—about an American man who had been consumed by an extreme order of sadhus and had lived in India for years—to make a point about Justin. "Why do you think he's dead?" Yon asked Frey and Skeels. "Maybe he wanted to become a sadhu."

After word of Justin's disappearance reached Suzie's longtime friends John and Kay Marikos in Oregon, John began staying up late, scouring the internet for any image recently posted by trekkers or tourists and geotagged to the Parvati Valley. There were hundreds from villages and viewpoints around the valley. He copied a note into the comments section of every one that felt relevant, asking if the person who had posted the image had seen an American named Justin. He searched under relevant hashtags, some of the same ones Justin had been using under his posts, to find any clues—a photo of him, perhaps, or maybe one taken near Kheerganga or Mantalai Lake that could provide a hint. John's memory kept flashing to when he and his wife had visited Suzie's old house outside Portland and seen the thirteen-year-old Justin constructing a lean-to shelter out of branches and leaves in the backyard and fashioning tools out of deer antlers. Then, late one night, as John scrolled through Facebook, a face appeared on his computer: Justin's.

John peered closely at the background of the photos on his computer screen. He had studied so many that detailed the trail to and around Mantalai Lake that he could approximate the location where the photograph had been taken. They hadn't been taken in the Parvati Valley's lush, lower gorges but in the high, treeless alpine area. The photographs were in a folder titled "With Friends Surrounded," uploaded on September 15 by an Indian man named Sunny Panchal. Two pictures included Justin: in the first he is standing next to Panchal, wrapped in his tan-colored shawl and clutching his flute–staff;

in the second he is standing next to Panchal's friend Nirmal Patel, who is twirling Justin's flute–staff between his fingers. In the pictures, both Panchal and Patel are smiling broadly, whereas Justin wears an expression that's half serenity, half exhaustion.

John passed the two photographs of Justin at Mantalai Lake to the main search group. Seeing the pictures fed the belief that Justin was still alive. The group tracked down Panchal and Patel, who relayed the story of meeting Justin while gathering supplies in the market in Kasol and later of their chance encounter with him near Mantalai Lake. After the two friends had left Kasol, they had joined a group of Polish backpackers for a trek to Mantalai Lake, across the Pin Parvati Pass, and down into the Spiti Valley. On the group's fourth day after leaving Kheerganga—where they had soaked in the hot springs knowing it would be their last opportunity for a proper wash for more than a week—the trail had been straightforward, a gradual ascent following the river. Soon, Patel had thought, they should see the waters of Mantalai Lake shimmering up ahead. It was the early afternoon of September 3.

As they had plodded on, the air thinning with every step, a tall man had appeared on the trail ahead of them. He had been wearing a black down jacket, brown pants, and a dark gray headband. He had carried a day pack on his back and a long bamboo flute–staff in his hand. The Indian men had recognized Justin instantly. Panchal had figured that it was likely they would run into one another somewhere on the trail. They had been eager to hear about Justin's journey, but what had struck them immediately was that he was alone.

Justin had told them about his pilgrimage, saying that he had carried firewood beyond the tree line for campfires and had subsisted on little food for days. The trekkers had shared some dried fruit and chocolate with him, then rolled a cigarette and smoked. As they had sat there in the heart of the valley, Patel recalled having passed a sadhu on the trail, about an hour before they had encountered Justin. In those days, it was not unusual to see pilgrims plying the route to Mantalai, so it hadn't instantly registered with him that he could be Justin's companion. Panchal recalled passing a sadhu as well, but said he never paid them much mind. The true definition of a sadhu had been lost, he thought, as more people used the image of these holy men to make money: "Practically, the best way to hide out from the world is to become a baba. But that's not the way for a real sadhu."

Tomasz Biskup, one of the four Polish trekkers, had been moving slower than the rest of the group that day, the effect of altitude weighing heavy on his lungs and legs. He had been trailing behind but catching up, when he had seen a man walking toward him along the trail, picking his way over the stones with a short walking stick as an aid. The man was not kitted out in a hiker's bright synthetics but draped in the faded saffron robes of a sadhu. As he had neared, Biskup had heard the man mumbling to himself. He had appeared stressed. "Namaste," the Polish man had said to the sadhu, but the man had passed by without the customary acknowledgment in return or even a glance in his direction.

As the group of trekkers had all perched on rocks on the valley floor, Justin had told the others that he and the sadhu were no longer together. After arriving at Mantalai Lake, he said, the sadhu had started acting strangely and the two had had a falling out, arguing over how long they should remain at the holy site. Rawat had wanted to descend almost immediately after arriving, but Justin had wanted to stay longer, for at least another week, in a nearby boulder cave. He had come so far already, why turn around immediately? But Rawat had been adamant that he wanted to descend and return to his hut in Kheerganga. He had poked Justin in the ribs with a stick, to try to prod him to descend the trail; Biskup recalls Justin complaining of a pain in his side. Justin had been so upset that he had lingered at Mantalai Lake for a few hours after the sadhu had departed. Once Rawat was out of sight, he finally began slowly trekking back down the trail. Justin had told the group that he was now on a journey of his own.

Panchal and Patel recall they had sensed that Justin was loath to leave the high mountains, so Patel had asked him if he wanted to join their group in crossing the Pin Parvati Pass and going down into the Spiti Valley. They had more than enough food and space in their tents to accommodate one more. Justin had politely declined, they remember. He had said that he wanted to descend to edit the video clips and pictures he had shot on his pilgrimage and upload them to his accounts.

After half an hour of resting and catching up, the trekking group had picked up their packs to leave; they had another hour or two to reach their camp location on the high side of Mantalai Lake, below the pass. Panchal had grabbed his camera, and they had taken pictures together—the photos John Marikos later stumbled across on Facebook. Justin had thanked the group for the snack and said goodbye. He had gathered his day pack and leather pouch and slung them over his shoulders, then picked up his flute. As he had turned and began down the trail, he had put the instrument to his lips and begun to play.

By the end of the first week of October, the search team hit the wall of what they could uncover from afar. It was time to get someone to India—eyes and ears in the valley and boots on the ground. Michael Yon had tipped the group onto Hilik Magnus, the head of the international search-and-rescue outfit based in Israel that had worked on missing-persons cases in the Parvati Valley for decades. In the quote that Magnus International provided to Skeels and Frey, the company proposed a "preliminary investigation" that included information gathering and analysis and a final summary report of any findings, plus a ten-day "on the ground search" during which a team of professionals would retrace Justin's movements and activities in the valley. "Main purpose of this part is to try and locate Justin and if not succeeded within this time, to set the ground for later focused on-ground searches in designated areas," the proposal read. "It is our hope that it will take us to Justin's belongings." The total quote was $20,000, plus $3,000 for local expenses and $3,000 to establish a network of "local informers." Flights to India for Magnus's team were extra. If the initial phase did not turn up Justin, alive or dead, the quote read, there would be additional per-day costs.

By then, the GoFundMe campaign had raised more than $20,000 from nearly three hundred individuals, including one donation that caught people's eye: an anonymous $5,000. But the money still wasn't enough to cover Magnus International's fee. Skeels had also been contacted by the team behind the search for Bruno Muschalik, who had read the early news reports of yet another traveler missing in the Parvati Valley. They had reached out to offer assistance, having been to India and the valley three times in the year since Muschalik had vanished and learned much about the region. When Skeels mentioned that the group had been in contact with Magnus International, one person close to the search for Muschalik issued a warning: proceed if you desire, but go with caution, as it is an expensive investment with no guarantee that anything new will be learned.

The thought of handing over the reins of a deeply personal search effort to an unfamiliar company left Skeels and Frey, as well as the rest of the search team, uneasy. They turned down Magnus International's quote and began to decide how to get trusted people into the Parvati Valley. They needed people who would have the family's best interest at heart and at least one person who was knowledgeable about the country. Skeels volunteered. He was the closest geographically, living in London, but more important, he had been to India before and had even ridden a motorcycle into the neighboring Spiti Valley. As a New Zealand national he could acquire a visa on arrival, cutting down on red tape. Frey had met Skeels only online and was initially skeptical as to why he would quit his job and volunteer to lead a search effort in India for someone with whom he had no deep friendship. But she let go of those qualms, recognizing that he was tenacious and resourceful.

Though Terry had traveled to India before, the travel restrictions resulting from his conviction made it challenging for him to receive permission to leave the country. It fell on Suzie to make the trip. She flew from Oregon to San Francisco and managed to obtain a travel visa for India within a few hours after pleading her case at the Indian Consulate. Visa in hand, she boarded a plane for New Delhi, meeting Skeels en route in London's Heathrow Airport. Sitting on the plane, Suzie sifted through possibilities in her mind: Did Justin walk off trail to refill his water bottle and slip on wet boulders? Did he simply lose his footing along the trail and fall into the churning waters? Was he injured? Was he the victim of a robbery gone wrong? She didn't let herself dwell on the darker scenarios for too long and instead turned her thoughts to the two September 3 photographs. They were the most promising lead yet, proof that Justin had reached his destination at Mantalai Lake.

Suzie believed that they were going to India not just to look for information about her son's last weeks in the Parvati Valley but to bring him home. When word from Humphreys had reached her about Rawat's claim that there had been an argument and confrontation at Mantalai Lake and that someone had been hurt, she began to wonder if it might have been her son, rather, who had seriously hurt someone else while defending himself in some way—and if he was hiding out because he was scared. Despite her ominous dream, there was no doubt in her mind: her son was alive.

INTO THE MIST

An orange sun glared above New Delhi's cityscape as Suzie and Jonathan Skeels boarded a small Air India plane and flew north, landing at the regional Kullu-Manali Airport, located in the dusty transit town of Bhuntar at the foot of the Himalayas. They had arrived in India the day before, October 12, and had met with representatives of the US Embassy, who, though they didn't have the staff to help on the ground, offered assistance, push and pull, when needed. The embassy couldn't staff a search, but Skeels had already been working contacts in the Parvati Valley who were awaiting their arrival. That night in Delhi, Skeels heard a knock on his hotel room door: a representative of the Polish Embassy wanted to speak to him. It was a stark reminder that a year after Bruno Muschalik had disappeared in the Parvati Valley, his father, Piotr, and the Polish Embassy were still on the case, still searching. The man from the embassy offered Skeels advice about who might be trustworthy in the valley, as well as who they should steer clear of, outfits known to offer search services while taking people's money and doing little.

After Suzie and Skeels landed in Bhuntar, they met Ashish Chauhan, the owner of a local trekking company called Himalayan Drifters, and his client Brijeshwar Kunwar, an engineer from Bangalore who was on holiday climbing a nearby mountain, who in the days before had connected with Skeels with an offer to help. They drove to the city of Kullu, to the district's main police station, a two-story, pale pink complex across from a large common where kids played pickup cricket and couples picnicked on the grass. Inside the station, they walked past a missing-persons poster for Muschalik pinned to a bulletin board, on their way to meet with Padam Chand, the superintendent of police of the Kullu district, one of twelve districts in the state of Himachal Pradesh, in which the Parvati Valley is located. He oversaw dozens of police stations throughout a largely rural district with more than half a million residents. Sitting in his wood-paneled office, slowly sipping a cup of tea, Suzie offered as much information as she knew: when her son had departed for his trek with a sadhu, when he had said he would return, the story of the trekkers who had encountered him on September 3 near Mantalai Lake. She hoped the police could help by launching a formal investigation.

Chand's office had registered dozens of missing-persons cases, under many superintendents, over the years. Few investigations, in the end, had turned up meaningful leads. He tried to temper their hopes and expectations of finding anything. Then, to everyone's surprise, he divulged that police had learned that a third person had joined Justin on the pilgrimage to Mantalai Lake. Until that point, based on everything Justin had written online, his followers and friends had assumed that he had embarked on his trek with only Rawat as his guide. Skeels and Suzie were taken aback.

Abruptly, Chand said something in Hindi to an officer in the room. The officer left and quickly returned, bringing with him a man who wore a faded saffron-colored wrap around his waist and a matching *pagdi* wrap around his head, a thin gray shawl draped over his shoulders, and prayer beads dangling from his neck. The man had a wispy black beard and small eyes, and when he raised his arms above his head to gesture, he flashed an emaciated stomach and large growths on his elbows. Suzie knew instantly who it was: Satnarayan Rawat, the sadhu from Kheerganga.

Suzie was completely unprepared for the encounter. She had been given no warning that she would be sitting within feet of perhaps the last person to see her son alive—forced to face someone her son had trusted and who had possibly betrayed him instead.

Skeels surreptitiously pulled out his iPhone, pointed the camera at Rawat, and hit Record.

The sadhu began to speak in Hindi, at times softly, at others growing more animated. Little of the interrogation was translated into English concurrently, so Suzie and Skeels were offered few opportunities to interject and ask a question. They would later receive the gist of what Rawat had said but never translated the video in full. It begins with Rawat describing his relationship with Justin in Kheerganga.

"He said, 'Baba, I want to learn yoga from you.' I said, 'Okay, if you serve the baba, then only you will learn yoga,'" Rawat told Chand in Hindi. "He stayed one month, day and night he did service."

Rawat said that he wanted to make a pilgrimage to Mantalai Lake and Justin had asked to join him. "So I said, 'If you want to come, then come.'" Rawat explained that he had arranged for a porter to join them, to carry their food. Justin had carried his own bag.

Gesticulating with his hands, Rawat narrated the stages of the trio's journey. They had departed Kheerganga on August 28 and walked slowly, he said. The trek typically takes four full days from Kheerganga to Mantalai Lake, but it had taken them a few days more to reach their destination. Rawat said they had arrived at Mantalai early in the morning of September 4, having spent the previous night an hour's walk below the lake, unwilling to push on for the final stretch as evening had fallen. "Now, sir, in Mantalai," the sadhu told the police superintendent in Hindi, "on the way back Justin said he won't go. So he stopped in Mantalai." Rawat said that as he and the porter had departed to begin making their way back down the valley, Justin had remained behind. Around 5:00 p.m., Rawat said, he and the porter had reached the stone and boulder bridge at Pandu Pul. They had made camp and cooked food. Later that evening, after dark, Justin had arrived, Rawat claimed, having decided to descend on his own. He said the three had slept the night there, made tea in the morning, and departed together as a group. After stopping at the meadows near Thakur Kuan for a late breakfast, Rawat had directed the porter to go on to the stone hut at Tunda Bhuj and begin preparing dinner. "I told the porter that you walk first, keep some food ready, and I'll reach slowly by the evening," Rawat told the police. "The porter went first, Justin followed, and I followed last." He said he had hung back because his knees were hurting. When he had reached Tunda Bhuj, he said, he found the porter there alone. Justin had not yet arrived, and even though there is only one trail, Rawat had somehow passed him. He said he had stayed some or all of the night with the lone sadhu who lives in the hut at Tunda Bhuj. "What happened to him, where he fell or not, I do not know," Rawat told the police, maintaining that he knew nothing about why, how, or where exactly Justin had disappeared; he had seen nothing and knew nothing. He said he had been back in Kheerganga on September 6.

Chand translated two sentences of Rawat's account into English. "This is today's version?" Skeels replied. He was referring to the fact that in late September, after Rawat had returned to Kheerganga, the sadhu had told Christofer-Lee Humphreys and Swapnashree Bhasi that the last time he had seen Justin had been farther down, near the hut at Tunda Bhuj, and he was turning around to head back up the valley toward Mantalai Lake. Rawat's story had changed.

Suzie quietly tried to ask a question, but police officers sitting behind her cut her off. As Chand continued to interrogate Rawat, Suzie remained stoic, flicking her attention from the empty cup of tea on the table in front of her to the folded hands in her lap to the flag of India on the wall behind the superintendent. But every time she heard Rawat mention her son's name, she winced. In that moment, confronted with Rawat, Suzie felt too overwhelmed to fully register much of what was happening, to understand the fragments that were translated, or to recognize and point out inconsistencies to the sadhu's face. When Chand asked Rawat why he hadn't reported that someone had gone missing, the sadhu claimed that he had been new to the valley and unfamiliar with the area.

Before an opportunity was given to Suzie and Skeels to ask their own questions, the interrogation ended as abruptly as it had begun, and Rawat was escorted from the room. Skeels ended the recording on his iPhone.

As he and Suzie gathered to leave, Chand called for his officers to bring in another man: Anil Kumar, the porter. Wearing jeans and an orange Nike hoodie, he stood where Rawat had and nervously answered Chand's questions. The interrogation was brief and not recorded, and once again Suzie and Skeels were left largely in the dark. All Skeels had been told after the questioning, he recalls, was that Kumar's account revealed inconsistencies about what had transpired on the descent from Mantalai Lake. "That's when it became clear that the stories didn't match up between the porter and the baba."

Before they left the station, Suzie was taken to another building to file a First Information Report, an official document that lodges a complaint about an alleged offense. It signaled the beginning of an investigation into the disappearance of her son. Beyond the two witnesses' accounts, there was no physical evidence to support any theory about what might have transpired. Justin had simply disappeared. "The mindset then: He's still alive," Skeels recalls. "That was everyone's mindset." His focus shifted from sorting out timelines and corroborating stories to getting into the high valley as soon as possible. Chand, however, seemed unfazed by the situation; he didn't appear to be taking the case seriously. During the interrogation of Rawat, Chand had to be reminded of the name of the missing person in question.

So Suzie concluded her First Information Report into the disappearance of her son with language that she felt would compel the police to act: "We suspect Baba or his porter have done something wrong or are not telling the truth and are potentially responsible for his kidnapping with intention to murder."

Justin's final post before leaving for Mantalai Lake concluded with the lines "Maybe Baba Life will be good for me" and "If I'm not back by then, don't look for me." The admonition was punctuated by a winking emoji, leading many of his followers to read his last line as a joke. But many others were certain that he had been absolutely serious. Skeels felt that sleeping in a mountain cave was a way for Justin to push and test himself physically, and that he had written about his curiosity with the sadhu way of life to build an alluring story line for his followers. "Justin led a life that people wanted to lead," Skeels says; there was pressure to satisfy those with high expectations. From the outset Skeels maintained that Justin's "don't look for me" line had been written in jest, but he acknowledges the power that those words had in influencing the fact that many people didn't leap to action sooner. Tracy Frey, on the other hand, saw Justin's last line as a call for help that he was at a low point and was reaching out into the void. Though some pointed out that before he had first hiked to Kheerganga to find a cave, he had written that he wanted to "wander alone" but not "renounce the world or become enlightened," they still believed that Justin's final words were a signal that he intended to vanish intentionally—a possibility with considerable precedent.

In January 2011, a man appeared at the Russian Embassy in Delhi saying he had been living illegally in the Himalayas for a decade and a half. Kirill Pomerantsev had visited India twice in his twenties and then on his third trip, at the end of his six-month tourist visa, had decided to overstay his visa in order to study and practice Hinduism while living in a cave in the Himalayas. "Indeed, I have spent 15 years here in India," Pomerantsev told RIA News after finally turning himself in. "My mind and heart were immersed in the Indian religion. I was 27 or 28 years old when I made the decision to remain here. Now I am 42 or 43. I was advised that if I wanted to achieve progress in my religious pursuits, it would be best to spend 12 years in the wilderness in order to reflect and read Hindu religious literature. This would make spiritual progress possible." Pomerantsev was deported from India and returned to Russia. That same year, Indian officials arrested a sixty-six-year-old French national named Mark Hamieau in a mountain village. He had neither passport nor visa and had reportedly been living quietly in the region for around thirty years.

Two of India's highest-profile cases of missing foreign tourists were both suspected, whether out of true likelihood or out of simple hope, to have ended in a voluntary disappearance. In August 2005, Ryan Chambers, a twenty-one-year-old from Australia, spent nearly two months backpacking in the country, beginning on the country's southern beaches before heading to Varanasi and ultimately arriving in the town of Rishikesh. He and a friend lodged in an ashram, took yoga classes, and visited the overgrown ruins of Maharishi Mahesh Yogi Ashram, where the Beatles had stayed. The friend began to worry when he noticed that Chambers had become unsettled, partly from lack of sleep, but also after Chambers had spent time with a sadhu. The next morning, Chambers vanished. He was last seen opening the metal gates of the ashram, wearing only a pair of shorts, and walking off into the early morning light. He left his passport, his money, and all his belongings in his room. A week after his disappearance, word circulated that the Australian backpacker had been spotted at a temple a short walk outside of town. "He was sitting down and he was delusional, which would have been exhaustion from lack of sleep," his father told the *Sydney Morning Herald*, based on firsthand accounts he had uncovered while searching for his son in India. "The priest fed him and gave him a drink, but he wasn't able to stay there so he left. And again the trail has gone cold." In a journal entry written in the days before he disappeared, Chambers had said, "If I'm gone, don't worry. I'm not dead, I'm freeing minds. But first I have to free my own." He, or his body, has never been found.

Seven years later, in February 2012, a twenty-eight-year-old Irish journalist, Jonathan Spollen, was on holiday in northern India when he disappeared—also in Rishikesh. He had spent time with sadhus, including one who was originally from South Africa, and, on a previous trip to India, with a yogi who had allegedly fasted for sixty years. Before embarking on a trek in the surrounding mountains, he called his family. "Don't worry, Mum," he said, "it's kind of like a spiritual journey." After that, he went quiet. His family routinely posted updates to the popular travel forum India Mike looking for help and updating a growing cohort of online searchers. Some tips emerged that he had been seen at a bakery in the Rishikesh area weeks after the date he had checked out of his guesthouse. One traveler said that she had met Spollen and chatted about the novel *Shantaram*, which they were both reading. Two others said they had spoken with Spollen about a group of foreigners who had become priests or sadhus and were living in a riverside cave outside town. But no concrete leads materialized. Then, in the middle of March, Spollen's backpack was found under the lee of a boulder in the forest above the town. Inside were his passport and some money. His sleeping bag was rolled out, with his copy of *Shantaram* laid on top. Speculation abounded: Spollen had drowned while swimming in the Ganges River; he had been attacked by a leopard in the forest; he had taken datura and fallen into an amnesiac state; he had been robbed and murdered. Yet without any evidence of foul play and the words he had told his mother hanging in the air—even though she later clarified on India Mike that her son had made the remark casually—many wondered if Spollen had renounced his life.

Months after Spollen vanished in the hills around Rishikesh, reports of sightings began to flow in from all across India. First it was in Dharamshala, then in Haridwar, then in Delhi. What seemed like a major tip came from south India around a year after Spollen's disappearance: a man claimed to have spent a few hours riding a bus outside the city of Chennai speaking with Spollen about spirituality. Spollen had appeared "very thin, with long hair, in slightly shabby saffron clothing and carrying a small brown bag on his shoulder," his family posted online. It bolstered the theory that he had become a sadhu and was wandering around India. "Until I know otherwise," his mother wrote on India Mike, "I have to keep in mind the possibility that . . . perhaps he is suffering from a form of India Syndrome." The family, however, was ultimately unable to corroborate the possible sighting. In the years after, Spollen's mother still held hope that her son was out there somewhere, telling CNN, "There's nothing I'd like more than to think he's meditating in a cave."

After Justin's three weeks of living in a cave in the Parvati Valley, many could not help entertaining similar thoughts about their friend. At one point, even though Humphreys was actively assisting the search team on the ground in the valley, he, too, wondered if Justin had perhaps gone to work on a cannabis plantation somewhere in the valley or had simply wandered off on his own without telling anyone. But he interpreted Justin's final words largely as a sarcastic comment meant to thrill his followers online. He felt that Justin had romanticized his stories to make them more extreme, more intense, or more compelling. "Learning yoga with a French man from Paris in a little village is not very interesting," he says. "But going high to Mantalai Lake in the altitudes of the Himalayas with a wild sadhu to learn asanas is a bit more of a good story." The claim that Rawat had cut off his penis, which Justin had posted online, wasn't true, but Justin had believed it when the sadhu had told him—as had Justin's followers when it was shared online. And the growths on Rawat's arms and knees weren't the result of intense yoga, as Justin had written, but a medical condition, possibly even cancer.

Justin's desire to live a life of legend and grand experiences led to slight bends in the truth as he presented his story online. For example, three full weeks passed between when he embarked on his solo trip to find a cave at Kheerganga and when he shared the experience online. "I've been living in some caves in the Indian Himalayas for the last couple weeks," he wrote then, alongside the photographs from inside his cave. But Andrey Gapon believed that Justin had descended from Kheerganga for a short period in the middle of his three-week stay in his cave—possibly to visit a festival, a gathering of sadhus, in Bhuntar or Kullu. Humphreys, though, remembers the festival visit as happening later, after Justin's weeks in his cave. He recalls seeing him collecting some of his belongings in Kalga before heading to a festival during his week of preparation for his pilgrimage to Mantalai Lake. If Justin had, in fact, left his cave in the middle of his three weeks in retreat, he had made no mention of it online, nor had he posted anything about it. He could easily have ridden his motorcycle through the Parvati Valley, his phone blinking with notifications. But as far as his followers were concerned, he had spent three weeks in solitude in a Himalayan cave developing a relationship with a sadhu—a much more impressive story.

Of all the travelers who crossed paths with Justin during his final international trip, none felt more indelibly marked by the encounter than Andrey Gapon. After last seeing Justin in Kalga, he remained in the village until his visa was nearing expiry. With newfound confidence from his experience in Kheerganga, he spent many nights in a cave that he had found tucked in the forest above Kalga. And every time someone returned from Mantalai Lake, he asked about Justin. After returning home to Russia in September, he watched the search for his new friend unfold online. Initially, he felt that there was "too much fuss" being made about Justin being late by a few days, or even a couple of weeks. "I didn't believe it," he says, when questions began to be raised about Justin disappearing. "He was so tough. I was sure he might still be meditating in a cave somewhere." Shortly after Justin's disappearance was made public, Gapon took a walk in the forest near his home, and on October 4 he posted a video to YouTube narrating the brief friendship that had blossomed in the Parvati Valley that summer. Fighting tears, he recounted how he and Justin had met and the story of seeing the cave Justin had cleaned and stocked with firewood for him. "I'm sure that we will find him, that he will show up very soon," Gapon said in the video. "There was a smile," he says, referring to the winking emoji Justin used as punctuation at the end of his "don't look for me" final blog post, "but he partly meant it. He was looking for something, for liberation. He was ready to play big, and when you play big, it's always all or nothing."

In fact, Justin had long been planning something bigger for the future. Since arriving in India, he had reconnected with Mike Spencer Bown, a Canadian traveler who had made a name for himself by traveling to every country in the world, which he would later document in a memoir, *The World's Most Travelled Man*. Justin didn't just want to swap road stories but was looking for advice on how to plan an extended solo expedition in the wilderness. Bown, who was originally from Ottawa but had grown up across Canada, was also an experienced wilderness survivalist, having completed many solo stints in the Canadian wilderness for months on end free of human contact. His longest stretch of solitude had been more than eighty days in the Slocan Valley in western Canada in the early 1990s.

Over several phone calls and sessions of back-and-forth messaging, Justin sought guidance on how to embark on something similar, what he might expect, physically and emotionally, if he were to remain for months on end in complete isolation in the wilderness. "An extended solo wilderness trip could be the best thing I can do at this point in my life," he messaged, noting he wanted to go "as primitive as possible. Maybe knife, clothing and a blanket." Bown counseled Justin on what tools and supplies he might need, including the importance of an emergency stash of food "as you do not want to accidently [*sic*] end up like the 'into the wild' guy in Alaska." Justin was particularly curious as to why people failed in their attempts, as the "guy in Alaska," Christopher McCandless, had.

Justin was also curious about the kind of transformations he should expect. Bown told him to prepare for a transition from Camp Mode—in which we are constantly social and connected to a family and a community in a city or a village—to Bush Mode, a state that can be found only after an extended period of time in solitude in the wilderness. "It's an entirely different way to be human," Bown explains. He told Justin about a pattern he had noticed among people who had done multimonth stints in complete isolation in nature. After ten days, time starts to distort. You begin to lose the awareness of what day it is, or exactly how many days have passed since you began. Around twenty-five days in, you begin to lose the habit of compressing thoughts into words, and your internal monologue evaporates. You run on intuition. At forty days, you enter into a kind of dream state in which days and nights blend together; you dream when you're awake, and you're aware of reality when you sleep. At sixty-five days, Bown told Justin, you begin to become more aware of the natural processes around you. You start to notice the life cycles of birds and animals and even subtle changes in plants fluctuating by day or night, in cool weather or hot. But the biggest change after two months is that you lose your "self." Your sense of being an individual relating to a community or society fades, and you become just another aspect of the nature that surrounds you. "He wanted to go all the way to the dissolving of self after sixty-five days," Bown recalls. "He wanted to experience the whole thing."

When Justin arrived in the Parvati Valley, he again reached out to Bown, messaging him that he was going on a "pilgrimage with a sadhu into the mountains for a few weeks" and saying that he was more determined than ever to embark on a long, solitary trip. To Bown, Justin seemed eager for a spiritually illuminating experience. Before leaving, Justin had mentioned that he hoped the trek was going to be a trial, a stepping-stone to something greater. And he put what he struggled most with into one word. "Loneliness," he messaged Bown. "I feel pretty good about wilderness basics and have done short trips but I'm always pulled back by loneliness, or lust for living with people, in the world. . . . But it feels like a personal flaw."

In early October, after Justin's September deadline to return came and went, Bown reached out. "Hi Justin. Are you okay?" he messaged. "It has been well over a month, more like a month and a half, and from what I've seen on your facebook page, you didn't take nearly enough food." But there was little worry in Bown's mind; he wrote the words assuming that Justin would read them. "We talked so much about him doing several months alone that I was one of the last to suspect that there was something really wrong," he realizes now. He assumed that Justin had simply found an ideal location for the solo that had long been forming in his dreams.

The thrum of a helicopter is not a welcome sound in the Parvati Valley, especially at the beginning of October at the height of hash-harvesting season. As Jonathan Skeels looked out the window at the terrain below, the trail was impossible to miss: a tan-colored snake flanking, and sometimes crossing, the gray-blue Parvati River. The occasional shepherd's track forked off the main route through the valley, but there was only one trail that led from Kheerganga to Mantalai Lake. Instead of contracting an expensive search outfit with their GoFundMe money, the search team had decided to hire a helicopter from a local heli-skiing company to conduct a reconnaissance flight. Skeels had climbed aboard in Manali, flown over the cannabis plantations around Malana, and then followed the river above the hot springs and camp at Kheerganga before entering the higher reaches of the Parvati Valley.

The sky was a cloudless blue as Skeels poked his GoPro camera outside the window of the helicopter above the stone hut at Tunda Bhuj. The tree line quickly faded below, replaced with slopes of alpine moraine and shrub-covered hills. The high mountain peaks, now framed by every window in the helicopter, were iced with snow. What would have taken nearly a week of hiking on foot to reach Mantalai Lake had taken the helicopter less than ten minutes. Sinuous glacial rivulets gave the landscape the look of a watercolor painting. Skeels couldn't help but imagine Justin calmly stepping out of a cave in the mountains, waving at them as they circled overhead, as if in a scene in a movie, having not shunned the world but simply stepped aside from it to test his mettle.

The entire flight there and back lasted less than an hour, and after returning to Manali Skeels began poring through his footage for any sign of his friend. He looked for smoke from a fire, a rock formation intentionally made to be seen from the air, or anything that might be a signal that Justin was still alive. Seeing the landscape from above, one prevailing theory that Skeels had held in his mind immediately dissipated. There was no way Justin had simply become lost. "There's no left or right turn," Skeels recalls. "It's just one trail up and one trail down." The territory was vast, though, and he realized that the only way to properly comb the area would be to search on foot. He also noticed that near Thakur Kuan there was a flat pad of grass where a helicopter could potentially land. He took a screenshot on his iPhone of the GPS coordinates. If they were to believe what Rawat had told them at the police station in Kullu, the last place Justin had been seen was in that area.

Meanwhile, the search team's social media campaign was paying off. Leah Lañojan, who had helped Justin start his "Adventures of Justin" Facebook page when he was in the Philippines, handed over log-in information so they could begin posting from that account. Tracy Frey led the online effort from the United States. The Go-FundMe page, of which Frey had assumed management, encouraged people to spread the word on social media using the hashtags #JustinAlexanderShetler and #LostInParvati, even providing ready-made tweets to be copied, pasted, and shared. One of Frey's main goals in her Twitter campaign was to get the attention of Sushma Swaraj, India's external affairs minister. Eventually, the minster acknowledged the situation. "I will ask for a report from Chief Minister Himachal Pradesh @virbhadrasingh.ji regarding #JustinAlexanderShetler," Swaraj tweeted to her millions of followers.

Then Skeels learned that Virbhadra Singh was just about to head to the Kullu area for Dussehra, a major annual Hindu festival. Skeels figured they would have a chance to petition the state's chief minister in person at the Kullu-Manali Airport; he wanted to ask to use the government's repurposed Russian helicopter to take a search team and land at Thakur Kuan. At the airport, Suzie and Skeels worked their way through the throng of greeters to make contact with Singh. The state minister had heard of the case of the missing American and agreed to let his pilots shuttle a few people into the Parvati Valley. Around midday on October 16, the orange helicopter took off from the airport with Skeels on board. Alongside him was Brijeshwar Kunwar, who had offered his mountaineering skills and familiarity with the area to help on the ground. With them were a few police officers from Kullu and two drone operators from Delhi, who had joined at the last minute.

A cool breeze swept down from the glaciers creaking at the head of the valley as the helicopter circled and landed on the meadow near Thakur Kuan. Skeels instructed the pilots to return to the airport and pick up a team of volunteer mountain guides that included Ashish Chauhan of Himalayan Drifters and Shiv Ram Thakur of Little Rebel Adventures. Earlier that summer, on August 11, as Justin had been living in his Kheerganga cave, Thakur had pulled over by the side of the road: a body had been spotted in the middle of the river, caught on some rocks and flotsam. Chhape Ram Negi, the valley's renowned "Mountain Man," had deemed the recovery impossible. Thakur was green to search-and-rescue but knew that the river flows higher during the day than at night, so he returned at 2:00 a.m. with a group of his guides, affixed a rope to the far bank, clipped in his harness, and pulled his way across until he was directly above the body. He completed the recovery by sunrise. A Kullu police official later confirmed, through DNA analysis, that the body was of East Asian descent. Thakur says the body was identified as that of a Japanese national, assumed to be Shota Sakai, the backpacker who had vanished in the valley sometime that June.

Skeels was desperate for exactly that kind of assistance in the high valley. But after a couple hours of scouring the nearby riverbanks around Thakur Kuan for any clues, he watched the helicopter return empty. The pilots had been told not to shuttle any of the skilled mountain guides into the valley and insisted to Skeels that it was time to go. Skeels protested. As the police climbed into the helicopter, he told them that he and Kunwar would continue searching downstream on foot. There were only a few hours of daylight remaining, but the hut at Tunda Bhuj was reachable before dark. Skeels and Kunwar began walking.

Most of the trail from Mantalai Lake to Tunda Bhuj is a gradual meander across moraine and alpine meadow, but there is one section, as the route approaches the tree line, where it traverses a rocky slope that slips down to the river. On the whole, Skeels recalls, it was a simple hike, but one section contained portions that required careful scrambling: the narrow gorge known as Pathar Ghati, or Stone Valley. The trail was uncomplicated, but a constant reminder of danger hummed like white noise in their ears: the thrash of the Parvati River below. "It's like death valley," Kunwar says, thinking back. "You have a river, and the current is so fast, and a lot of boulders in between. You can easily die. It was that fast and that dangerous a spot."

Kunwar and Skeels leapfrogged down the bank of the river, following the trail while scanning the riverside and grassy slopes for anything out of the ordinary. Skeels felt as if he were walking a crime scene like an amateur detective. But there was no bullet trajectory to analyze, no fingerprints to dust for, no broken glass that might offer a clue. The passing of time had acted like a swab, the torrential monsoon like bleach: it had been more than a month since Justin had last been seen along the trail by the group of trekkers who had taken his picture below Mantalai Lake. Rain had fallen. Mud and rocks had slid down the mountainside. The river had swollen and receded and swollen again. The footprints of hikers, pilgrims, and shepherds had long since obscured anything that could be gleaned from the path.

The sun was setting early at the bottom of the valley, and Skeels knew that they were running out of daylight. He passed Kunwar and jogged ahead along the trail. At around 4:00 p.m., Kunwar reached a section where the path bent around a slight corner that ran close to a cliff edge, a steep fifty-foot rock shelf sloping down toward the river. He peered down, scanning the boulders along the raging waters and a small patch of grass below. He stopped. Something black and glistening stood out among the vegetation. *A jacket?* he thought. And then he saw it. He cried out over the roar of the Parvati River to Skeels, "I saw the flute!"

Skeels hurried back along the trail, following the sound of Kunwar's shouts, to find the Indian man making his way down toward the river. "Oh, my god," Kunwar said as the pair carefully picked their way through sparse knee-high grass, between a small evergreen rhododendron bush and a white-barked birch tree, and down to the riverbank. There, fifteen feet up from the milky waters, was a black waterproof backpack cover bundled with a light gray wool scarf and a collapsible black umbrella tucked inside. Nearby lay a blue canister of dental floss and a dark gray wool headband. A couple feet away was a red butane lighter. And sticking straight upright in the grass, like one of the Shiva tridents on the shores of Mantalai Lake, stood a bamboo flute that had been converted into a walking stick.

Staring down at Justin's belongings, found around a dozen miles, less than a full day's walk, from where hundreds of backpackers had gathered and reveled in guesthouses and tents at Kheerganga, was crushing for Skeels. He knew it wasn't everything that Justin had carried with him—there was no day pack or machete, none of his electronics or clothes—but what they had found was clearly his. Justin had purchased the gray wool scarf in Kathmandu; Andrey Gapon had presented him with the lighter the day they had last seen each other in Kalga; and the bansuri flute–staff was unmistakably the one Justin had purchased in Varanasi and had carried with him ever since. Skeels began to curse, convinced he knew who was responsible. "Fucking baba!" he cried out.

With darkness approaching, no police around, and no idea of when he might be able to return this high in the valley, Skeels decided to collect the evidence. He took photos and GoPro video of the scene, noting the placement of each item and the location of the spot along the trail—and then carefully placed Justin's smaller items in his day pack and carried the flute–staff in his hands. Before leaving, he allowed himself a moment to absorb the scene.

Several of his previous theories immediately evaporated. Having just walked the path himself, he knew that the trail was straightforward and simple to follow: keep the river in your ears, and you will find the way. Apart from two sections that required a moment of scrambling—both located below where Justin's belongings had been found—there was nothing along the trail that a sure foot couldn't handle; the possibility that Justin had lost his footing and plunged into the river now appeared to Skeels to be nearly impossible. It had also become clear that Justin had not simply walked off the trail to refill his water bottle and slipped into the river. Nobody would scramble down this scree-and-bramble slope to collect water at the dangerous river's edge when numerous streams cut across the trail and there were other, much easier access points to the river. The theory that Justin had been caught in a landslide—he had noted that it was "landslide season" in his final blog post—also faded.

Skeels turned his attention to Justin's belongings. Could Justin have fallen or been pushed into the river elsewhere and the items been deposited at this site by the waters? But that didn't make sense. It explained the randomness of the belongings—a backpack cover, a butane lighter, a roll of dental floss, the flute–staff—but not the arrangement. If Justin had lost his footing while traversing the boulder bridge of Pandu Pul, higher up, or at any other point, his body and his day pack would have been carried downriver. If his things had broken free, they would have been strewn about, not found in a single area; there was simply no way such a grouping of items would have collected in such a way along such a bank. The items, furthermore, had been found well above that season's high-water mark, clearly identifiable by a line where all soil and grass had been washed away. Had Justin been robbed and pushed, then? Rawat was head-and-shoulders shorter than Justin, skinny and frail. But, Skeels thought, it wouldn't have taken much effort to nudge a person off the trail where it ran close to the cliff. He could see no evidence of a struggle, no disturbed earth or broken branches. But the items were also the sorts of things that another person might deem worthless. Where were his day pack and leather hip bag? His iPhone and machete? Skeels scampered back up to the trail, to the spot above where Kunwar had first spied the flute, to survey the area. Someone could have discarded the items from there, hoping they would disappear into the river's churn; or, Skeels thought, perhaps someone had scurried down from the trail to the more secluded spot along the river's edge to rifle through Justin's bags.

There were two other curious aspects of the items. How could Justin's gray scarf and black umbrella have possibly ended up tucked inside the waterproof backpack cover if not placed that way by someone? And how had Justin's flute–staff ended up in such an odd position? It hadn't been lying down in the grass like the other items or lodged in a thicket; it had been standing upright, as if it had been spiked into the ground as a walking stick might be as its owner took a break to sit or as if cast off from the trail above to land upright in the soil. Skeels wondered if Justin might have come down to the river's edge to contemplate life. Or if someone else, someone guilty of something, had sneaked off the trail to think about what he had just done.

Darkness had come to the valley as Skeels and Kunwar walked on in silence through the evening, carrying Justin's belongings. The moon, a day from full, lit the trail. They reached the hut at Tunda Bhuj close to midnight, guided by an orange flame that shone through the window. Inside, sleeping on the dirt floor, was a small team of state police officers—a search party that had walked up the valley. With them was Humphreys. He and Skeels, after weeks of communicating and coordinating online, were finally meeting in person. For weeks, Humphreys had held out hope that Justin would be found alive. "I didn't think he was dead," he recalls. "I was still hoping that maybe he was injured somewhere and we could still stumble upon him." But now, seeing the flute, his hope began to flicker.

There was one other person with the party, asleep on the floor, whom Skeels recognized with surprise. The man had bushy eyebrows and a black mustache. It was the porter, Anil Kumar. The last time Kumar had been in the high valley, he had been accompanying Justin and Rawat to Mantalai Lake. Skeels guessed that the police had made him return to retrace his steps.

Before the sun peeked above the mountains and the others awoke, Skeels and Kunwar set out on the last leg of their return to Manali as quickly as possible. Questions for the porter burned in Skeels's mind, but he had news to relay to the search team in the United States and items to return to an anxious mother. Skeels and Kunwar hurried down the trail past Kheerganga and Kalga to the road head, where they hired a taxi.

In Manali, Suzie was waiting at her hotel, having sat out on her balcony all morning, gazing at the mountains partially hidden by the clouds. She had listened to the theme song from the film that she and her son had watched together seven times after it had come out,

The Last of the Mohicans: "No matter where you go I will find you/If it takes a thousand years." There was a knock on her door, and Skeels presented her with what he had found along the river. Suzie gripped the flute–staff tightly in her hands, this object from India that her son had carried wherever he went. She had given Justin his first instrument, a mandolin, when he had been a teenager, and now she was holding his last. Suzie knew that the flute–staff had been a talisman for her son, a symbol of two things he had held dear—music and exploration—fused into one. He had used it to ground himself, to write music, and to walk steadily. And she knew that he would not have parted with it easily.

The Kullu police requested that Suzie turn over the items found along the riverbank, in case they held clues to their investigation. But it was hard for her to let them go, knowing that once they entered police hands, it was unlikely she would ever see them again. So she and Skeels hatched a plan. They took Justin's flute–staff to a musical instrument shop in Manali with the intention of fabricating a duplicate that they could hand over to the police instead. They figured that any important clues—fingerprints, for example—were unlikely to remain on the staff, given how much time had passed. At the shop, Suzie purchased a flute of the same size and a section of bamboo to affix to the end. They tied red string around one end, just like Justin's. But when they tried, as he had done, to bring the two pieces together, the decoy flute split down the middle. The two shared a moment of levity, laughing at their crumbling plan, as they realized that Justin's talisman could not be replicated.

The greatest hope for information or clues remained with Rawat. After being questioned in the presence of Suzie and Skeels in Kullu, the sadhu had been held in remand behind iron bars in a small cell in the police complex in Manikaran. Now Suzie began preparing for a moment when she might be able to question the sadhu directly on her own terms. If Justin, Rawat, and Kumar had departed Kheerganga for Mantalai Lake on August 28, as the sadhu had said, Suzie wanted to know what her son had done in the week after leaving Kalga on August 22. Had he returned to his cave? She wanted to know when and where, exactly, Rawat had last seen him. Why had he changed his story? The sadhu had previously claimed that he, Justin, and Kumar had reached Mantalai Lake on September 4, but if that were true, how could Sunny Panchal and Nirmal Patel have seen Justin descending from the lake and taken his picture the day before? Had Rawat simply miscounted the number of days in August, or was this yet another inconsistency in his story?

Suzie also wanted to know why the police had dragged their heels for ten days until she and Skeels had arrived. Why hadn't they apprehended Rawat and Kumar immediately? Why hadn't they quickly launched a concerted search into the high valley?

According to one person who worked closely with Suzie and Skeels on the ground in India, the Kullu police were "unequipped and unmotivated" to commit to a sustained search and made an effort only in order to appease the family and the US Embassy, which was exerting pressure on the police department. The department was well aware of the Parvati Valley's history of foreign tourists dropping off the map. The steps the department took, including eventually arresting Rawat and Kumar and agreeing to send officers on the helicopter organized by Skeels into the high valley, were made under pressure by an embassy unlike any it had ever felt for a previous missing-persons case. Suzie echoes feeling the police's indifference. "I was fighting for my son's life," she says. "I was fighting for them to consider that he was really missing."

After Humphreys had filed a report with the police in Manikaran on October 3, it had taken five days before a group of officers had hiked to Kheerganga to speak to the sadhu they had been told had last been with Justin. The police had listened to Rawat's story but had felt enough confidence in his account that they had left him in his hut near the hot springs. It wasn't until the Kullu police had begun receiving calls from the office of the state minister, mentioning pressure by the US Embassy and stating that family members were en route to India, that they had finally picked up Rawat and brought him down from Kheerganga. He had been detained but not arrested and allowed to live in Manikaran, likely sleeping in one of the temples, until he had been placed in a police vehicle and driven to Kullu to be presented to Suzie and Skeels. Additional Superintendent of Police for the Kullu district Nishchint Singh Negi, whom Chand had appointed as the supervising officer for the investigation into Justin's disappearance, later acknowledged that his department had officially arrested Rawat—two days after the interrogation at the police station on October 15—based entirely on the complaint lodged by Suzie.

Suzie handed over her son's flute-staff on the condition that the police would arrange a second interrogation of Rawat. Along with her questions, she had written a letter that she wanted to read to him—to try to connect with him on a level that he might understand, on a spiritual level. She intended to refer to the karma of his actions and remind him that no court on Earth was going to try him like the one he would face after he died. "I was going to appeal to his higher self," she says.

Suzie never had the opportunity to ask her questions and make her statement. Just after 7:00 p.m. on the evening of October 21, the on-duty police officer in charge of watching Rawat stepped outside the Manikaran police station to relieve himself. When he returned inside and checked on Rawat in his cell, he found the sadhu dead.

14
STONE VALLEY

Justin didn't try to hide the fact that he had smoked hash in the Parvati Valley. The Kullu police saw Justin's Instagram pictures of him and Rawat smoking a chillum and speculated that he was one of the many who were drawn to the valley solely for its hash and succumbed to the power of the drug. "Initially, my notion was that he had taken some drugs and gotten lost," Additional Superintendent Nishchint Singh Negi recalls matter-of-factly. "We have so many instances of that, people falling in the river." Though superintendents of police in India are often politically appointed, the midlevel officers, such as Negi, are the officers who more often run and coordinate investigations. Perhaps, Negi speculated, Justin was hiding out around Malana, the isolated hash epicenter of the valley. Justin had been familiar with the village: while trekking in the Annapurna Mountains in Nepal earlier that year, he had met a hiking guide who had come from Malana, who had told him about its isolation, its mythical founding, and its legendary hash. Justin had subsequently written online about a desire to visit the village.

The Kullu police weren't the only ones who wondered if drugs had played a role in Justin's disappearance. The few who knew that Justin had been carrying the brick of hash and also knew of his willingness to show it assumed that it might have made him a target. Humphreys understood that the local police presume that the Parvati Valley's missing foreigners are all people who have become entangled in the drug trade. So before he had hiked to Kheerganga to question Rawat and before he'd filed the official police report at the Manikaran station, the first thing he had done was visit the Om Shanti guesthouse in Kalga, where Justin had left his large green backpack for safekeeping. Humphreys knew that what had been left tucked carefully inside, if found by the police, would derail—if not completely defeat—any potential search effort. The police might believe that Justin had been not a consumer but a trafficker. The guesthouse owner recognized Humphreys as a friend of Justin's and given him access to the backpack, and Humphreys had removed the brick of black hash and stashed it in the forest outside the village.

The search team in the United States was surprised to learn that Justin had traveled with such a quantity of hash, knowing it was risky to do so in a country that could put him in prison for more than a decade if he was caught. When they discovered that Justin had made two ATM withdrawals, both dated in August in the Parvati Valley, further questions were raised. The first was a withdrawal of $299.30 worth of rupees from an ATM at Pinki Tours & Travels, which has a branch in Kasol, on August 6. Did the date confirm that Justin, despite not revealing it to his followers online, had, in fact, left his cave in the middle of his three weeks of supposedly uninterrupted off-grid retreat? Or had he trusted someone with his debit card as he had his motorcycle keys with Andrey Gapon? The second ATM withdrawal, this time for $393.02 worth of rupees, was on August 17, when he had been resupplying in Kasol before departing for Mantalai Lake with Rawat. The withdrawals struck some as unusual: Why would a backpacker, known to travel modestly, need so much money within such a short period of time? And why, in the second instance, would he have withdrawn enough money to live in a guesthouse in the Parvati Valley for more than two months if he was embarking on a pilgrimage with no paid accommodation, no restaurants, and no foreseen expenses?

As the Kullu police learned more about Justin's background, the simple drug tourist narrative turned more complicated. In public, Superintendent Padam Chand was trying to absolve his department of responsibility for yet another missing backpacker. "Usually foreigners' arrival is registered compulsorily at guesthouses and hotels," he told the Indian media organization Mid-Day. "But Justin was staying in jungles and mountain areas, so we did not know of his arrival, as the location he was staying in is a no man's land." Chand told Indian media that his department was "probing the case from both accidental and homicidal angle[s]," yet behind the scenes, according to one person with intimate knowledge of the search, he was trying to stop local media from reporting on the case of Justin and the death of Rawat in an effort to diminish any further negative attention to his jurisdiction.

The day Suzie and Skeels arrived at the Kullu police station, Chand had told them that a likely possibility was that Justin had wanted to disappear—as so many other foreign tourists had in the valley—and it was possible that he might simply reappear soon. Over the years, the department had located and deported dozens of foreign tourists who were living there illegally beyond the expiry of their visa. Some had married locals. In private, the Kullu police had become convinced that Justin was yet another foreign backpacker who had dropped off the grid to live long term in the Parvati Valley.

According to a report in Mid-Day, after Rawat's body was found in the Manikaran cell, the inspector in charge at the Manikaran police post did not call a local doctor. Nor did any other member of the police. Instead, the police drove Rawat's body to the district hospital in Kullu, where the sadhu was officially declared dead. It was determined that Rawat had untied his dhoti from around his waist, looped it around the bars of his cell door, and hanged himself.

Many people accepted the suicide as an admission of guilt, saying that Rawat had known the police had him and could not imagine a life in prison. But others sensed a different possibility in this region so dependent on tourists coming into the valley to lodge in guesthouses and eat in restaurants, to hire trekking guides and purchase marbles of hash. The story of a murderous sadhu would have sent shock waves through the industry. If evidence had been found in Rawat's possession—Justin's iPhone, machete, or backpack, for example—the lifeblood of the valley might dry up. The Kullu police, instead, maintained that Rawat had killed himself not out of guilt but out of shame. Additional Superintendent Negi later explained that Rawat had declared to police before he died that the arrest and custody had ruined his reputation as a sadhu, that all the respect as a holy man that he had accumulated was now gone. There would be no police report released publicly about the effects of the incident on tourism and no need to update their initial suspicions; people who wanted to take the suicide as an admission of guilt could live with that theory, and nothing needed to be announced officially.

When Suzie heard the news of Rawat's death, she was horrified. But she also suspected that the police weren't releasing the full story. "My first thought was that he didn't kill himself," she says. Skeels found it a strange coincidence that the sadhu had died approximately forty-eight hours before his scheduled release. The police, after all, had no hard evidence that implicated Rawat. The department was accustomed to media attention over missing foreign tourists in their jurisdiction, but this case had drawn more international attention—including from the powerful US Embassy—than any other. Now Rawat could no longer be summoned for questioning; he could no longer plead his innocence; he could no longer try to convince people that the "argument" at Mantalai Lake had never amounted to anything serious. With his death, there would never be an admission that one of the valley's legendary holy men might have killed a foreign tourist, pushed his body into a river, and stolen and sold his valuables. The local police could control the narrative of what might have happened.

The Kullu police conducted an analysis of Rawat's body, including an autopsy by the state medical department the following day. "No wound, bruise or injury visible on body," the official autopsy report read. But it noted a "depressed pressure abrasion" on the upper part of the neck that ran from one earlobe to the other. "In our provisional opinion," the report concluded, "the deceased died due to asphyxia as a result of antemortem hanging. However final option will be given after viscera chemical examination." The viscera—the abdomen's large internal organs—was sent away to be tested for possible traces of poison; Rawat's dhoti was sent away, too, to determine if its tensile strength was sufficient to be used as a method of hanging. The garment was found to be capable of bearing 72 kilograms (159 pounds) of weight—"Easily hence death is possible by hanging," the autopsy read, for someone as small and thin as Rawat.

After Rawat's death, Mid-Day reported that the Kullu police had allegedly violated several guidelines of India's National Human Rights Commission: the autopsy had been performed by nonforensic surgeons, and no forensic experts had analyzed the crime scene—the cell—immediately following the death. Most crucially, the officers had failed to notify the commission within twenty-four hours, as is required after a death in police custody. The NHRC and its requirements date back to 1993, when India's secretary general noted that "Failure to report promptly would give rise to presumption that there was an attempt to suppress the incident." Four years after that, in 1997, a former national chief justice reiterated the need for the NHRC to be notified quickly: "A number of instances have come to the Commission's notice where the postmortem reports appear to be doctored due to influence/pressure to protect the interest of the police/jail officials."

Any death of a suspect or accused in a jail in India is labeled a "custodial death"—whether by natural causes or illness, during hospitalization, by suicide, or as a result of physical assault by police. A Human Rights Watch report noted that, in 2015, approximately 6 percent of all deaths in police custody in India were due to "physical assault by police" while around a third were listed as suicide. "However," the report continued, "in many such cases, family members allege that the deaths were the result of torture," and that "usually, torture is likely" after a suspect is first taken into custody. "Police in India routinely violate domestic and international laws governing due process for arrest and detention," the report read. "Many law enforcement officials view the use of force to obtain confessions and information as an acceptable and necessary tool for investigating crime and enforcing the law."

A couple of days before Rawat died, Humphreys had visited the Manikaran police station and spoken with an officer there. The sadhu was being held in a cell inside.

"Don't worry," the officer said. "If the baba is guilty, he will confess."

Humphreys had asked the officer not to hurt Rawat but to verbally interrogate him to reveal the inconsistencies in his stories.

"Don't worry, he will confess," the officer had responded.

"I knew what that meant," Humphreys recalls. "Two days later, I came down the mountain and he was dead."

When pressed, two police officers who were close to the case later acknowledged to me that they had known "force" had been used while Rawat was held at the small Manikaran station but stopped short of admitting that any police actions had led to his death. The sadhu had hanged himself, they insisted.

After a week in India, Suzie was beginning to feel the leads slipping away. "I wasn't out for vengeance at all costs. I wanted answers," she says. But Rawat's death haunted her. "I was very bitter because I felt we lost the last thread of hope of finding Justin—and finding out what truly happened."

Soon after, police officer Daya Ram Singh, who was installed as the lead officer at the Manikaran station after the death of Rawat, received a call that Suzie wanted to conduct a formal questioning of Anil Kumar. After being brought along on the trek to retrace his steps above Kheerganga, the porter had been released without charge to live in Manikaran. But mounting pressure had led Singh to formally arrest the man on October 24. Two days later, Kumar was placed in a police vehicle and driven to the police station in Manali, near where Suzie was staying.

Skeels had regretted not at least trying to interrogate Kumar when he had seen him in the hut at Tunda Bhuj, the night he had found Justin's belongings. Skeels was skeptical of the porter. For one thing, Justin had never mentioned that he and Rawat were hiring a porter to assist them. It didn't fit the tone of the journey: simple, ascetic, monklike—a disciple following a guru on a pilgrimage. And importantly, when Skeels had spoken with Nirmal Patel and Sunny Panchal about their chance encounter with Justin on September 3, not only had they seen no porter that day, but Justin had mentioned that he had carried firewood from the tree line to Mantalai Lake—an odd thing to do if there had been a porter in the group. Even though he had no evidence, Skeels had become convinced that the porter had been appended to the story by Rawat to add a corroborating witness to the sadhu's account.

Inside the Manali police station, Kumar, wearing jeans and a black jacket and a toque, was brought into the office of an inspector for questioning. Skeels hit "Record" on his iPhone.

Suzie and Skeels had brought the manager of Suzie's hotel to act as an unofficial translator, through whom they were prepared to interview the porter, but the inspector quickly took charge of the interrogation. Kumar removed his toque and clutched it behind his back as he nervously answered the inspector's questions.*

Anil Kumar was originally from Uttarakhand, a state that neighbors Himachal Pradesh to the southeast. He said he had come to the Parvati Valley earlier that year to find employment as a porter for trekking companies and found the environment familiar to that of his home state, featuring similar mountainous terrain, remote valleys, and spiritual destinations. He had found consistent work,

---

* Little of what the porter revealed was translated in real time for Suzie and Skeels; the hotel manager wasn't able to keep up with the pace of the questioning and deferred to the inspector. Most of the details included in this scene were later drawn from a translation of Skeels's video.

enough to rent a room in the small roadside village of Barsheni, where buses perform a tight turnaround near the end of the drivable road half a mile before Kalga. Because he lived near the beginning of the trail, he was also sometimes hired by camp and café owners in Kheerganga to haul loads of groceries or blankets or camp equipment on his back up the seven-mile trail. Kumar said that while resting in Kheerganga in late August, he had been approached by Rawat to accompany him and an American tourist on a trek to Mantalai Lake. Rawat had told him that he would take care of Kumar's wages: 3,000 rupees ($45) for the trip in exchange for carrying some food and for cooking for the trio—2,000 rupees up-front and another 1,000 after completion of the trek. Kumar agreed. It's likely that Rawat had some money from donations by tourists and pilgrims who had visited his hut in Kheerganga, but even so, he would not have been flush. It's more likely that Justin had paid something, a portion of a fee, to the sadhu up-front and Rawat used that to pay Kumar's initial payment. Justin had never written about that or mentioned to anyone that he was paying Rawat to be his guide. What he had posted online had sounded as though they had a spiritual and personal connection rather than a business understanding. It is possible that he had omitted the fact that he was paying for the sadhu's services precisely because it would have revealed the relationship to be transactional rather than authentic.

Kumar told the inspector that he had never trekked to Mantalai Lake before. He hadn't known the way so had been relying on the sadhu to be the guide. "How is that route?" the inspector asked.

"It has some steep incline. There are some places of worry. And there is some fear of falling," Kumar responded.

"And if the person falls, where will he go?"

"Into the river."

The first three days from Kheerganga had passed uneventfully, Kumar said: they had walked slowly during the days and in the evening had affixed their tarp to boulders to create a lean-to-like shelter under which they had cooked and slept. Their first night had been near Tunda Bhuj; their second night had been somewhere in Stone

Valley; their third night had been at Thakur Kuan. It was a challenge to communicate, with Justin knowing only a few words in
Hindi and Rawat knowing only a few in English, but Justin had
used a translation app on his iPhone that didn't need cell service
to ask questions so he could learn what he could. When they had
taken breaks from hiking, the sadhu had shown Justin how to meditate. After they had reached Mantalai Lake, they had gone to make
offerings at the small waterfront Shiva shrine. Then, as Kumar had
prepared food, Justin had wandered around the lake for hours. It had
looked to Kumar as though he was sitting on the rocks, practicing
his meditation.

When Justin had returned, he had told Rawat that he wanted to
remain at the lake for a few days or longer. The inspector pressed,
but Kumar refused to admit that any confrontation had occurred
between Justin and the sadhu. He simply noted that the American
had been "stubborn" in wanting to remain there.

"What did he want to stay back for?" the inspector asked.

"Nothing, really," Kumar responded. "A cave. Some rocky paths."

Kumar didn't clarify how or when the trio had departed Mantalai Lake, but he said that the last time he had seen Justin was the
next day, over tea at Thakur Kuan, when Rawat had told him to go
ahead to prepare food at Tunda Bhuj and await their arrival. It was
customary for porters in trekking groups to forge ahead of their cli-
ents in order to begin setting up camp. Kumar had set out. He had
reached the hut at Tunda Bhuj while there was still daylight, but
the sun had long set by the time the sadhu had arrived on his own.
The porter had expressed his concern. "I asked the baba, and he said
[Justin] got left behind and that maybe he's clicking pictures. So I
said, 'Okay, he must be clicking pictures.'" Kumar said that around
8:00 p.m., he had gone to look for Justin in the dark, retracing the
path back up the valley. He said he had spent an hour looking for the
American that evening but had eventually had to give up. Justin had
been nowhere to be found. The next morning, Kumar and Rawat had
made their way through the forest to Kheerganga, the sadhu telling
him not to worry about Justin, Kumar said. "I was worried, but the

baba said, 'There is nothing to worry about, and he'll come in two to three days.' That's why I didn't pay much attention and went back to work." Still, Kumar said, he had told the sadhu that if Justin didn't arrive, he would notify the police that someone was missing. "No, no," Rawat had told him, "he'll come."

Suzie and Skeels were provided with only a bare-bones version of Kumar's account, which they understood now largely aligned with Rawat's. But Skeels remained suspicious: after the brief interrogations of the sadhu and the porter at the police station when they had first arrived in Kullu, while Suzie had been filing the First Information Report, Skeels had spotted the men speaking together in an outdoor holding area. In his mind they had been synchronizing their stories.

As the questioning went on, Kumar reminded the inspector that he had helped with the on-foot search party. Another police officer who was taking notes in the room pointed out that if Kumar had been guilty of something, he could easily have run away after early September. But the inspector at times became impatient with Kumar's evasiveness, threatening him at one point with ten years in prison and at another—perhaps trying to catch the man in a lie—demanding that the porter speculate as to what he thought could have happened to Justin. Kumar offered that the American could have walked off the trail or possibly turned back up the valley; he could have embarked on another trek; he could still be at Mantalai Lake.

Toward the end of the hour-long interrogation, the inspector looked at the porter and made a suggestion. "Put the whole thing on the baba. He's not here. Why don't you put the whole thing on him?"

Kumar paused and didn't respond. The inspector moved on.

"Do you want to say anything to them?" he asked Kumar at one point, and the porter turned to face Suzie. "I'm sorry," he said in Hindi. "I didn't do anything. My job was of a porter. I was carrying their stuff and making food. I was serving them and feeding them, and I was doing all their work."

Daya Ram Singh, the officer who had formally arrested Kumar, later explained that the porter was of a low caste and would have followed any orders from anyone above him on India's social hierarchy. If Rawat had given him a command, he would have obeyed it without question or comment. Yet despite his social status, which might have acted as a barrier to speaking up, and despite Rawat telling him not to, Singh said that Kumar had, in fact, been the first person to alert authorities—days or even more than a week before Humphreys had filed a report at the police station in Manikaran. In India, many issues are dealt with and often settled not by the police but by the village or town *panchayat*, a kind of local government. Reports of a disturbance or even a crime are often lodged there first, and its members then decide if the issue requires police. After Kumar had returned from Mantalai Lake, he had hiked out to catch a bus to Manikaran, where he had gone to speak with the head of the town's *panchayat*. It's unclear whether or not a lower police officer was ever informed about a possible missing foreign tourist or if the elected official didn't deem the situation serious and, knowing the history of the valley, assumed the tourist would simply reappear in time. Additional Superintendent Negi recalls that the first time he heard that an American tourist had gone missing was on the second or third day of the Dussehra festival, around the time Suzie and Skeels arrived at the police station on October 13.

In the end, the police believed Kumar's story. After his interrogation in Manali, he was held in remand for two weeks at the Manikaran station before being let go on the grounds of insufficient evidence or cause for suspicion. He left the valley shortly after being released from police custody, presumably returning to his home state of Uttarakhand and melting into India's masses.

Suzie struggled to find sense in how the police had treated the two key witnesses relating to her son's disappearance. Even though Kumar had accompanied officers beyond Kheerganga to retrace his steps to Tunda Bhuj and beyond, that was hardly a sign of good faith. "Well," she says, "arsonists and murderers do return to the scene of the crime."

Above Kheerganga, there was only one person who had made the high valley his permanent home: the sadhu who lived alone in the hut at Tunda Bhuj. For fifteen years, Bhinder Baba, as he was called, had prepared cups of tea and bowls of instant noodles in his wood-fired, open-air kitchen for trekkers and pilgrims in need of respite on their way to and from Mantalai Lake. Passersby rested on the grass out front amid a small garden and bushes of aromatic lemon balm, some sleeping overnight in the curtained-off back room beside the altar to Shiva. During the six-month tourist high season, from spring to fall, it was rumored that the sadhu earned around 50,000 rupees ($650) in donations for his food and the use of his roof, not an insignificant amount of money for someone living an ascetic life. As the sole permanent resident, Bhinder also became a relay point for gossip and news from those going up and down the valley.

Bhinder's account differed from that of Rawat and Kumar. He recalls seeing Rawat and a foreigner pass by his hut on their way to Mantalai Lake but noted that they hadn't stopped, unusual for a party on their way up the valley. Despite both of them being sadhus and in close proximity, Bhinder says that he and Rawat had never actually met. "When I stayed here, he stayed in Kheerganga," Bhinder recalls, through a translator. "We didn't even exchange greetings." Rawat, however, had told the Kullu police during his interrogation that he had met Kumar at Tunda Bhuj when they had realized Justin hadn't arrived and had stayed some of the night in Bhinder's hut. But Bhinder rejects that account. "He didn't stay with me at all while coming down. He just kept on going. I didn't even see his face."

Bhinder was not the only person who had encountered Rawat on his descent from Mantalai Lake. Ali Hussein had been living in a seasonal camp just below Tunda Bhuj. There, in the remote pastures of the Parvati Valley, the small community of Gujjar shepherds raised buffalos and sold milk and *paneer* to the cafés in Kheerganga. One day during the first week of September, Hussein had completed another daily delivery, leaving his horse, laden with empty metal milk containers, to graze in a meadow. As he walked toward his family's wooden-pole-and-tarp camp, something had caught his eye. He had recognized Satnarayan Rawat sitting under a copse of trees. About a week before, one late afternoon, the sadhu had arrived with a porter and a foreign tourist and had asked permission for the trio to sleep within the camp. Hussein had told them that they could affix their tarp to the outside of his tent. Come morning, the sadhu had purchased some buffalo milk so they could make tea during their journey up the valley. Then the trio had set off to continue toward Mantalai Lake. Hussein remembers the foreign tourist well, a tall man who had carried a long flute that he had used as a walking stick; he had seen Justin inside Rawat's hut many times when he had dropped by to sell milk to the sadhu that August.

This time, however, Hussein had been struck to see the sadhu alone. Shortly thereafter, he had noticed that the porter had arrived and joined him, but the foreigner was nowhere to be seen. Unusually, the sadhu and the porter had not been camping within the buffalo herders' camp or socializing with the Gujjar, as they had done on their way up the valley, but instead had been sitting across the meadow and on the other side of the trail, far from anyone else. Rawat had purchased milk from Hussein many times before, but that evening and the next morning, he didn't. When Hussein had entered his camp, his sister-in-law had told him that she had passed Rawat on the trail and had inquired about the whereabouts of the "foreigner" who had been with him before. In contrast to what Rawat would later say—that Justin had returned to Mantalai Lake or that he had gone missing along some vague point along the trail—this time he had offered a specific location. After seeming to ignore her question, Rawat's face had changed, and he had said gruffly, "He's in Stone Valley."

Justin's large green backpack had been collected from the Om Shanti guesthouse in Kalga and brought to where Suzie was staying in

Manali. She carefully removed each item, placing it on the white bedspread in her room, looking for anything that might offer a clue. Justin had yearned for a life of adventure that would inspire others to pack a backpack and see the world. That was his dream. "He lived it," Suzie recalls thinking, "and how can I say that was the wrong thing to do?" To her, the motive behind his perpetual seeking was simple. "In the end," she says, "it was all about looking for love and acceptance."

Inside Justin's backpack were her son's passport, multiple passport photos, and credit cards. There were several changes of clothes and a small collection of souvenirs, including the bull's horn he had found in the forest near his Kheerganga cave, a package of multicolored prayer flags he had purchased in Nepal, and a couple of small pouches containing beaded bracelets and silver amulets—gifts, possibly. There was a jump rope he had used to exercise while on the road and a dopp kit of basic toiletries. There was a stocked waterproof medical kit bulging with an extensive miscellany of survival items including antiseptic creams, cold pastilles, Imodium, and water purification tablets.

Stowed carefully inside the backpack were also several documents: a glossy certificate for the completion of the Bhachek Primary School, the one Justin had helped build in Nepal that spring; the insurance and purchase documents for Shadow, his Royal Enfield motorcycle; and a lined piece of paper folded into eighths that revealed a single-page love letter that someone had hidden in his backpack just before he had left the United States. "How could I not fall in love?" the letter read. "Whether this leads to a sincere friendship or relationship, I'd hold them both dearly. I wanted to say this all in person but I was never quite sure if the timing was right, or how you'd even react. Truthfully, ever since we met I knew there was something different about you, and I'd be lying if I didn't say I constantly thought & hoped you'd stick around." It was signed "Manda."

Jonathan Skeels took a guess as to the author and sent a message to a woman on Facebook. "Is this by chance your signature?"

"Yes it is," Amanda Sansoucie, who had been quietly following the search online, replied. "Did you guys find him???"

There was another piece of lined paper inside Justin's backpack, too, one torn from a notebook, upon which he had drawn three illustrations of a *nag chhatri*, a rare Himalayan trillium plant. Found across the mountain range in forested areas from 8,000 feet in elevation up to where the tree line fades to inhospitable moraine, the plant is identified by its three leaves and a single purple flower that blooms in the shape of a star. Its rhizome is pulled from the ground, dried, and used in Ayurvedic medicine as a painkiller, an anti-inflammatory treatment, and an aphrodisiac. *Nag chhatri*'s known qualities, coupled with its rarity, have made it highly coveted, and several mountain states in India have banned the harvest and trade of the plant. But its value and power as a panacea have spurred many to seek it out in the high meadows and forests of the Himalayas.

Justin had sketched the plant in three stages of growth: with its initial trillium of leaves, then with a closed bud, and then with the open flower in bloom. Above the drawings he had scribbled a mantra of sorts: "Happiness comes from the freedom and capability to dream a life into reality."

15
FOOTSTEPS

The discovery of Justin's belongings along the banks of the Parvati River represented a ray of hope for some members of the search team back in the United States. They wondered if further clues might be left in the area. Toward the end of October, Tom McElroy, Justin's old friend from the Tracker School, decided to fly to India to see if his skills could turn up any evidence of his friend's whereabouts or final movements. He knew that the chance of finding anything was slim, that the most crucial and most fruitful time for a tracker is within the first forty-eight hours after a disappearance. As their former teacher, Tom Brown, Jr., had once written, "The place where you lose the trail is not necessarily the place where it ends," and McElroy wanted to see the exact spot where the path had run cold.

Jonathan Skeels organized another helicopter and convinced a group of police officers and officials from the state forensic science laboratory to accompany him. Suzie joined for the trip. They landed once again on the flat meadow at Thakur Kuan. "I felt no fear. I felt peaceful," she remembers about the bumpy helicopter ride into the mountains. "I just was relishing the splendor, the magnitude of the beauty." She remained at the meadow as the others made their way downriver. Soon—before the water flowed below Kheerganga, where it would mix with steaming water from the camp's hot springs; before it pushed through the hydroelectric dam beside the orchard village of Kalga; and before it rumbled under the prayer flag–draped bridges at Manikaran and Kasol and rushed out of the valley—it would pass through the narrow gorge of Stone Valley.

Skeels led McElroy and the officers down along the Parvati River. Even though it was only late October, winter was already arriving. The brooks that had once dribbled into the river now formed clusters of icicles and mounds of white ice. The team soon came across a green jacket on the hillside, but it appeared to have been there for many months and DNA later retrieved from inside failed to match that of either Justin or Rawat. Some of the police officers scrambled around the hillside looking for any kind of evidence, but many spent their time posing for mountain selfies; others made a fire to keep warm.

McElroy walked the stretch where Justin's flute–staff had been found. He examined the rock shelf that slides toward the river and noticed small shrubs with branches broken and bent and what he deemed to be an impact site of crushed vegetation at the bottom. Something heavy had tumbled down from the trail to where the flute–staff had been found, he thought. After nearly two months since his friend would have been in the area, however, it was hard to reach any certain conclusions. But he was sure of one thing: knowing his friend's wilderness and survival skills, McElroy didn't believe for a second that he might have simply slipped off the trail.

"You couldn't help but think that he was going to wander around the corner, all skinny and emaciated, and say, 'Tom! What are you doing here? I can't believe you're here!'" McElroy recalled the year he had volunteered to caretake the Tracker School's land in New Jersey when he was eighteen, living in the bush and surviving on his wilderness skills. His parents had figured he would last a few weeks, but weeks had gone by and their son hadn't emerged for months. McElroy's parents had been getting close to notifying the police when he had found a pay phone in a state park and called home. Standing on the banks of the Parvati River, looking up to the peaks around him, the patches of alpine meadow among the ash gray cliffs, the mountain passes leading to new lands and new adventures, it was impossible for McElroy not to imagine his friend reappearing as he used to after excursions into the bush when they were young. Standing beside a mythical river in the Himalayas, walking through a land of eagles and snow leopards and holy lakes—it felt fitting for the final known steps of his old friend's journey.

Back at Thakur Kuan, Suzie sat by the banks of the river, watching the water laden with fine particles of time-ground rock sparkle in the sunlight. "To have walked in a path that I know my son was on was a phenomenal experience," she recalls. "I can see why he wanted to be there: the majesty of the Himalayas is beyond words." But her presence on that day was more than just an attempt to understand the natural forces that had drawn her son to these mountains. "It was special to me to follow in his footsteps," she says. "I brought him into this world. I had to be where he took his last footsteps, so that I could try to see what he saw." Over the two frenetic weeks that she had spent in India, she had oscillated between believing that her son was still alive and trying to bring herself to accept that he was gone.

She looked up the valley to where her son had wanted to go and down the valley to where some of his scattered possessions had been located. She thought of a quote from Joseph Campbell, the comparative mythologist who had outlined the Hero's Journey, which had resonated so strongly for her son since he was a boy: "People say that what we're all seeking is a meaning for life. I don't think that's what we're really seeking. I think that what we're seeking is an experience of being alive, so that our life experiences on the purely physical plane will have resonances within our own innermost being and reality, so that we actually feel the rapture of being alive."

Suzie had traveled across thirteen time zones to a country she had never imagined visiting and was now looking up at mountains that were part of the tallest range in the world and thinking about the boy who had loved high places; and looking down to the river, thinking about the boy who had loved the water. As she sat on a flat rock, the roar of the river in her ears, a shadow flitted over the stones. She glanced up. A great bird, which looked like an eagle, soared above her, its wings barely moving as it caught warm updrafts, lifting it higher and higher toward white-capped peaks.

As November arrived, temperatures began to drop throughout the Parvati Valley. Tourists fled out of the mountains to warmer climes, and the camp at Kheerganga began to be dismantled. That area, once buzzing with backpackers and pilgrims, drumbeats and revelry, was slowly restored to a high mountain pasture. Late monsoon rains had rinsed away the footprints of those who had come, and snow was soon to cover the trails. With the tourists gone, the sadhus packed up their few belongings and left the high mountains as well. Their search for neophytes would continue elsewhere on the subcontinent.

Like many mothers and fathers before her who had gone searching for a loved one who had disappeared in the Parvati Valley, Suzie boarded a plane and left India without answers. They had found no body to repatriate; there was no confession; there was little resolution. Before she had departed the hotel in Manali where she had been staying, the manager had organized a *puja*, a small ceremony, to honor her son. Oil lamps had been lit. Fruit had been offered. Hindu mantras had been read. Suzie had sat cross-legged on the floor, hands folded together in her lap.

Upon arriving back in the United States, she posted one last update for those who had been following the search efforts:

The final search before winter sets in has concluded, and we are heartbroken to say that there has been no further trace of Justin. While the investigation into his death is still ongoing, we now believe his body has been lost to the river, and we are deeply saddened to mourn the loss of his light in the world.

 . . . We know it is deeply difficult and painful to move on without a real trace of him, and without answers that would help any of us to understand what really happened here. We have struggled with this question ourselves, and ultimately we have all asked what Justin would want us to do. We know he would want all of us—his family and his friends—to focus on what we each can accomplish in this world. He would want us to seek out adventure, to find beauty in the smallest and largest things, and to celebrate each other. . . . May we each spend our own lives following and finding kinship in his footsteps.

In the wake of Justin's disappearance, people had emerged from all corners of the globe, claiming they had known him well. They said they had been a best friend or a girlfriend, a longtime follower, or an acquaintance who had shared a memorable moment with him on the road. They had known him as Justin the Outdoorsman, Justin the Musician, Justin the Motorcycle Rider, Justin the World Traveler, or Justin the Instagram Star. And through each of those lenses they saw him distinctly, as an idol or an explorer, as a survivalist or a photographer, as a partner or a friend. Some wanted travel inspiration and exotic pictures. Some wanted survival tips and stories of adventure. Some wanted friendship, companionship, or love.

And now many didn't accept that that was the end of Justin's road:

"They won't find his body cause he's alive somewhere. One day he'll return when he wants to. I believe to be true," one follower posted on Facebook.

"I'm assuming why you are gone missing it's because you are finding new worlds, so I can not wait to hear all about it," another wrote.

"It's not time, he has so much more to do, so much more to teach and even learn. And hence I believe that personally, he is still there."

"Don't worry he will be back all right."

"I don't think he wants to be found at this moment."

"I still believe you are somewhere with us in the World."

"I hope this isn't real and somewhere Justin Alexander is sitting there playing his flute."

"There's a lot of us praying you're safe and are just deep in meditation in a cave somewhere high in the hills."

"If anyone could Justin could. Keeping a candle burning and hope alive here as well."

Many of Justin's closer friends wanted to believe that he had found the isolation, the meaning, the peace that he had long sought and was taking the first steps of a new journey alone. "Honestly, I thought that he probably just dropped off the map to figure out where he was in life," says Amanda Sansoucie. After everything the two had talked about while walking and riding his motorcycle around the scrublands of Nevada, that seemed to her not only possible but likely. It was a hope shared by many I had spoken with over the years. "It's good to leave a little window of hope. Life's weird. Maybe something that nobody has imagined happened. Maybe in a year's time he'll come back down," Christofer-Lee Humphreys told me six months after Justin had disappeared before admitting that the odds were slim. "But why not leave that little window open? If there's one guy who could jump through that window it would be him." Linda Borini echoed the sentiment: "I will look over my shoulder for the rest of my life, wondering. There is part of me that believes that he could still be around."

At first, Tracy Frey, too, willed herself to believe in the possibility that Justin might still be alive. "There's nobody else who I've ever met who really spent his life preparing to survive anything. And some of that was forced on him, and some of that he sought for himself." Over time, she came to accept the unlikelihood of that possibility despite an absence of closure. "Sure, there was some world where he had gotten far more disconnected or deeply despondent than anybody realized," she says. "There are enough possible scenarios that I want to believe that one of them could be true, but I don't. But I'd love to be wrong."

Anne Osbaldeston, who had taught Justin at the Wilderness Awareness School in Washington State when he had been a teenager and who had helped with the search early on, remembered a moment from Justin's school days when classes had concluded for the year and she had led the students in an exercise called "Appreciation." The students had sat in a circle and taken turns sharing something about another person, something that they appreciated or that had inspired them. Everyone had fawned over Justin, she recalls, marveling at how good he was at climbing trees, how fast he was at making fires, how kind he was, how skilled at hiding. Through it all, Justin had sat quietly, with his head down. After the others had finished, he had looked up and said, "I wish I knew that guy."

"It was his Achilles heel," Osbaldeston says. "He couldn't see it himself. It was so telling for who he was, because you would never know it looking at him day to day. He would literally be swinging branch to branch, starting fires in pouring rain. The hardest things we would throw at them he was always the best at." Yet he had struggled to see who he truly was. "Really there was such a longing in him to not just be good at things but to be *good*. To be who he was meant to be in the world, to be someone he could respect. And I think that was elusive for him. To his last adventure—the last adventure we know of, anyway—he was searching for that deeper well."

As someone who had traveled to India at a similar period in his life, Terry Shetler had a different perspective on his son's journey, recognizing the many people who have arrived in India as tourists and ended up finding a new life. "It's what I would've done," he told me before reciting a story from the Mahabharata about an ancient king named Shantanu. The legend goes that Shantanu was walking by a river when he saw a beautiful woman. They fell in love and married under her condition that he never question any of her actions. When she gave birth to a baby, she threw the child into the river. Shantanu was devastated but could not ask why she had acted that way. Six more children were born, and again his wife threw each of the babies into the river. After the birth of their eighth, however, Shantanu, in pain, broke down and questioned her. She revealed herself to be Ganga, the goddess of the Ganges River; she had killed the children because they were the reincarnations of seven of the eight elemental deities, all of whom had been cursed. But Ganga promised Shantanu that she would save their eighth child, a son, from the river; she took him to the heavens instead. For many years, Shantanu waited for his son's return. Finally he did reappear as a young man named Devavrata, part mortal and part divine, who became a warrior of legend with the ability to choose the time of his death.

It was hard for Terry to watch the search effort in India from afar. But he recalls finding comfort in the belief that his son was still alive throughout, and a kind of disconnection from the search on the ground. He says he never spoke with Jonathan Skeels or Tom McElroy while they were in India, or the others who helped search for his son. "I felt that it was kind of futile, that Justin did not want to be found."

Terry has made peace with the fact that, whatever happened, his son ended up culminating his journey where he did: in nature, in the mountains, in India. Terry hasn't fully given up on the idea that his son might return, like the eighth son of Shantanu, after many years, or maybe in another life. There is a part of him that believes his son has already been reincarnated. "A good death, evidently, is a death doing what you love. And that could've happened," he says. "The only life that's worth living is one that you love."

Justin's black Royal Enfield motorcycle had been found near the dam below Kalga and taken to the police station in Kullu. When Skeels went to pick it up, it roared to life on the first try. With Humphreys and McElroy in a support vehicle, Skeels rode north, higher into the mountains. The three men had decided to leave the Parvati Valley behind and ride the motorcycle on Justin's intended journey over the Tanglang La, the 17,480-foot pass, and down into Ladakh. It was a road that eventually, after many turns, would lead to Kashmir and the temple where Justin's father had experienced a moment of realization. As Skeels navigated the road over the pass, strapped to the back of the motorcycle, with a white star painted over each ear, was Justin's helmet. Justin had managed to bring three friends from three phases of his life together, riding through the Himalayas to write the last chapter of his Indian story.

With the family and friends gone, the investigation into Justin's disappearance wound down. The Kullu police effectively closed the case, and the Indian media stopped publishing stories shortly after Rawat died. But in the Parvati Valley, whispers remained. As in years past, rumors and murmurs filled the voids left by unanswered questions about the latest traveler to have mysteriously disappeared in the Parvati Valley. Whispers floated throughout the Kheerganga camp that the sadhu had robbed Justin and pushed him into the river: "Baba killed him" and "He was thrown into the water." Several people remember chatter that Justin had been seen in Malana, the famed isolated village that sheltered many foreign nationals looking to hide away from the world. Others heard that Justin was still living in a cave at Mantalai Lake. Those people referenced a story from earlier that summer of a foreign tourist who had been living in a shelter built of stones in the lee of a boulder at the lake's edge. The shelter was often used by shepherds passing by and trekking groups on their way to or from the pass. The man in question had spent more than a month living at Mantalai Lake, eventually falling ill after allegedly being bitten by a stray dog. He had died that August in a hospital in Kullu. He had dressed like a sadhu and had become known in the valley as the "Russian baba."

In early January 2017, four months after Justin disappeared, the Kullu police submitted a report of their investigation to the US Embassy in New Delhi. It was forwarded to Skeels, who had been waiting for one piece of possibly key information. During the second interrogation of Anil Kumar, the police had inquired about his personal cell phone. The porter had said that he had taken pictures with his phone during the trek with Justin but it had been ruined after he had returned to Kheerganga. Skeels hoped that it could still contain photographs or text messages that might offer a clue as to what had happened. A representative from the embassy, however, told Skeels that the state forensics laboratory had been unable to retrieve anything relevant to the case from the phone.

Without having located a body, the Kullu police would have to wait the required seven years to officially close the missing-persons case. But in the conclusion of its report, the department borrowed language from Suzie's initial missing-persons report: "At this stage," the document reads, "we cannot conclude the possible reason of death, but we presume that he might have been abducted by someone with the intention to kill him." It was a recognition, at least, that foul play was a possibility.

The report, signed by Superintendent Padam Chand, however, supported Rawat's initial account of events—that Justin had returned on his own back up to Mantalai Lake and possibly continued on into the Spiti Valley, speculating that "may be [sic] he left alone on that trekking routes without telling [Rawat and Kumar]." As evidence that Justin might still be alive, the Kullu police pointed to his own words, quoting the lines from Justin's "don't look for me" final post in their report. Justin was a spiritual seeker who had voluntarily disappeared; he had pushed himself beyond his capabilities in the mountains; he had been exhibiting more extreme signs of India Syndrome; his fascination with "baba life" had finally tipped over into emulation.

The report also noted the results of tracing Justin's iPhone through its IMEI number, a unique code that can track a smartphone independent of its SIM card being removed or switched. The IMEI number, found by Robert Gutierrez on a receipt in his business's records, revealed twenty-four attempts to locate the phone through the Find My iPhone service between September 20 and October 14, 2016. Several pings had come from New York City; others from a city in China. "No reactivation has taken place," the report noted, "which may sign that he is still in possession of his phone."

For years, the Kullu police have maintained an internal document used to keep track of the international tourists who have disappeared in and around the Parvati Valley. It is not exhaustive, but the two-page chart provides the names, corresponding nationalities and passport numbers, and estimated locations of last known whereabouts and last seen dates for the cases the department in some capacity investigated dating back to the early 1990s. Odette Houghton, Marianne Heer, Gregory Powell, and Ian Mogford. Ardavan Taherzadeh, Nadav Mintzer, Alexei Ivanov, and Francesco Gatti. Daniel Mountwitten, Amichai Steinmetz, Bruno Muschalik, and Shota Sakai.

That fall, Justin Alexander Shetler was added to the list of the vanished—his status, like the others': "Untraced."

Justin's web domain, adventuresofjustin.com, eventually fell out of service after payments were missed. But his social media accounts remain online. As long as the platforms exist, so, too, will the content. His trail left in pixels and bytes is indelible. Years after his disappearance, followers and strangers who have found inspiration in his story and are unaware of what transpired still comment on his "Adventures of Justin" Facebook page as if he will respond and even send private messages asking where he is heading next. Maybe that was exactly what Justin wanted: his story, captured in images and words, enshrined forever, like a personal eulogy, in the universe of the internet.

Justin's final post to Instagram, his four hundred thirty-ninth, was uploaded from the Parvati Valley on August 21, 2016: a black-and-white portrait taken by Nirmal Patel at the café in Kasol. In the photograph, Justin's forehead is wrapped in a dark woolen headband, the one later found along the banks of the Parvati River. In the caption he explained that he was resupplying for his "baba trek" and listed the few supplies and food items he was taking. He appeared to be the epitome of self-reliance and independence. "Solitude makes me appreciate human connection all the more," he wrote. There are few portraits on Justin's social media in which he faces the camera; he is most often seen in profile, in action, or with his eyes hidden behind sunglasses or motorcycle goggles. But in his final picture, he stares directly at the viewer. His eyes catch the light, and his mouth betrays the faintest smile. In his bio at the top of his Instagram page he has added, "Currently living in a cave in India."

EPILOGUE

*And when he has spent the third part of his lifespan in
the forests in this way, he may abandon all attachments and
wander as an ascetic for the fourth part of his lifespan. A man who
has gone from one stage of life to another, made the offerings into the
fire, conquered his sensory powers, exhausted himself by giving alms
and propitiatory offerings, and then lived as a wandering
ascetic—when he has died, he thrives.*

—The Laws of Manu, 33–34

Three years to the week after Justin Alexander Shetler disappeared,
I traveled to the Parvati Valley. I had leads to pursue and people
I wanted to interview. I also hoped to find Justin's cave. I carried
with me photographs and videos that Justin had posted online and
a hand-drawn map that Andrey Gapon had sent, noting the cave's
approximate location in the forest near Kheerganga.

It was the summer high season in the valley, and tourists packed
the guesthouses and cafés in Kasol and Manikaran and in the more
remote villages throughout the valley such as Kalga and Tosh. It was
my second trip to the Parvati Valley, and both times I encountered
foreigners who had made this corner of India their home. Near Kalga,
I was directed to a creek-side cottage and a woman who was garden-
ing outside. She was known to spend half a year in the valley. She

was wearing gray-brown woolens and a patterned apron traditional of Himachali women. "I don't want to talk," she warned me off in a British accent when I approached her. "I just want to live in peace." In Manikaran, I sipped chai with a tall man originally from France who was wearing long red robes and leaning on a thin walking staff. His dreadlocked hair was tied back, his wispy beard touched his sternum. The only name he was willing to offer was Baba-ji.

In Malana, villagers fed me stories about "Glenu," the legendary Italian who had lived nearby for decades until his deportation; one local man pointed to the wooden house on the far side of the glen that Galeno Orazi had called home for so many years. The Malanese were intensely wary of an outsider's probe, and I was warned against asking too many questions in the valley. "It's very easy to go missing, as you know," the man cautioned with a sideways look.

The previous March, I had flown to San Francisco by invitation of Justin's mother and close friends to attend a celebration of his life. For some time after Justin's disappearance, various people who had known him found their own ways to honor their friend. In the small Thai village outside Lampang where Justin's adoptive family lived, the news of his disappearance was met with sorrow and disbelief. Sitthikorn Thepchanta remembers his mother not accepting that Justin could be gone. Until she died in 2017, she believed that one day he would stroll into the village, backpack over his shoulders, as he had done so many times before. Every month since, when a monk performs a ritual walk around the village, members of Thepchanta's family place green chicken curry, Justin's favorite Thai dish, into the monk's bowl to honor their friend's life. Others celebrated Justin in the way that perhaps seemed most fitting of all: online. They gathered on Facebook at a set time and shared stories of their friend. They lit candles in China, Mexico, Thailand, France, Australia, India, wherever they were. Participating in the event were people who had known him well, as well as people he had never met. For many, a conclusion to his story remained elusive even years after his disappearance.

No formal funeral or memorial had been held until that March

2019. As a light rain fell on the sequoia, eucalyptus, and pine trees, around fifty people gathered in a circle at the Miwok Shelter in Huddart Park in the forested hills southwest of San Francisco, near where Justin had lived between 2003 and 2009. They were people who had worked with him at the Riekes Center, played onstage with him in Punchface, or tracked animals with him at the Wilderness Awareness School in Washington. In the circle stood Aaron Alvarez, Justin's mentee at the Riekes Center; Aidan Young and his father, Jon Young, from the Wilderness Awareness School; Layla Brooklyn Allman from the San Francisco music scene; and Tracy Frey. Each one, in his or her own way, had felt magnetically drawn to Justin, and many still, even two and a half years after their friend's disappearance in India, couldn't accept that he was gone. "I wouldn't be surprised if Justin just showed up right now, at his own service," Aidan Young said.

Suzie told stories of Justin the toddler and Justin the teenager, a keen and curious kid who had wanted nothing more than to find solace in nature. The day before, Frey had met Suzie at a nearby hotel and presented her with a worn gray shawl made of Indian wool and a long, thin item wrapped in newspaper: Justin's flute–staff. Frey had spent months badgering the Kullu police to release Justin's belongings, which had finally arrived more than two years after they had been recovered. Suzie announced to the circle that she hoped to one day change her last name—her maiden name is Runyon, but she had gone by her second husband's surname, Reeb, even after their divorce—to Alexander. As she spoke, she clutched the gray wool shawl that lay across her shoulders with one hand and in her other hand gripped her son's Indian flute–staff, which she occasionally leaned on for support. She had come to see the instrument as his memento mori, a symbol of the inevitability of death. But it was one that also held life: it could still be put to the lips and played.

After Justin's disappearance, some people felt compelled to follow in his wake. Christofer-Lee Humphreys purchased his own bansuri flute to which he affixed a piece of bamboo, which he carried in honor of his friend. And Ashish Chauhan, the owner of the trekking company Himalayan Drifters, which aided in the search, embarked on a trek in the Parvati Valley in honor of Justin. "I am planning for a fortnight of survival hiking up in the Parvati Valley without carrying any kind of food or shelter. I have a perfect cave in mind," he posted online. "May he find peace wherever he might be." Andrey Gapon returned to India several times after Justin disappeared, and each time, he was able to find more balance in his life. He says a personal transformation began during that summer of 2016 in the valley, a transformation that, in large part, he ascribed to Justin. "He was brave enough to follow his heart not his mind. The mind always calls for safety. The heart knows that life is not only about safety; it is also about adventure and challenge. People who live life and meet all the challenges of life, of course the chances are higher that the quantity will be less. If there was no risk, he wouldn't be Justin."

After Justin disappeared, Bishal Kapali, the Nepali man Justin had supported financially for years, launched an NGO called the Justin Eco Foundation "to bring back happiness in the heart of the most vulnerable Nepalese communities: orphans, elderly people, defenseless women, disabled and marginalised people, and everyone deeply affected by the devastating earthquake in 2015." Kapali wanted to do something that would honor his friend's spirit. "I want to prove that anybody can be Justin," he explains. "If you are positive, you're going to find positivity in everything." When Kapali wanders the narrow streets of Kathmandu after sundown, he often wonders if his friend might appear around the next corner. "He might be somewhere," he says. "He might be doing meditation in some cave. Maybe he decided to be a yogi for a while, who knows. Even though they found some of his stuff, you never know."

A handful of people opted for a permanent tribute by tattooing a small version of Justin's eagle tattoo or his motto, "Be kind, and do epic shit," onto their arms or bodies. "I will never be like Justin," says Stefano Vergari, Justin's friend from Milan, who had both tattoos, one on each wrist, inked to mark Justin's birthday the March after he disappeared. "But I have something that reminds me that this is the way I want to live." Whenever someone asks him about his tattoos, he recounts the story of his friend who went to the Himalayas to better understand the world. Sitthikorn Thepchanta, the Thai man who still sees Justin as his brother, tattooed the eagle onto his left arm, the outline filled in with feathers as if seen from above; Justin had told him he wanted to see what the eagle saw when it flew, high above the world, gliding from one wind to the next.

I intentionally returned to the Parvati Valley during the exact month when Justin had lived in his cave and trekked to Mantalai Lake. I wanted to see the valley as he had seen it. But much had changed in the area since Justin's trip and since the first time I had visited in early 2017 to report on his disappearance. A new wave of Indian tourists, part of the country's bourgeoning middle class keen to partake in domestic tourism, was cresting. A place like the Parvati Valley, an overnight bus ride from Delhi, had become highly attractive to those looking to escape the crowded, polluted capital for a breath of mountain air. To accommodate the influx, dozens of hotels had popped up along Kasol's riverbank, extending the town both up and down the valley. And more remote destinations, such as the villages of Kalga, opened new homestays and services for tourists.

I left my large backpack in a guesthouse in Kalga, as Justin had done, and hiked the four hours up to Kheerganga. When I had visited in 2017, it had been winter and the camp had been quiet, operating at a bare minimum for off-season pilgrims. It had been easy to spot Satnarayan Rawat's stone hut a few steps down the hill from the steaming hot springs. The faded saffron pennant had still fluttered from a long pole outside. Inside, ashes from Rawat's fire had been wet, as had the grass mats on which Justin and other curious onlookers had sat before the sadhu. On a wall, pinned to the wood beams, were posters of three Hindu gods and goddesses. It had struck me that those three images represented three forces of Justin's life: who he was, who he wanted to be, and what he sought. One was of Saraswati, the Hindu goddess of music, art, and wisdom, depicted sitting in a lotus flower and playing a sitar. Another was of a three-headed, six-armed deity named Dattatreya, who, in this avatar, is a monk, a master of yoga, and a wandering ascetic who has renounced possessions to live as a reclusive sadhu in the wilderness and a protector of animals. The last poster was of Vishnu, the second third in the Hindu trimurti, representing order, preservation, and balance between good and evil, between the forces of creation and the forces of destruction.

The year after my first trip, in 2018, the camp, long the ultimate destination for travelers in the Parvati Valley, had been closed. Under order by the Himachal Pradesh state court, the owners of the temporary cafés and guesthouses that they had erected each spring had been forced to dismantle their establishments for good; the cluster of tarp-and-pole structures that had made up the temporary village had been deemed to be too destructive to the sensitive alpine environment. "It had turned into a hotspot for parties. A lot of trash was being produced here," Pradeep Sangwan, the founder of a local trekking organization that focuses on cleaning up the valley, told the *Times of India*. "Its face had changed in the past 10 years. This move will help Kheerganga return to its original self." But the pilgrims and tourists still came. They were required to obtain a permit from the Forest Department to pitch a tent there, but few bothered with the bureaucracy. They simply camped on the meadow below the hot springs or sought out the boulder caves hidden in the forest.

In 2019, though, the full camp had reappeared, bigger than ever. That summer, as I climbed the familiar hillside toward the hot springs, a high-season hum reverberated around the area, with pilgrims and tourists dipping into and out of canvas tents. Many café and guesthouse owners had struck deals with the police to receive permission to erect rows and rows of canvas and tarpaulin structures, increasing the overnight capacity of Kheerganga to thousands. As I approached the top of the hill, I noticed another significant change: Rawat's hut was gone. The building had been torn down. The flag was gone. The posters were gone. The building's stones and wood had been repurposed elsewhere.

But much in the Parvati Valley had remained the same, including the rate of mysterious disappearances and strange deaths. Over the years, sources in the valley connected with the region's search-and-rescue operations had sent me pictures and videos from dozens of other operations, many involving recovering bodies from the Parvati River. In December 2017, a thirty-five-year-old backpacker from Israel named Matan Orgad vanished after leaving his backpack in a guesthouse in Kasol and setting off on a hike. In early January 2018, his body was found in a river near Grahan village. The following April, a twenty-three-year-old engineer from New Delhi named Aman Awasthi went missing near Malana. Awasthi's father had received text messages from his son's phone requesting that he wire money to him. Then the phone had been turned off. More than a month later, police found Awasthi's walking stick and backpack—and then discovered his body in a gorge near Malana. His father was convinced of foul play. "I am doubtful about the entire sequence of events," he told the *Hindustan Times*, "and want an investigation to be conducted in this matter as it is not a simple accident."

Less than six months after Justin disappeared, Yunus Khan, the deputy commissioner in Kullu, announced the launch of a web-based app for tourists in the region in a bid to offer assistance to those who might encounter trouble while in remote mountainous regions. By signing up, tourists would enable the police to track their movements via the GPS in their phones. But registering was a step that interested few free-footed backpackers. And in a region with spotty cell service, the app was reportedly rarely used.

During my first visit to the Parvati Valley, thigh-high snow in the forest around Kheerganga had put an end to my search for Justin's cave. This time, with humid days and skies that cleared once the morning fog burned off, I set out to try again. I left the bustling camp and quickly made my way across a grassy hill carrying the scrawled map that Andrey Gapon had sent me. I passed sheep grazing on the hillside, crossed a stream, and hiked up into the forest. I quickly emerged into a clearing below Garam Gufa, the cave in which Swapnashree Bhasi had lived that summer. Through the pine trees I could see dozens of truck-sized boulders that had tumbled down from the mountain and come to rest in the forest. The map was vague, so I turned to my phone to study the pair of photographs Justin had taken inside his cave. I began methodically poking my head into any cavern or dark hole formed by boulders in the hope that something would appear familiar. Each one was dark and damp, but some held evidence that a creature—whether human or animal—had taken refuge inside. A scrap of plastic. A piece of forgotten clothing. The smell of musk.

Cave after cave failed to yield a match to what I saw in the photographs. Then I noticed one, formed by a fractured boulder, that required me to scramble up a slab and enter the opening a couple feet off the ground. Inside, the cave was spacious, not quite tall enough to stand erect but deep enough to easily lie down and sleep. I pulled out my phone again and scrolled through the photographs. I lingered on the one that Justin had shared of the inside of his cave, the one in which he sits by the fire reading his book, the entire scene cast in a warm orange glow. It was the photograph that had remained as the banner image of his personal Facebook account, an image that he had clearly held dear.

But the features of the cave where I was crouching weren't lining up with the pictures; the opening was on the wrong side. And then it struck me: Justin had flipped the photo horizontally before he had posted it. My eyes flickered from the images to the walls of the cave as everything began to align. The flat rock that he used as a shelf to hold the few belongings he had brought. The unique zigzagging quartz vein in the wall of granite behind him. I compared what I saw to the final video Justin had uploaded to his blog and the distinct V-shaped opening of the cave was an exact match. I inspected the entrance, and there was even soot from his evening fires still caked on the wall and roof. It was Justin's Himalayan cave, effectively the last place he had called home.

I imagined Justin lying down here to sleep with a fire crackling near the entrance while the monsoon pelted the soft ground outside, as he thought about the many steps that had brought him to this point along his search. How daring, I thought, crouched in the cave, to attempt even a single night alone here, never mind several weeks. Looking out into the forest through the opening in the rock, I thought back to my own first backpacking trip to India, how I had set goals for what I hoped to experience, what I had hoped my own pilgrimage around the country might reveal, and how those expectations had never fully materialized. It struck me that at the core of Justin's travels and life were motivations that I recognized. He valued the connection between people, both face-to-face and on the internet, but sought a calm place in the maelstrom of the world where he could understand the road behind him and where his future would become clear before him. They are questions that can be answered only by stepping back to find space, tuning out to find quiet, or climbing higher to find perspective. They are questions that can spark a shift in thinking or a complete change of direction. And they are questions that compel people to fill a backpack, buy a plane ticket to India, embark on a pilgrimage, and seek a mentor or a mountain. But Justin had taken things a step further. He had climbed mountains and scoured valleys, followed rivers to their sources and paths to their end. He had done what many others have done—only pushed to the furthest extreme. And, in the end, he may have ended up exactly where he wanted to be.

The following day, I hired a mountain guide and struck out at dawn to hike beyond Kheerganga toward Mantalai Lake. As we walked, I felt the pull of the world's tallest mountain range, once produced by the immense pressure of two continents colliding; I understood viscerally why so many pilgrims had trudged along this path to touch the glacial waters that fed into a holy river. I passed through the camp of Gujjar buffalo herders where Justin, Rawat, and Kumar had slept their first night beyond Kheerganga. I stopped in at the hut at Tunda Bhuj and watched the resident sadhu serve tea to a group of pilgrims resting on the grass outside. I followed the trail along the edge of the valley above the river, passing through the final forests before the tree line. And finally, I entered the narrow gorge known as Stone Valley and arrived at the point in the trail above where Justin's belongings had been found along the banks of the Parvati River.

There are some people who prefer standing at the base of a mountain looking up rather than climbing to the top of the mountain to look down. They ascend to where they feel comfortable and go no further, knowing their limits or held back by fear. But Justin did not stop. He sought the mountaintops and the clouds, the beauty and mystery and knowledge that appear only at the extremities of the world. At the pinnacles and peaks can lie fame and recognition and a sense of pride of achievement. And in those heady heights reside higher states, spiritual or physical or simply a clearing of the clouds—a fleeting sense of perspective as you are given a view of both the trail just climbed and the trail ahead. But there is much to be found along the hard path as well, in the act of moving upward and toward something bigger than ourselves, to somewhere closer to the heavens, from a place of darkness to a place of light.

Justin tried to live with intention. He visualized his life as a journey and devoted everything to realizing his dream. When he quit his job in Miami, the decision may have surprised some, but it was in fact part of a calculated plan that had been years in the making. In one of his few personal journals that remain, written in the waning months of 2010 during his first year working for the startup based in Miami, he penned a plan. The one-page entry was a collection of goals, motivations, and intentions that he called "The Hero Project." "If I could do anything in life, what would it be?" he wrote. "If I were infinitely wealthy what would I do? What is it, that just thinking about it, makes me excited to be alive? These all have the same answer: I would make myself into my own hero. Meaning I would create an imaginary hero, someone I wish I could be, and then become him." He then listed qualities such a hero would possess: someone who is "strong, fast and fit" and lives "the old way," a "world traveler" who is both an "expert at self protection and protection of others" and a student of meditation. Even as he worked his glamorous job, seemingly relishing his outward success, he saw it as a means to an end. He wrote that the work was a way to save as much money as possible so that he could fulfill the dream of realizing a life he had always wanted. He concluded that he would start a "travel blog and document the process of self transformation . . . so I will forever remember my adventures."

I believe that Justin did have some sort of transformative experience at Mantalai Lake. In the photographs taken by Sunny Panchal and Nirmal Patel on September 3, he is neither grinning nor frowning. He isn't posing or pretending or posturing for the camera. He appears calm and stoic—wool shawl draped around his shoulders; gray headband wrapped around his head—as if unaffected by the high mountain elements. He looks, in some ways, like a different person.

There are Buddhist *beyul*s, hidden valleys offering refuge and realization, across the Himalayas; some will remain hidden forever, but others will be discovered. There are Hindu *tirtha*s, literal and metaphorical fords across holy rivers, where the gossamer divide between the tangible and the spiritual becomes thin enough to pierce. And there are the mythical gates of Shambhala, where one passes from a land that is known into a land that is unknown. It is possible that Justin reached Mantalai Lake and at a place of Shiva, the supreme transformer of the world, found what he was looking for. His Indian journey had begun at a river, floating calmly along the languid Ganges at Varanasi, watching the orange flames from dozens of cremation pyres rise in the night. And it had culminated beside another holy river. Maybe he had a revelation while sitting near the source of the Parvati River, cross-legged in a sit spot while listening to the minute motions of nature, and finally felt what he had been brought up to seek: "the spirit that moves in all things." Maybe he had a vision, like his idol Stalking Wolf, one that revealed to him his own possible futures, his ways forward, emerging like a reflection from the nascent waters. Siddhartha Gautama spent forty-nine days sitting under a tree before he attained enlightenment and became the Buddha. Justin Alexander Shetler entered the Parvati Valley on July 19 and most likely disappeared the day after he was last photographed near Mantalai Lake on September 3, forty-eight days later. Was Justin, too, on the brink of an epiphany?

I left the trail and scrambled down the slope toward the river's edge, to the spot where Justin's flute–staff had been found upright in the grass, to where the red butane lighter that Andrey Gapon had given him had been recovered. The river was deafening, the water moving so quickly and so violently that it lost form and became abstract and intangible.

Of course, it's also possible that Justin's "spiritual journey" and the moment of realization he had been searching for never materialized. He had constructed the story in his mind, whether for himself or for those who would read about it later, and it was not unfolding as he had imagined. We don't know whether he had been aware that Rawat was going to hire a porter. He could have assumed that he was embarking on a pilgrimage with only a sadhu and it could have been a disappointment for Justin, someone proud of being self-sufficient, to learn that Rawat had decided to hire another man for help. It could have felt like a tarnishing of the story. Justin had also committed to spending weeks meditating and living at the lake, in another cave surrounded by mountains and mist. But he had been instructed by his guide to leave. He had never been one to turn around, climb down, give up, but it's likely that in the end, he spent only a few hours at his destination. Perhaps that was the source of the confrontation that transpired between him and Rawat: Justin had expected the journey to be grander, and it was not.

Maybe Justin's realization wasn't about himself but about the man he trusted to guide him. Maybe, with each foot in elevation they gained, the smoky halo above the sadhu began to dissipate and Justin began to see that the holy man was unable to provide him with anything he sought. Though Rawat purported to be a guru, perhaps Justin had realized that the man held no special ability to help him move from the darkness to the light. Instead, what Justin found may have come less from the mountains or his guide and more from taking the time, step by step, to look inward. What had begun inside his cave at Kheerganga may have culminated inside the cave shelter on the shore of Mantalai Lake—the one the "Russian baba" had lived in for months earlier that summer. There Justin could have found the healing, the peace, and the calm in his heart that he had sought for so many years of his life. In some Buddhist communities across the Himalayas, caves are not only places of spiritual power but also sacred abodes of healing—places to cleanse one of *sgrib*, often translated as "shadow." Justin could have emerged to watch the sun creep down the cliff walls to illuminate the valley floor and feel the warmth and possibility of a new beginning.

Or perhaps what Justin sought had never been there to begin with, no matter how high he climbed or how far he walked. After all, spirituality is a path without end; even enlightenment is just another beginning. What India may offer, in the end, may have less to do with reality and more to do with one's perception of the country, a land dreamed up and built up by those on the outside looking in. Is it more metaphysical than the forests of Washington State? Is it more spiritual than the western coastline of California? Does it bring you any closer to enlightenment than the woods in the Pine Barrens of New Jersey? Maybe at the end of his trail Justin found nothing— the harder he tried, the clearer it became that he was grasping at mist, chasing fleeting tendrils higher and higher into the mountains.

At the end of Joseph Campbell's Hero's Journey, the hero's return to civilization after the apotheosis of the quest is not always certain. After the realization, the hero faces choices: to emerge as a newly made "master of two worlds"—spiritual and material—to pass the "runes of wisdom" onward; or to give up "all attachment to his personal limitations, idiosyncrasies, hopes and fears" and to remain. Or, as Campbell wrote, to "retire again into the heavenly rock dwelling, close the door, and make it fast."

I looked up to the mountains and the gaps in between and wondered if, this time, Justin could have forsaken his belongings, even those he held dear, and heaved them down into a gorge before continuing on and up, higher into the valley. The pass to the Spiti Valley lay just beyond Mantalai Lake, and his weeks living in a cave would have been preparation, a test, for such a journey. He would have walked past the lake and up to the pass, where he would have left the conifer forests and mountain meadows of the Parvati Valley behind and stepped into another land. Looking down to the arid terrain marked by trails that forked to whitewashed monasteries perched on tawny hilltops, to new valleys and new mountains, he would have felt as if he were passing from one world into another. There is only one road into the Parvati Valley, but there are many paths out.

Every summer, the annual monsoon returns to this part of the Indian Himalayas, filling the valley with rain and cloud. The Parvati River surges, swollen and turbulent once again, and flows down from the great peaks past villages and pilgrimage centers where bathers come to wash away their imperfections and sins. As reliable as the rains, the tourists, from around India and from around the world, return, too. Many are aware of the valley's dark history, but the pull is too strong and the possible rewards are deemed to be worth any risk. Alongside the keen and wide-eyed are families and friends making reluctant journeys to the Parvati Valley to follow the shadows of lost loved ones through the mountains.

Every day, pilgrims and tourists travel through the towns of Kasol and Manikaran and Kalga and walk beyond Kheerganga into the upper reaches of the Parvati Valley. They pass a certain spot along the trail, unaware of what was once found there or what might have transpired along this section of the river. They continue on, heads down, until they reach a point where they can finally stop and raise their heads to the light illuminating the mountains, in their journeys to Mantalai Lake and beyond.

ACKNOWLEDGMENTS

I'm exceptionally thankful for the many people who took the time to speak with me, to share their memories and their experiences with Justin. This book, at its heart, follows the story of someone who was lost, and I recognize and appreciate how open and honest those quoted were with me. I wish to express my particular gratitude to those who spoke to me so many times, in particular Suzie Reeb and Terry Shetler, as well as Tracy Frey, Tom McElroy, Andrey Gapon, Amanda Sansoucie, Nishchint Singh Negi, Christofer-Lee Humphreys, and Linda Borini. A particular thank-you to Jonathan Skeels, who provided photographs, videos, and many hours of his time since we first met in Manali in early 2017 regarding the search in India. And to the countless others—friends, acquaintances, and connections of Justin—some named in this book and some not—I'm so grateful for their sharing what they remembered about him from various points in his life.

An enormous thank-you to the people of the Parvati Valley, who, despite the complicated history of their home, see the beauty that it so clearly holds above all else. It is a place of irresistible energy and mystery, and I will surely be back. In particular to Raju at the Snow Line guesthouse, who provided the perfect mountain-view base to report and write on two occasions, and to Shiva Thakur for expertly guiding me around the valley.

Thanks to Erin Berger, who edited my feature article for *Outside* magazine, titled "Lost in the Valley of Death," of which elements appear in this book. To Shreya Kalra for helping with translations and research in newspaper archives in Hindi. And to my early draft readers—writers, editors, and journalists whose work I so admire, including Kate Harris, Carmine Starnino, and Kevin Patterson— for providing such thoughtful feedback and support along the way. A special thank-you to Stephanie Nolen, former South Asia bureau chief for the *Globe and Mail*, who, in 2012, agreed to take me on as an intern based in New Delhi and who taught me so much about reporting.

I am infinitely grateful and fortunate to have been able to work with such wonderful and talented editors: Jennifer Barth at Harper and Lynn Henry at Knopf Canada. And to my agent, Stuart Krichevsky, for his kindness, feedback, and championing of this book from our very first phone call and throughout.

To my father, whose stories inspired me to first travel to India in 2008, and to my mother, who was certain long before I was that I might write a book set there. And to my wife, Élise, who was beside me with her heart and her support along every step that was this book's journey, and to our son, Sacha, a Sagittarius, a future traveler, who was born amid drafts.

NOTES ON SOURCES

AUTHOR'S NOTE

The *Times of India* article referenced was Suresh Sharma's "US Man Missing in Kullu Wanted to Live Hermit's Life," published on October 17, 2016. I pitched a 5,000-word feature article to *Outside* magazine on December 1; the pitch was accepted on December 15, and the article was published on December 13, 2018, as "Lost in the Valley of Death." Portions of the article appear in this book.

PROLOGUE

The scene inside Justin's cave in Kheerganga was re-created based on personal observation, as well as on media Justin posted online, namely the photographs he posted to Instagram on August 13, 2016, and the video titled "Himalayan Caves and the Naga Baba" that he uploaded to his YouTube account on August 19, 2016, as well as to his social media accounts, and embedded above his final blog post. The video shows him descending into one cave and lighting a fire within his principal cave, which shows its distinct V-shaped opening.

The Parvati Valley's nicknames have appeared in many publications over many years, including the *Guardian* on April 20, 2002, and the *Lake Oswego Review* on October 8, 2016. The number of missing international tourists comes from an internal document maintained by the Kullu police titled "Country Wise [*sic*] List of Missing Foreigners Since 1991," as well as extensive research into newspaper archives of the *Times of India*, the *Hindu*, and the *Indian Express*, among others.

CHAPTER 1: TRAILHEAD

Much of the description of the Parvati Valley came from personal experience, observation, and reporting during two trips, in March 2017 and August–September

2019. The scene of Justin in Kalga the day he returned to Kheerganga to begin his trek to Mantalai Lake came from several interviews with Andrey Gapon.

CHAPTER 2: VISIONS

The details of Justin's early life came from many interviews with Suzie Reeb and Terry Shetler. The life of Stalking Wolf was written about in many books by Tom Brown, Jr., most extensively in *Grandfather: A Native American's Life-long Search for Truth and Harmony with Nature* (New York: Berkley, 1993). Chris Kenworthy had died many years earlier, so her tutelage of Justin came from Suzie Reeb's recollection as well as from Chris's husband, Bill. Jon Young narrated Justin's first arrival at the Wilderness Awareness School in a speech during the March 10, 2019, service for Justin in San Francisco, California, and it is also mentioned in Young's book *What the Robin Knows: How Birds Reveal the Secrets of the Natural World* (New York: Houghton Mifflin Harcourt, 2012). The details of Justin's time at the WAS came largely from interviews with Jason Knight, Aidan Young, Doniga Markegard, Matt Wild, and Anne Osbaldeston.

The second quote from Tom Brown, Jr., comes from *The Tracker: The True Story of Tom Brown, Jr.* (Hoboken, NJ: Prentice-Hall, 1978). The history of the Tracker School came from Brown's own books as well as Tom Dunkel's "Walk Like an Apache," published in the July 1987 issue of *New Jersey Monthly*; Richard Wolkomir's "A Natural Man," published in the June–July 1984 issue of *National Wildlife Magazine*; and Robert Hanley's "Woodsman's Skill in Tracking Led to Rape-Robbery Suspect in Jersey," published in the *New York Times* on November 3, 1977. Some of the criticism of Brown and the question over Stalking Wolf's identity has been posted on Wildwood Survival Forums and on the website Tracker Trail (http://trackertrail.com), as well as in Aaron Lake Smith's "Getting Back to Basics at a Primitivist School," published in *Vice* on May 14, 2015, and in Thomas King's *The Inconvenient Indian: A Curious Account of Native People in North America* (Toronto: Doubleday Canada, 2017).

The information relating to Justin's years at the Tracker School came from interviews with former instructors and students, including Doniga Markegard, Dan Stanchfield, Tom McElroy, Tracy Frey, Aidan Young, Brittany Ceres, and Liam Purvis.

Justin's early spiritual background came from interviews with Suzie Reeb and Terry Shetler, as well as John and Kay Marikos. Quotes about the spirituality of Stalking Wolf, Tom Brown, Jr., and the Tracker School came from Tom Brown, Jr.'s, *The Vision: The Dramatic True Story of One Man's Search for Enlightenment* (New York: Berkley, 1988).

CHAPTER 3: LET IT GO

Tracy Frey, Aaron Alvarez, Layla Brooklyn Allman, and Gary Reikes, among others, provided information relating to Justin's years in San Francisco. Details of Justin's trip to Nepal in 2006 came from interviews with Tashi Ghale and Kishwor Sedhai. How that trip gave Justin "purpose" came from a podcast interview titled "From Homeless to Retired at 31—World Nomad Justin Alexander," published in *OpenWorld* magazine on September 16, 2014: "From that point on," he said, "I had purpose again." Justin's trip to Thailand was described in interviews with Sitthikorn Thepchanta.

Information on Punchface, including the band's description, came from bios uploaded to sites including MySpace, Broadjam, and Sonicbids. Lyrics to songs, including "Liberate" and "Firefly," were published with the permission of former band member Ryan Tapley. The quote about the band's rise came from a review in the April 2009 issue of *Fringe* magazine titled "Punchface: Hot in Their Own Way" by Eric Davis. Many of the band's shows were documented on Facebook and MySpace.

Information about Justin's years in Miami, Florida, came from interviews with sources including Robert Gutierrez, Ashley Keenan, Bishal Kapali, Stefano Vergari, Suzie Reeb, and Terry Shetler.

CHAPTER 4: FIRST STEPS

Justin published his first blog post, titled "I'm 32, and Last week I Retired," to his website, Adventures of Justin, in January 2014. Many of the descriptions of his life on the road after quitting his job came from what he posted online on Instagram, Facebook, YouTube, and his blog. One of the books he carried was Rolf Potts's *Vagabonding: An Uncommon Guide to the Art of Long-Term World Travel* (New York: Villard Books, 2002). His "highest ideal" quote came from a Q and A with Lavi Nair for *Lavi Was Here* titled "Stories from the Road: Justin Alexander," posted on July 6, 2015. "I feel like belonging . . ." came from a podcast episode of *Tangentially Speaking* with Christopher Ryan titled "143—Justin Alexander (Nomadic World Traveler)," released September 14, 2015. *Baraka*, directed by Ron Fricke, was released in 1992 by Magidson Films. "I wasn't really proud . . ." came from episode 143 of *Tangentially Speaking*. The history of other similar seekers came from Henry David Thoreau's *Walden* (Boston: Ticknor and Fields, 1854), David Robert's *Finding Everett Ruess* (New York: Broadway Paperbacks, 2011), and Jon Krakauer's *Into the Wild* (New York: Villard Books, 1996). "Walking that razor's edge" came from episode 143 of *Tangentially Speaking*, referencing W. Somerset Maugham's *The Razor's Edge* (New York: Doubleday, 1944). The legend of the Apache Native American community was told to me by Matt Wild. The seven-part series of Bill Moyers interviewing Joseph Campbell was titled *Joseph Campbell and the Power of Myth*, broadcast on PBS in 1988 shortly after Campbell's death in October 1987. The Hero's Journey was distilled and quoted from Campbell's book *The Hero with a Thousand Faces* (New York: Pantheon Books, 1949).

Justin's motorcycle journey around the United States was re-created using his social media posts, videos, and blog posts, as well as numerous interviews with people he met and crossed paths with along the way, including Linda Borini, Jonathan Skeels, Justin Chatwin, Tracy Frey, Amanda Sansoucie, Aidan Young, Layla Brooklyn Allman, Indhi Korth, Robert Gutierrez, and Tom McElroy, among many others.

The "I think people are drawn . . ." came from his August 2015 blog post titled "Motorcycle Adventuring in America." Henry David Thoreau wrote "To live at home . . ." in a letter to Harrison Blake, in Joseph J. Moldenhauer's "Thoreau to Blake: Four Letters Re-edited," in *Texas Studies in Literature and Language* 8, no. 1 (Spring 1966). "I've experienced so little . . ." came from a Q and A with HighExistence titled "15 Questions on Travel, Life, and Adventure Answered by the World's Coolest World Traveler." The account of the robbery was documented in a blog post titled "18,000 Motorcycle Miles Through the American West," published in December 2015. The Jack London quote that Justin reproduced on Instagram comes from *Jack London's Tales of Adventure*, edited by Irving Shephard (New York: Doubleday, 1956), but no document of the quote exists. "Maybe I'll be single . . ." comes from the podcast interview Justin gave with *OpenWorld* magazine.

CHAPTER 5: ALOBAR

Justin's travels in the Philippines, Thailand, and Nepal were re-created through what he posted to Instagram and Facebook as well as interviews with sources including Leah Lañojan, Christopher Ryan, Sitthikorn Thepchanta, Linda Borini, Bishal Kapali, Hank Stowers, Kishwor Sedhai, Tashi Ghale, and Jacqueline Woo. The second episode of *Tangentially Speaking* featuring Justin was partly recorded in Thailand, titled "167—Adventures of Justin Alexander (Return Visit)" and released February 18, 2016. Stowers and Justin discussed the novel *Shantaram* (Melbourne: Scribe Publications, 2003). The references to "gymnosophists" came from Ulrich Wilcken's *Alexander the Great* (New York: W. W. Norton, 1932), and the quote from Marco Polo came from chapter 26 of *The Travels of Marco Polo* (Edinburgh: Oliver & Boyd, 1845). The history and culture of sadhus came from publications including Kirin Narayan's *Storytellers, Saints, and Scoundrels: Folk Narrative in Hindu Religious Teaching* (Philadelphia: University of Pennsylvania Press, 1989), Baba Rampuri's *Autobiography of a Sadhu: A Journey into Mystic India* (Rochester, NY: Destiny Books, 2005), John Campbell Oman's *The Mystics, Ascetics and Saints of India; a Study of Sadhuism, with an Account of the Yogis, Sanyasis, Bairagis and Other Strange Hindu Sectarians* (London: T. Fisher Unwin, 1903), Sondra L. Hausner's *Wandering with Sadhus: Ascetics in the Hindu Himalayas* (Bloomington: Indiana University Press, 2007), Bansi Dhar Tripathi's *Sadhus of India: The Sociological View* (Bombay: Popular Prakashan, 1978), and Dolf Hartsuiker's *Sadhus: India's Mystic Holy Men* (Rochester, NY: Inner Traditions, 1993). The account of Mohan Singh was documented in Shankhadeep Choudhury's "Indian Holy Man's Roll of a Lifetime Stopped at Border," published in the *Los Angeles Times* on September 25, 2004.

CHAPTER 6: PILGRIMS

My personal experience in India noted in this chapter took place during my first trip to the subcontinent between August 2008 and May 2009. As a teenager I had read Mark Twain's *Following the Equator: A Journey Around the World* (Hartford, CT: American Publishing Company, 1897). The Beatles' time in India in 1968 has been well documented, including in Ajoy Bose's *Across the Universe: The Beatles in India* (New Delhi: Penguin Random House India, 2018), as well as in Allan Kozinn's "Meditation on the Man Who Saved the Beatles," published in the *New York Times* on February 7, 2008. Rory MacLean's *Magic Bus: On the Hippie Trail from Istanbul to India* (London: Viking, 2006) thoroughly narrated the Hippie Trail years. Early guidebooks from that period include *Across Asia on the Cheap* (Melbourne: Lonely Planet, 1973) and *Head East* (West Somerville, MA: Head Guide Publications, 1973). Marco Polo documented his journey to the Indian subcontinent in *The Travels of Marco Polo*. The history of the Theosophical Society was noted in Alex Norman's "The Turn East: 'New' Religious Consciousness and Travel to India After Blavatsky," published in *Journeys and Destinations: Studies in Travel, Meaning, and Identity* (Newcastle upon Tyne: Cambridge Scholars Publishing, 2013), 129–57. Philip Goldberg's *American Veda: From Emerson and the Beatles to Yoga and Meditation: How Indian Spirituality Changed the West* (New York: Harmony Books, 2010) was an excellent source for the influence of Indian culture on the West. Notes on Ralph Waldo Emerson came from papers including Dale Riepe's "Emerson and Indian Philosophy," published in *Journal of the History of Ideas* 28, no. 1 (January–March 1967), and Russell B. Goodman's "East-West Philosophy in Nineteenth-Century America: Emerson and Hinduism," published in *Journal of the History of Ideas* 51, no. 4 (October–December 1990). Emerson's quote "The first books . . ." can be found in *Journals and Miscellaneous Notebooks of Ralph Waldo Emerson*, vol. 10, edited by William H. Gilman, Alfred R. Ferguson, George P. Clark, and Merrell R. Davis (Cambridge, MA: Harvard University Press, 1960). The Henry

David Thoreau quote comes from *Walden, Or, Life in the Woods* (London: J. M. Dent, 1908).

Two books that heavily influenced travelers to visit India were Paul Brunton's *A Search in Secret India* (London: Rider, 1934) and Paramahansa Yogananda's *Autobiography of a Yogi* (New York: Philosophical Library, 1946). George Harrison's inspiration from *Autobiography* was noted in John O. Mahony's "'A Hodgepodge of Hash, Yoga and LSD,'" published in the *Guardian* on June 4, 2008. Hitendra Wadhwa wrote about Steve Jobs in an article in *Inc.* titled "Steve Jobs's Secret to Greatness: Yogananda," published on June 21, 2015. More details of Jobs's travels in India came from Walter Isaacson's *Steve Jobs* (New York: Simon & Schuster, 2011). The note about his memorial service came from Marc Benioff, the CEO of Salesforce, in "Marc Benioff Explains Steve Jobs' Spirituality and Chides Apple," published by CNET on September 10, 2013. Records of Westerners who moved to India are documented in Malcolm Tillis's *New Lives: 54 Interviews with Westerners on Their Search for Spiritual Fulfilment in India* (Varanasi, India: Indica Books, 2004), first published in a shorter format as *Turning East* (New York: Paragon House, 1989), and in the 2001 documentary *Last Hippie Standing*, produced and directed by Marcus Robbin. Baba Rampuri (William A. Gans) recorded his life in *Autobiography of a Sadhu: A Journey into Mystic India* (Rochester, NY: Destiny Books, 2010), originally published as *Autobiography of a Blue-Eyed Sadhu* (New York: Bell Tower, 2005), as did Alfred Emmanuel Sorensen in *Dancing with the Void: The Innerstandings of a Rare-Born Mystic* by Betty Camhi and Gurubaksh Rai (San Diego: Blue Dove Press, 2001). Records of famous seekers who visited Kalimath Ridge and Almora are noted in books including Robert Greenfield's *Timothy Leary: A Biography* (Boston: Harcourt, 2006), Deborah Baker's *A Blue Hand: The Beats in India* (New York: Viking, 2008), and Robert Thurman and Tad Wise's *Circling the Sacred Mountain: A Spiritual Adventure Through the Himalayas* (New York: Bantam Books, 2000), as well as Shikha Tripathi's "The Highs of Kasar Devi, Where Bob Dylan, Cat Stevens, and Nehru Vacationed," published in *National Geographic Traveller India* on September 14, 2016.

Information on India Syndrome came from several interviews with Régis Airault and Sunil Mittal. Airault provided an advance copy of the English translation of his book *Fous de l'Inde: Délires d'Occidentaux et sentiment océanique* (Paris: Éditions Payot & Rivages, 2000).

CHAPTER 7: SOLITUDE

Justin's travels from Varanasi to the Parvati Valley were re-created through his posts to his Instagram, Facebook, and YouTube accounts and on his blog, as well as through interviews with sources including Brianna Welsh, Alexander Gurov, Parakram Hazarika, Linda Borini, and Christofer-Lee Humphreys.

Descriptions and history of Varanasi came from personal experience, as well as Diana L. Eck's *Banaras: City of Light* (New York: Alfred A. Knopf, 1982). Information about pilgrimage, *tirtha*, and the Khumb Mela came from books including Surinder Mohan Bhardwaj's *Hindu Places of Pilgrimage in India: A Study of Cultural Geography* (Berkeley: University of California Press, 1973), Ian Reader's *Pilgrimage: A Very Short Introduction* (Oxford: Oxford University Press, 2015), and Diana L. Eck's *India: A Sacred Geography* (New York: Three Rivers Press, 2012).

Numerous spiritual memoirs, set in whole or in part in India, have been published over the years, including Elizabeth Gilbert's *Eat Pray Love: One Woman's Search for Everything Across Italy, India, and Indonesia* (London: Bloomsbury, 2006), Marilyn Stablein's *Sleeping in Caves: A Sixties Himalayan Memoir* (Rhinebeck, NY: Monkfish Book Publishing, 2006), and Sarah Macdonald's *Holy Cow: An Indian Adventure* (New York: Bantam Books, 2002). The quote by Rudyard Kipling comes from his novel *Kim* (London: Macmillan, 1901). The Dalai Lama wrote about *beyul* in his introduction to Ian Baker's *The Heart of the World: A Journey to Tibet's Lost Paradise* (New York: Penguin Books, 2004). The story of Padmasambhava came from Yeshe Tsogyal's *The Lotus-Born: The Life Story of Padmasambhava* (Hong Kong: Rangjung Yeshe Publications, 2004). Legends of Shambhala were found in Victoria LePage's *Shambhala: The Fascinating Truth Behind the Myth of Shangri-la* (Wheaton, IL: Quest Books, 1996), Edwin Bernbaum's *The Way to Shambhala: A Search for the Mythical Kingdom Beyond the Himalayas* (Los Angeles: J. P. Tarcher, 1989), James Hilton's *Lost Horizon* (London: Macmillan, 1949, first published 1933), and Talbot Mundy's *Om: The Secret of the Abor Valley* (New York: Avon Books, 1967, first published ca. 1924).

Many of the descriptions of the Parvati Valley are based on personal experience and reporting. Dilaram Shabab's *Kullu: Himalayan Abode of the Divine* (New Delhi: Indus Publishing Company, 1996) was an excellent source for the history of the Kullu and Parvati Valleys. The history of Malana relied in part on Richard Axelby's "Hermit Village or Zomian Republic? An Update on the Political Socioeconomy of a Remote Himalayan Community," published in *European Bulletin of Himalayan Research* 46 (2015): 35–61; Rajiv Giroti and Indu Talwar's paper "The Most Ancient Democracy in the World Is a Genetic Isolate: An Autosomal and Y-Chromosome Study of the Hermit Village of Malana (Himachal Pradesh, India)," published in *Human Biology* 82, no. 2 (April 2010): 123–41; Molly Charles's "Drug Trade in Himachal Pradesh: Role of Socio-Economic Changes," published in *Economic and Political Weekly* 36, no. 26 (January 2001): 2433–39; and Kevin Fedarko's "Bad Trip" in *Outside* magazine's January 2005 issue. The accounts of bus accidents in the Parvati Valley were reported in "36 Die as Bus Falls into River in Kullu," published in the *Times of India* on September 9, 2002; "6 Killed, 29 Missing as Bus Falls into Himachal River," published by the Indo-Asian News Service on July 23,

2015; and Dipender Manta's "Kullu Bus Accident Leaves More Than Physical Scars," published in the *Hindustan Times* on July 31, 2015.

CHAPTER 8: THE VALLEY OF DEATH

The accounts of the tourists who have disappeared in the Parvati Valley since the early 1990s were based on interviews, newspaper and magazine articles, blog and forum posts, and police records. I interviewed Piotr Muschalik and Gra Studzinska Cavour for the account of Bruno Muschalik, which was also reported on in Suresh Sharma's "Polish Girl Drives Online Search for BF Missing in HP," published in the *Times of India* on August 28, 2015; and Beata Czuma's "Gdzie jesteś, Bruno? Wkraczał w dorosłe życie. Zaginął w dolinie cieni," published in *Wiadomośki* on July 19, 2019. Many of the early disappearances were recorded in an internal document maintained by the Kullu police titled "Country Wise [*sic*] List of Missing Foreigners Since 1991" and were confirmed and described through reports and interviews. Details of the account of Odette Houghton came from an article her father published in *That's Life* magazine, accessed via the Australian Missing Persons Register (http://www.australianmissingpersonsregister .com). The disappearances of Marianne Heer, Gregory John Powell, and Ian Mogford were reported in articles including Jason Burke's "Death Valley," published in the *Guardian* on December 6, 2003, and Sandra Laville's "Lost in a Valley at 'the End of the World,'" published in the *Telegraph* on September 3, 2005. The details of the disappearance of Ardavan Taherzadeh came from a Wattpad post by Danyael Halprin titled "Missing in India" and the documentary *Missing in Kullu* (SWPictures, 1997). The account of Nadav Mintzer came from Jenny Booth's "Valley of the Gods Is a Place of Death," published in the *Sunday Times* on October 4, 2003; that of Maarten de Bruijn came from translations of Jan Poesen's "Dag van vermisten: Vader gaat terug naar Himalaya," published by *EenVandaag* on August 28, 2015, and Gerben van 't Hof's "Niemand snapt hoe het voelt als je kind vermist is," published by AD on April 9, 2014; that of Alexei Ivanov was mentioned in "Death Valley," published in the *Guardian*; that of Francesco Gatti came largely from his blog at http://francescogatti.blog.excite.it/; that of Daniel Mountwitten came from Hilary Leila Krieger's "Death Valley," published in the *Jerusalem Post* on October 17, 2005; that of Amichai Steinmetz was recorded in Sara Yoheved Rigler's "The Search for Amichai," published on Aish.com on September 13, 2009, and "Missing Israeli's Father Ends Search in Himachal," published by the Indo-Asian News Service on October 19, 2009; that of Vladislav Kesternov was noted on the Kullu Police crime blog on May 19, 2011; and that of Petr Slanina came from Suresh Sharma's "2 Foreigners Found Dead in Himachal Pradesh," published in the *Times of India* on August 7, 2013. The account of Martin Young and his family was reported by the BBC in Jill McGivering's "India's Valley of Death" on September 4, 2000; that of Dror Sheck in Shelly Paz's "Slain Backpacker Dror Sheck Laid to Rest," published in the *Jerusalem Post* on July 18, 2007; and that of Alessandro Tesi in "Italian Found Dead at Guesthouse in Kullu," published in the *Hindustan Times* on January 30, 2012.

The story of Charles Sobhraj was documented in Richard Neville and Julie Clarke's *On the Trail of the Serpent: The Life and Crimes of Charles Sobhraj* (New York: Random House, 1979). Information about datura was found in Marcello Pennacchio, Lara Jefferson, and Kayri Havens's *Uses and Abuses of Plant-Derived Smoke: Its Ethnobotany as Hallucinogen, Perfume, Incense, and Medicine* (Oxford: Oxford University Press, 2010); C. Claiborne Ray's "Poisonous Plants," published in the *New York Times*, August 13, 2018; *Missing in Kullu* (SWPictures, 1997); and Vishal V. Koulapur et al.'s "Poisoning Due to Datura—a Rare Case Report," *Indian Journal of Forensic and Community Medicine* 2, no. 1 (January–March 2015): 64–66.

In 1956, Colin Rosser presented his dissertation on Malana titled "The Political System of a Himalayan Community" at the School of Oriental and African Studies at the University of London; he also published "A 'Hermit' Village in Kullu" in the *Economic Weekly* in 1952. The *Strain Hunters* documentary episode titled "Strain Hunters India Expedition" was broadcast in October 2010. The story of Galeno Orazi ("Glenu") is mentioned in P. Krishna Gopinath's "Malana: The Valley of Cannabis," published in the *Hindu* on June 9, 2018; the article about Orazi's arrest was titled "Italian Suspect in Drug Trade Arrested Near Malana," published in the *Indian Express* on November 4, 2010. Foreigners who have lived long term in the Parvati Valley have been well documented in articles including "Death Valley" in the *Guardian*, "The Skunk Invasion," published in *Outlook* on June 24, 2002, and Dipender Manta's "The Curious Case of Missing Foreigners," published in the *Himachal Tribune* on December 1, 2018.

The search-and-rescue operations in the Parvati Valley were outlined in interviews with police officers including Nischchint Singh Negi, trekking company operators including Chhape Ram Negi, Shiv Ram Thakur, and Ashish Chauhan, and search-and-rescue outfit owners including Yechiel "Hilik" Magnus.

The warnings about the Parvati Valley were included in *Lonely Planet: India*, 16th ed. (Oakland, CA: Lonely Planet Publications, 2015) and *The Rough Guide to India*, 9th ed. (London: Rough Guides, 2013).

The disappearance of Shota Sakai was documented in the Kullu police's internal document and confirmed with interviews with a friend of his and a fellow traveler who had met him on the road.

CHAPTER 9: THE CAVE

The description of the trail from Kalga to Kheerganga, as well as the camp itself, is based on personal experience over two reporting trips. Justin's three weeks living in his cave were re-created based on what he later posted online, as well as interviews with people he met there, including Roy Roberts, Andrey Gapon, Christofer-Lee Humphreys, and Swapnashree Bhasi. Justin's financial situation was based on interviews with Robert Gutierrez, Linda Borini, Bishal Kapali, and Stefano Vergari, among others. Bhasi also wrote about her experience living in a cave at Kheerganga in a Q and A for Indian Women Blog (https://www.indian womenblog.org) titled "IWB Talks to the Girl Who Shaved Her Head, Slept in Caves & Swept Floors to Find Herself," published on October 23, 2017.

Satnarayan Rawat's name was published in several media outlets as "Satyan-arayan Rawat," but I've used the name as it is spelled on the official report composed by the Kullu police, as well as how it appears on his autopsy report.

Justin posted the quote from Sterling Hayden's *Wanderer* (New York: Alfred A. Knopf, 1963). References to caves in literature appear in Dan Millman's *Way of the Peaceful Warrior: A Book That Changes Lives* (Tiburon, CA: H. J. Kramer, 2000); Don Miguel Ruiz's *The Four Agreements: A Practical Guide to Personal Freedom* (San Rafael, CA: Amber-Allen Publishing, 1997); E. M. Forster's *A Passage to India* (London: Edward Arnold, 1924); Tom Brown, Jr.'s, *The Vision: The Dramatic True Story of One Man's Search for Enlightenment* (New York: Berkley, 1988); and Vicki Mackenzie's *Cave in the Snow: Tenzin Palmo's Quest for Enlightenment* (New York: Bloomsbury Publishing, 1998). The book Justin was reading in his cave was Eric Weiner's *The Geography of Bliss: One Grump's Search for the Happiest Places in the World* (New York: Twelve, 2008).

Justin's quotes "Religion is a very . . ." and "path to truth" came from the podcast interview he gave for *OpenWorld* magazine. Religion and spirituality came up in many interviews with sources, including Suzie Reeb, Terry Shetler, Tracy Frey, Kishwor Sedhai, Brittany Ceres, Layla Brooklyn Allman, and Indhi Korth, who narrated her and Justin's trip to South America.

CHAPTER 10: FINDING FREEDOM

The time between Justin's three weeks in his cave and his return to Kheerganga to embark to Mantalai Lake was re-created through interviews with sources including Nirmal Patel, Sunny Panchal, Archana Singh, Andrey Gapon, Christofer-Lee Humphreys, Villas Bambroo, Linda Borini, Suzie Reeb, and Terry Shetler. It also relied on what Justin posted online.

CHAPTER 11: SEARCHING

The departure of Justin from Kalga to Kheerganga and his trek to Mantalai Lake with Satnarayan Rawat were re-created based on personal experience and observation as well as interviews with at least a dozen trekkers who had hiked all or parts of the route, including Andrey Gapon, Sunny Panchal, Nirmal Patel,

Swapnashree Bhasi, Villas Bambroo, Brijeshwar Kunwar, and Tomasz Biskup. Video and photographs taken by Jonathan Skeels, Andrey Gapon, and many travel blogs and social media posts also helped. Several guidebooks including Minakshi Chaudhry's *Guide to Trekking in Himachal: Over 65 Treks and 100 Destinations* (New Delhi: Indus Publishing Company, 2003) were helpful in describing the route.

Other information in this chapter came from interviews with several people including Suzie Reeb, Tracy Frey, and Amanda Sansoucie. The ex-girlfriend wished our interview relating to Justin's history to remain anonymous. The lyrics of "Let It Go" were published with the permission of former band member Ryan Tapley.

Justin posted the video described, titled "Himalayan Caves and the Naga Baba," to his YouTube account on August 19, 2016, as well as to his social media accounts and embedded above his final blog post.

CHAPTER 12: ALARM

The first days of alarm and the beginning of the search effort, in both the United States and India, were described to me in interviews with many sources including Suzie Reeb, Linda Borini, Christofer-Lee Humphreys, Andrey Gapon, Villas Bambroo, Swapnashree Bhasi, Tracy Frey, Tom McElroy, Jonathan Skeels, Robert Gutierrez, and John and Kay Marikos. Many of the early internal communications among the search team were provided by Jonathan Skeels and Tracy Frey. Michael Yon described his brief conversations with the search team, as well as his search for Gary Stevenson, which he wrote about for *Vice* in a September 30, 2006, article titled "American Aghori." The earlier interview with Stevenson was conducted by Hannah Thomas and originally published in the *Student*, the newspaper of the University of Edinburgh, in 2005, and excerpted by *Harper's* magazine and published in its January 2006 issue.

The next stage of the search included interviews with sources including Sunny Panchal, Nirmal Patel, and Tomasz Biskup. Jonathan Skeels provided the search-and-rescue quote from Magnus International Search & Rescue.

CHAPTER 13: INTO THE MIST

The on-the-ground search in India was described during numerous interviews with Jonathan Skeels and Suzie Reeb, as well as other sources in India, including Ashish Chauhan, Brijeshwar Kunwar, Nishchint Singh Negi, Christofer-Lee Humphreys, and in the United States, including Tracy Frey, Tom McElroy, Linda Borini, and Robert Gutierrez. Much of the internal communication was detailed in Slack, WhatsApp, and Facebook messages provided to me by several sources. Skeels provided the video of the interrogation of Satnarayan Rawat, which I later had translated in full. Even though Skeels had recorded the sadhu's interrogation, he did not record the first interrogation of Anil Kumar, the porter; what was said is based on interviews with Skeels, Reeb, and Kunwar. (Anil Kumar's name was published in several media outlets as "Anil Singh," but I've used the name as it is spelled on the official report composed by the Kullu police.) Skeels provided a copy of the First Information Report filed by Suzie Reeb.

The account of Kirill Pomerantsev was reported in "Russian Hermit Is Expelled After 15 Years in India," published in *Russia Beyond* on February 27, 2011; the account of Mark Hamieau is documented in Suresh Sharma's "The Kullu Police Have Arrested Mark Hamieau, a French National Under Foreigners Act at Thela Village of Kullu. He Was Found Without Visa and Passport," published in the *Times of India* on March 1, 2011; and Suresh Sharma's "Himachal Pradesh Becoming Unsafe for Tourists; Police Have No Details," published in the *Times of India* on June 6, 2013. Ryan Chambers's story was based on numerous reports including "Lost on a Journey to Free His Mind," published in the *Sydney Morning Herald* on September 19, 2005. Details of the story of Jonathan Spollen came from numerous articles including Scott Carney's "Death on the Path to Enlightenment," published in *Details* magazine on September 26, 2012; Roland Hughes's "The Disappearance of Jonathan Spollen," published by the BBC on February 27, 2017; "Mother of Missing Irish Man in India Still 'Determined' to Find Him Two Years On," published in thejournal.ie on February 4, 2014; and Jessica Ravitz's "Lost and Found: Missing in Rishikesh, India, the 'Land of Gods,'" published by CNN on June 7, 2014. Many of the details relating to his case and the search came from posts on the travel forum India Mike (https://www.indiamike.com), in particular the thread "Have you seen Jonathan Spollen? Missing in Rishikesh since February 3rd, 2012."

Andrey Gapon uploaded a video titled "About Justin" to his YouTube account on October 4, 2016. Mike Spencer Bown, the author of *The World's Most Travelled Man: A Twenty-Three-Year Odyssey to and Through Every Country on the Planet* (Madeira Park, BC: Douglas and McIntyre, 2017), provided details of his conversations with Justin as well as the messages between them over the two years they had been in contact.

The search in the high valley and the discovery of some of Justin's belongings in Stone Valley were described by Jonathan Skeels and Brijeshwar Kunwar and re-created using video and audio recorded by Skeels. The two drone operators, a father and son, had been called up from Delhi by Skeels, and they had slowly followed Skeels and Kunwar down the valley but had not been present when Justin's belongings had been found.

The lyrics from "I Will Find You," the theme song from *The Last of the Mohicans*, was written by Dougie MacLean, composed by Trevor Jones and Randy Edelman, performed by Clannad, and released in 1992.

The account of Satnarayan Rawat's death was included in the final report issued by Kullu police about Justin's disappearance and told to me by two Kullu police officers.

CHAPTER 14: STONE VALLEY

The later weeks of the search were re-created based on interviews with sources including Suzie Reeb, Jonathan Skeels, Nishchint Singh Negi, Tracy Frey, and Daya Ram Singh. The Kullu police's response was based on interviews with police officers, principally Nishchint Singh Negi and Daya Ram Singh, as well as several others who spoke to me anonymously. It was also based on statements given to the media, including articles on Mid-Day: Vinod Kumar Menon's "Missing American Trekker Justin Shetler's Mother to Return Home Alone," published on November 2, 2016, and Menon's "Missing Trekker's Pals Ride to Ladakh to Fulfil His Dream," published on November 8, 2016. The speculation about drugs came from interviews with the members of the search team, as well as records of internal communications.

Mid-Day reported on the death of Satnarayan Rawat in Menon's "Curious Case of Missing US National and Dead Sadhu," published on October 24, 2016, and Menon's "US National Missing: Sadhu's Death Points to Grave Lapses," published on October 30, 2016. The autopsy report conducted on Rawat was provided by two sources. Information on custodial deaths came from the transcript of a letter by India's National Human Rights Commission on December 14, 1993, and the Human Rights Watch report titled "'Bound by Brotherhood': India's Failure to End Killings in Police Custody," published on December 19, 2016. Information regarding the interrogation of Satnarayan Rawat was provided to me by two police sources, and was also mentioned in Ariel Sophia Bardi's "Death on the Hippie Trail," published in *Slate* on January 2, 2017.

The video of the second interrogation of Anil Kumar was provided by Jonathan Skeels and translated in full. Bhinder Baba's account was based on an interview conducted in his hut at Tunda Bhuj, where I also interviewed Lal Hussein, the brother of Ali. I interviewed Ali Hussein farther down the trail near the Gujjar camp.

The contents of Justin's large backpack, recovered from the Om Shanti guesthouse in Kalga, were documented by Jonathan Skeels.

CHAPTER 15: FOOTSTEPS

Suzie Reeb, Jonathan Skeels, Tom McElroy, and Tracy Frey, among others, described the final days of the search in India, and many others offered their thoughts on what might have happened to Justin.

The quote from Joseph Campbell was given during the interview for the PBS series with Bill Moyers and transcribed in their coauthored book, *The Power of Myth* (New York: Anchor Books, 1991). "The place where you . . ." comes from Tom Brown, Jr.'s, *The Tracker*.

The Facebook comments from Justin's followers regarding his disappearance were posted predominantly under Reeb's final update on Facebook, titled "IN CELEBRATION OF JUSTIN ALEXANDER SHETLER."

The story of the "Russian baba" was told to me by several sources in the valley, one of whom had met him, and his death was reported by the *Tribune* in an article titled "Russian Attacked by Stray Dogs, Dies," published on August 16, 2016.

The Kullu police's final report into Justin's disappearance was provided to me by Jonathan Skeels as well as by a local police officer.

Justin's web domain, adventuresofjustin.com, fell out of service the year after he disappeared but subsequently reappeared in part online by what appears to be a cryptocurrency company, likely because of the domain name.

EPILOGUE

The personal observations were based on the two trips I made to the Parvati Valley to report for my article in *Outside* magazine and for this book. I also flew to San Francisco in March 2019 to attend a celebration of life for Justin. The description of Bishal Kapali's organization was found at justinecofoundation.com.

How the Kheerganga camp had changed between 2016 and 2019 came from personal reporting as well as Siddarth Banerjee's "Now, Cafés and Camps Booted out of Kheerganga," published in the *Times of India* on May 27, 2018. The account of Matan Orgad was reported on in "Israeli Missing for a Month Found Dead on Hiking Trail in India," published in the *Times of Israel* on January 3, 2018; and the account of Aman Awasthi in Abhishek Behl and Saurabh Chauhari's "Missing Delhi Trekker Found Dead in Himachal Pradesh's Malana," published in the *Hindustan Times* on April 21, 2018. The web-based app was reported on in Sanjeev Kumar's "Trekkers to Get Safety via Online Portal," published in the *Statesman* on January 25, 2017, and in "GoKullu.com website to help keep tab on trekkers," published in *Himachal News* on January 26, 2017. The notion of caves as places of healing was drawn from Holley Moyes's *Sacred Darkness: A Global Perspective on the Ritual Use of Caves* (Boulder: University Press of Colorado, 2012), a collection that includes "Caves as Sacred Places on the Tibetan Plateau" by Mark Aldenderfer. The Joseph Campbell quote comes from *The Hero with a Thousand Faces*.

ABOUT THE AUTHOR

HARLEY RUSTAD is the author of *Big Lonely Doug: The Story of One of Canada's Last Great Trees*. His writing has appeared in numerous publications, including *Outside*, the *Guardian*, the *Globe and Mail*, and *Geographical*. He is a features editor and writer at the *Walrus* magazine, a faculty editor at the Banff Centre for Arts and Creativity's mountain and wilderness writing residency, and the founder of the Port Renfrew Writers' Retreat. A fellow of the Royal Geographical Society, Rustad is originally from Salt Spring Island, British Columbia.